ISSUES IN HUMAN RIGHTS PROTECTION OF INTELLECTUALLY DISABLED PERSONS

Medical Law and Ethics

Series Editor
Sheila McLean, Director of the Institute of Law and Ethics in Medicine, School of Law, University of Glasgow

The 21st century seems likely to witness some of the most major developments in medicine and healthcare ever seen. At the same time, the debate about the extent to which science and/or medicine should lead the moral agenda continues, as do questions about the appropriate role for law.

This series brings together some of the best contemporary academic commentators to tackle these dilemmas in a challenging, informed and inquiring manner. The scope of the series is purposely wide, including contributions from a variety of disciplines such as law, philosophy and social sciences.

Other titles in the series

The Legal, Medical and Cultural Regulation of the Body
Transformation and Transgression
Edited by Stephen W. Smith and Ronan Deazley
ISBN 978-0-7546-7736-9

Bioequity – Property and the Human Body
Nils Hoppe
ISBN 978-0-7546-7280-7

Altruism Reconsidered
Exploring New Approaches to Property in Human Tissue
Edited by Michael Steinmann, Peter Sýkora and Urban Wiesing
ISBN 978-0-7546-7270-8

The Child As Vulnerable Patient
Protection and Empowerment
Lynn Hagger
ISBN 978-0-7546-7252-4

Disclosure Dilemmas
Ethics of Genetic Prognosis after the 'Right to Know/Not to Know' Debate
Edited by Christoph Rehmann-Sutter and Hansjakob Müller
ISBN 978-0-7546-7451-1

Issues in Human Rights Protection of Intellectually Disabled Persons

ANDREAS DIMOPOULOS
University of Liverpool, UK

ASHGATE

Published by

Ashgate Publishing Limited
Wey Court East
Union Road
Farnham
Surrey, GU9 7PT
England

Ashgate Publishing Company
Suite 420
101 Cherry Street
Burlington
VT 05401-4405
USA

www.ashgate.com

British Library Cataloguing in Publication Data

Dimopoulos, Andreas.
Issues in human rights protection of intellectually disabled persons. -- (Medical law and ethics)
1. People with mental disabilities--Civil rights.
2. Mental health laws--England. 3. Mental health laws--Wales. 4. Mental health laws--Germany.
I. Title II. Series
346'.0138-dc22

Library of Congress Cataloging-in-Publication Data

Dimopoulos, Andreas.
Issues in human rights protection of intellectually disabled persons / by Andreas Dimopoulos.
p. cm. -- (Medical law and ethics)
Includes bibliographical references and index.
ISBN 978-0-7546-7760-4 (hardback) -- ISBN 978-0-7546-9505-9 (ebook) 1. Mental health laws--Europe. 2. People with mental disabilities--Civil rights--Europe. I. Title.

KJC1020.D56 2010
342.408'7--dc22

2009047844

Transfered to Digital Printing in 2012

ISBN 978-0-7546-7760-4

MIX
Paper from responsible sources
FSC® C018575

Printed and bound in Great Britain by the MPG Books Group Ltd, UK

Contents

List of Tables

Preface

This book aims to examine several conceptual difficulties in liberal human rights theory which are linked to intellectual disability. The first issue is the theoretical problem of accommodating non-autonomy within liberalism. The second issue relates to English law, and concerns the critique of common law best interests. The final issue touches upon the European Convention on Human Rights and the necessity of updating the Convention through the means of a disability protocol. These issues are treated as themes running through the argumentation of the book rather than being dealt with in separate chapters.

The term 'intellectual disability' has been used throughout the book to draw attention to the cognitive impairment of the person. We felt that this term is more in line with the distinction that the social model of disability draws between the impairment of the person (the biological factor) and her disability, which is brought about by exclusionary social practices. The more appealing term 'learning disabilities' has therefore not been used.

Even though much of the argumentation of the book is based on or inspired by disability rights theory, the analysis remains very much a legal argument as to how human rights theory may include persons with intellectual disability as equals in liberal legal systems. Intellectual disability poses a rather different set of legal issues when compared to other forms of disability. This book tries to reflect these differences and present a convincing argument as to how these differences may cohere with current human rights practices.

Acknowledgements

My first expression of gratitude goes to the great teachers I met during my studies: Ken Mason and Graeme Laurie in Edinburgh and John Bell in Cambridge. Special thanks are owed to Sheila McLean for accepting this book to appear in Ashgate's Medical Law and Ethics series. Further thanks are due to the editors at Ashgate, and Alison Kirk in particular. For moral support, my thanks go to Giorgos Leloudas.

To my parents, Christos and Paraskevi

Introduction

Theories of liberalism are based on the assumption that the individual is an autonomous agent. Contested questions of public morality have been answered in liberal theory by recourse to concepts such as autonomy and consent. What is more, human rights within liberalism have also been inextricably linked to autonomous choice. Negative rights especially, as the inalienable rights of man, were primordially conceived of as areas of freedom where the state could not interfere and where the citizen was empowered to act independently.

On the contrary, the present volume shifts the focus of attention in liberal theory from autonomous agency to cases where the individual is not autonomous, or has contested autonomy. The analysis examines the legal position of persons with intellectual disability within liberalism and human rights theory, as the paradigm case of contested autonomy in the context of liberal theory. The question here is whether and how the human rights of persons with intellectual disability are being exercised by the bearers of the rights themselves and/or protected by third parties.

The analysis shows convincingly that persons with intellectual disability are currently enjoying a low protection of their human rights. In several instances, such as involuntary sterilisations or donations of regenerative organs and tissue, legal safeguards against abuse are in practice unacceptably low.

The adoption by the General Assembly of the United Nations of the Convention on the Rights of Persons with Disabilities (CRPD) in late 2006 is hoped to provide the much-needed benchmark against which current practices in relation to persons with disabilities will be measured and will eventually change for the better.

Even though the rights protected by the CRPD do not make any formal distinction between intellectual disability and other forms of disability, this volume attempts to gauge the potential impact of the CRPD on issues of intellectual disability and human rights protection.

In further contrast to the CRPD, we will focus on intellectual disability as a rather distinct (but not separate) issue within the greater disability rights debate. An important argument in this volume is that intellectual disability poses a distinct set of human rights challenges when compared with other types of disability. This difference lies in the character of intellectual disability. Intellectual disability is stereotypically considered to diminish the autonomy of the person and thereby undermine the position of the person with intellectual disability as an *active* bearer of human rights. In other words, intellectual disability means contested autonomy, which is the prerequisite of liberalism, and as such, intellectual disability requires a reworking of our understanding of liberalism.

Even though the CRPD does address many of the specific issues that intellectual disability raises in respect of human rights protection, further thinking is required in order to buttress the position of persons with intellectual disability as equal bearers of human rights within liberalism.

With this analysis of the current state of things as a theoretical backdrop, the aim of this volume is to present a theory as to how persons with intellectual disability can be allowed to flourish in a liberal setting through the exercise of their human rights, even though they may be perceived as non-autonomous. Here, we borrow elements from the disability rights movement as well as human rights theory, in order to develop a legal argument as to how persons with intellectual disability may fit within liberalism and human rights.

In order to better understand the parameters of this question, we take a close look at the position of persons with intellectual disability in the English legal system, and comparatively, at German law. Immediately, the initial question behind this analysis becomes apparent. When everything in liberal legal systems is structured on autonomy and consent, and one is presented with an individual whose autonomy is contested, how can a liberal political community respond in a way which, firstly, grasps the issues at stake and secondly, respects that difference?

Historically, an early liberal response to this question has been paternalism. Persons without autonomy, or contested autonomy, were denied rights as they were considered unfit to control their exercise. Subsequent changes in social attitudes, and the renewed emphasis placed on autonomy and consent in relation to ethical questions posed by the rapid expanse of medical science, have now eroded the acceptability of paternalistic attitudes, even for persons with contested or no autonomy. Through the relentless efforts of the disability rights movement, paternalism has become increasingly harder to justify, whereas more freedom of choice has been granted to persons with disabilities.

The driving force behind the disability rights movement has been a new way of engaging with disability. Persons with disabilities have been stereotypically portrayed as sick and deviant, whereas their lives have been described as a personal tragedy. In contrast to this medical model of disability, the social model advanced by the disability rights movement describes disability as social oppression. Disability is the product of social exclusionary practices. People *become* disabled when faced with economic, environmental or cultural barriers which society places in their way.

This novel way of conceptualising disability has indeed had a liberating effect on disabled persons. The blame is rightly put on an exclusionary and indifferent society, whose practices must change. The person with disability is a blameless victim, who must stand up and fight for her rights.

Naturally, the social model of disability applies with equal force to persons with intellectual disability. However, the general description of disability as social oppression fails to focus on the distinguishing feature of intellectual disability. Here, the disabling feature, the exclusionary practice is a legally important criterion, the prerequisite for valid legal actions: whether the person has autonomy or not. It follows, at least for this volume, that a different way of conceptualising liberalism and human rights is required, so that the exclusionary criterion of autonomy is suitably modified or even removed from liberal theory, at least in respect of persons with intellectual disability.

To make matters worse, the issue of contested autonomy in the case of intellectual disability has been phrased in a dichotomy between claims for freedom and the need for protection. Persons with intellectual disability may sometimes lack the intellectual capacity or social skills and experience to prevent serious harm to their person, and their freedom must be curtailed accordingly. However, framing the question according to these terms does not help to advance the claims of persons with intellectual disability for more freedom, but rather inadvertently serves to justify paternalistic attitudes. In many instances, a so-called objective answer as to whether a person with intellectual disability is in need of protection may be hard to find.

However, the argument of this volume is that a principled approach to issues of intellectual disability is indeed possible. Since the disabling feature of intellectual disability is legal – the prerequisite of autonomy – a different legal analysis of autonomy is required. The argumentation adopted transposes the dichotomy between claims for freedom and the need for protection in a more rigorous legal vocabulary. The claim of the disability rights movement for more freedom is replaced by human rights, and the need for protection of vulnerable persons, such as persons with intellectual disability, is regarded as interference with these rights.

In other words, the theoretical issue shifts from a clash between freedom and protection to an analysis of what it means for persons with intellectual disability to hold human rights. The question changes in order to ascertain to what extent the intellectual disability of a person may justify an interference with her rights. This is a question which is designed to protect areas of freedom held by persons with intellectual disability from unnecessary intrusions. Moreover, conceptualising the issue of intellectual disability in human rights terms introduces a more nuanced analysis, since concepts such as proportionality immediately come into play. In the context of the English legal order, this analysis is particularly relevant after the incorporation of the European Convention on Human Rights (ECHR) in the Human Rights Act (HRA) 1998.

Parallel to this line of argumentation runs a broader enquiry, as to whether a legal framework of liberal theory can be found to support this human rights reasoning. Can a legal theory of liberal equality be found for persons with intellectual disability? Liberal theory bases equality on equal moral worth. Women, or black people, whose rights were being suppressed for centuries, gained their status as equal participants in liberal society as they convincingly put the argument forward that they are autonomous moral agents. Persons with intellectual disability however may have limited understanding of morality, or limited autonomy, or both. Their inclusion as equals in theories of liberalism underpinned by the importance of autonomous moral agency is therefore doubtful.

We will overcome this problem by engaging with the theory of liberal equality proposed by Ronald Dworkin.[1] This volume argues that Dworkin's ethical individualism can be modified to accommodate persons with intellectual disability as equals in liberal theory. The theoretical issue develops into an analysis as to how a liberal political community can set down a legal framework which is inclusive enough to ensure equality for persons with intellectual disability on the same footing as autonomous persons.

The principles which support these two lines of enquiry differ from the usual language of autonomous agency that liberal theory uses. Since there is contested autonomy, or no autonomy in the case of persons with intellectual disability, a different way of conceptualising liberalism and human rights is required. The argument has to be structured differently, but also in a way which coheres with liberalism.

As a solution to this issue, we will present an interpretive argument based on human rights theory. Human rights form an inextricable part of contemporary liberal theory, where, in the case of negative rights, the autonomous exercise of a human right is protected against state interference. In human rights declarations and related human rights documents, it is stressed that all persons are equal in dignity and rights. Human dignity is regarded as the normative fountainhead of human rights. It follows that in cases where there is no autonomous exercise of human rights, the residual principle of human dignity has to be applied in order to answer how these rights are to be protected and exercised.

Article 3 of the CRPD reinforces this argument, since human dignity features at the top of the list of principles underlying the CRPD, together with autonomy. Moreover, we will argue that this human dignity argument applies with equal force in the case of the ECHR. Human dignity may be used as a general principle in the interpretation of the ECHR in order to provide a higher standard of human rights protection to persons with intellectual disability. Finally, however, the argument of this volume is that an additional disability protocol to the ECHR is needed in order to bring the ECHR more in line with the developments in international human rights law which were brought about by the CRPD.

Part I develops these ideas and presents the arguments in relation to intellectual disability, liberalism and human rights. Chapter 1 defines intellectual disability. It provides a brief presentation of social policy relating to persons with intellectual disability. The social model of disability is also analysed in relation to intellectual disability. Chapter 2 moves on to present the challenges intellectual disability poses to liberalism. It presents the normative content of human dignity for this volume. It develops the human dignity argument we will advance, as well as a theory of liberal equality for persons with intellectual disability, based on human dignity.

---

1 R. Dworkin, *Sovereign Virtue: The Theory and Practice of Equality* (Cambridge, MA: Harvard University Press, 2000).

We will claim that, even though human dignity is philosophically complex, the principle has been used rather simplistically in human rights law: what does it mean, after all, that all human beings are equal in dignity and rights? Subsequently, we will analyse how liberal theory can ensure equality for persons with intellectual disability, by engaging with the theory of liberal equality advanced by Ronald Dworkin.

Part II turns to the current legal practice, which relates to the protection of human rights of persons with intellectual disability. In respect of international law, Chapter 3 examines the CRPD and attempts to gauge its potential impact on the rights of persons with intellectual disability. Chapter 4, on the other hand, scrutinises the existing case law of the European Court of Human Rights (ECtHR) in relation to intellectually disabled applicants. The argument of the volume is that the ECtHR has not been able to develop a coherent and fully fledged interpretation of human dignity in its case law, and for this reason, problems of human rights protection arise when the ECtHR is faced with disabled applicants.

Chapters 5 and 6 are devoted to a comparative analysis of national law. Chapter 5 furnishes an analysis of English law relating to persons with intellectual disability. We will argue that the challenges of intellectual disability are not adequately addressed by English law. The incorporation of the ECHR by means of the Human Rights Act 1998 has radically changed the legal position of persons with intellectual disability. This has not filtered into the provisions of the Mental Capacity Act 2005.

Chapter 6 compares the position of English law in respect of persons with intellectual disability to that of the German legal system, which is squarely based on the principle of human dignity and the protection of constitutional rights. We will claim that German law has developed a coherent legal framework in order to protect the rights of persons with intellectual disability, even though there are several German court judgments which offer hardly any protection to persons with intellectual disability.

The final part of this volume brings the analysis to a close by providing illustrations as to how the human dignity argument we have advanced makes a difference in the law. In Chapter 7, we revisit the sterilisation case law from the human dignity perspective to argue that important safeguards are still missing from the approach of English law. The application of German law in relation to authorised sterilisations is also criticised. The importance of human dignity is further examined in the context of the CRPD.

The volume concludes in Chapter 8 by arguing that a disability protocol should be added to the ECHR. This protocol should clearly flag disability as a sensitive issue within the rights protected by the ECHR. Furthermore, the protocol could prohibit non-consensual sterilisations for non-medical reasons, and set down restrictions to non-consensual transplantations. Most importantly however, adopting a new protocol on disability would also provide a unique opportunity for the Council of Europe to set down a minimum standard for positive rights for persons with disability and intellectual disability, which would be enforceable through the ECtHR.

PART I
The Protection of Human Rights for Persons with Disability in Theory: Intellectual Disability as a Distinct Issue

Chapter 1
Intellectual Disability as a Distinct Issue

The Distinguishing Features of Intellectual Disability

The Terminology of Intellectual Disability

Without denying the medical and psychological sides of intellectual disability, modern psychology insists that intellectual disability is a socially constructed concept.[1] What it means, how it is measured, and therefore who counts as having an intellectual disability, is historically and culturally contingent. To this day, definitions of intellectual disability vary greatly across countries, according to an array of ideological, political, economic and cultural factors.

For example, from medieval times until the end of the nineteenth century, the social environment, the medical profession and the courts have defined intellectual disability in terms of deficits in what is now described as adaptive behaviour. It was only in the twentieth century that the medical profession insisted in conceptualising intellectual disability as a deficit in intelligence.

Since intellectual disability is socially constructed, the persons regarded as having an intellectual disability will depend on the classification system used by society and the medical profession. The most comprehensive and widely accepted definition and classification system has been devised by the American Association on Mental Retardation (AAMR). According to the 2002 AAMR definition:

> Mental retardation is a disability characterized by significant limitations both in intellectual functioning and in adaptive behavior as expressed in conceptual, social, and practical adaptive skills. This disability originates before age 18.

The AAMR definition then proceeds to furnish several assumptions, which underlie this understanding of intellectual disability. Five assumptions are essential to the application of the definition:

> (1) limitations in present functioning must be considered within the context of community environments typical of the individual's age peers and culture;
> (2) valid assessment considers cultural and linguistic diversity as well as differences in communication, sensory, motor, and behavioral factors;

---

1 C. Hatton, 'Intellectual Disabilities: Epidemiology and Causes' in E. Emerson et al., eds, *Clinical Psychology and Persons with Intellectual Disabilities* (Chichester: John Wiley and Sons, 1998) at 20.

> (3) within an individual, limitations often coexist with strengths;
> (4) an important purpose of describing limitations is to develop a profile of needed supports;
> (5) with appropriate personalized supports over a sustained period, the life functioning of the person with mental retardation generally will improve.[2]

In this sense, intellectual disability is defined as the combination of fundamental difficulties in intellectual functioning and of deficiencies in certain daily life skills. These limitations relate to the present functioning of the person, and are culturally contingent. But intellectual functioning alone is insufficient to classify someone as being intellectually disabled. In addition, there must be significant limitations in adaptive skills – the skills to cope successfully with the daily tasks of living. The concept of adaptive behaviour is linked to what skills would be appropriate for a person's age and culture.

The assumptions that underlie the AAMR definition are very important because they constitute an effort to reduce the social stigma of being labelled as intellectually disabled. For instance, it is stressed that the purpose of describing the limitations of a person is to provide more accurate support, tailored to the needs of the person. Moreover, the assumptions related to the AAMR definition make it clear that intellectual disability is not necessarily a life-long condition, and depending on the support that society provides, these persons may not be regarded as having intellectual disability all their lives.

Although the 2002 AAMR classification system does not define levels of intellectual disability, the concept of different degrees of severity of intellectual disability is almost in universal use. These classifications are based on standardised IQ scores, although consideration must also be directed to adaptive behaviour when making a judgement about the level of the person's intellectual disability. The International Classification of Diseases produced by the World Health Organisation is the most widely used (see Table 1.1).[3]

Table 1.1 Classification of intellectual disability

Level of intellectual disability	IQ
Mild	50–69
Moderate	35–49
Severe	20–34
Profound	<20

2 Available at <http://www.aamr.org/intellectualdisabilitybook/content_2678.cfm?navID=282>.

3 Available at <http://www.who.int/classifications/icd/en/>.

The White Paper *Valuing People: A New Strategy for Learning Disability for the 21st Century*[4] cites rough estimations concerning the general prevalence of intellectual disability in the UK:

> Producing precise information on the number of people with learning disabilities in the population is difficult. In the case of people with severe and profound learning disabilities, we estimate there are about 210,000: around 65,000 children and young people, 120,000 adults of working age and 25,000 older people. In the case of people with mild/moderate learning disabilities, lower estimates suggest a prevalence rate of around 25 per 1,000 population – some 1.2 million people in England.[5]

These figures were updated by the follow-up to that White Paper, *Valuing People Now: A New Three-year Strategy for People with Learning Disabilities*.[6] According to the similar data presented by this policy document, it was estimated that in the UK:

> there were 985,000 people with learning disabilities, including 190,000 aged under 20, 127,000 aged 65 or over, and 795,000 adults (defined as over 20 and under 65). Of these, 224,000 were people in England known to social services. The remaining 761,000 people had mild to moderate learning disabilities, may not be known to services, and may not need very much additional support beyond their own families, friends and social networks. However, without information about and access to a range of mainstream services, and help at points of crisis, their needs may escalate to the point where their support networks break down.

It was also estimated that the total number of adults with a learning disability (aged 20 or over) will increase by 8 per cent to 868,000 in 2011 and by 14 per cent to 908,000 by 2021.

This short presentation of modern psychology in the field of intellectual disability illustrates that persons with intellectual disability are a very diverse group, with widely different characteristics and needs. Even though exact statistical data do not exist, persons with intellectual disability form a substantive minority in the English population.

In psychological terms, the disability of persons with intellectual disability consists of low IQ and a lack of adaptive skills; this makes them vulnerable and dependent for help. It is now time to examine how society has responded to this vulnerability.

---

4 Secretary of State for Health, *Valuing People: A New Strategy for Learning Disability for the 21st Century*, Cm 5086 (London: The Stationery Office, 2001).

5 Ibid. at 15.

6 Department for Health, *Valuing People Now: A New Three-year Strategy for People with Learning Disabilities*, Gateway Reference 10531 (2009).

Social Policy Relating to Intellectual Disability: Normalisation, Self-advocacy and Valuing People

Normalisation Despite the problems which intellectual disability poses to liberal societies, welfare provision and care for persons with intellectual disability are being provided by many social welfare systems. Historically, however, the prevailing social attitude in Europe towards persons with intellectual disability – or to use the language of the past, the feeble-minded – has always been alienation and exclusion from the community. It was only after the extensive atrocities committed under Nazi Germany towards persons with intellectual disability that social attitudes began to change. This, however, did not mean that official discrimination towards intellectual disability perished with the Nazi regime. On the contrary, large-scale policies of involuntary sterilisation of persons with intellectual disability were still being carried out in Scandinavian countries for many years after the war.[7]

But it became slowly evident in these countries that the quality of life of persons with intellectual disability that were alienated in special homes or asylums was very low. Slowly, a movement concerning the welfare of these persons emerged around 1960, under the wider influence of other similar social movements, such as the civil rights movement in the United States. The social dimension of this movement, known as normalisation, is very evident. Normalisation sought to make normal the life of persons with intellectual disability. The basic aims of the movement were to ensure that persons with intellectual disability enjoyed the same quality of life as everyone else, that they had a lifestyle broken down into time periods of work, leisure and holidays, and that they were awarded the same rights as normal people.[8]

The grounding of normalisation in basic human and civil rights was reflected in the incorporation of normalisation elements in the 1971 UN Declaration on the Rights of Mentally Retarded Persons.[9] For instance, Article 4 of the Declaration holds that 'If care in an institution becomes necessary, it should be provided in surroundings and other circumstances as close as possible to those of normal life.' Thus, normalisation did not develop as an isolated ideal, but reflected the prevalent liberal trends of many liberal societies at that time to respond to the demand for equal rights for a number of disadvantaged or minority groups.

During the period in which the concept of normalisation was being developed in Scandinavia, significant changes were also beginning to occur in North America, most notably the civil rights movement and the new label theories in sociology. The North American version of normalisation reflected a growing emphasis upon the importance of the way in which disadvantaged people are portrayed

---

7 See p. 181 footnote 10.

8 S. Whitehead, 'The Social Origins of Normalisation' in H. Brown and H. Smith, eds, *Normalisation: A Reader for the Nineties* (London: Routledge, 1992) at 47.

9 *Declaration on the Rights of Mentally Retarded Persons*, GA Res. 2856(XXVI), UN GAOR, 26th Sess., Supp. No. 29, UN Doc. A/8429, 93.

or perceived by the public. This is the reason why this theory of normalisation stresses the importance of the physical presence of persons with intellectual disability, so that they become socially visible and cannot be ignored by society. Consequently, community settings, rather than segregated institutions are of paramount importance. On the other hand, issues of immediate relevance to the quality of life of disabled or disadvantaged groups, such as personal well-being or happiness, and the expression of individual choice, were considered secondary to the social status of the devalued or disadvantaged group as a whole.

In recent years, normalisation has been gradually abandoned in favour of a different approach towards disability. The social model of disability has gained immense popularity among persons with disabilities. It also forms the backbone of the recent UN Convention on the Rights of Persons with Disabilities. Yet the influence of normalisation principles can still be seen in the provision of welfare for persons with intellectual disability.

For instance, the aims of the North American normalisation movement are evident in a 1999 US Supreme Court judgment, effectively saying that institutionalisation can be regarded as unlawful discrimination:

> Institutional placement of persons who can handle and benefit from community settings perpetuates unwarranted assumptions that persons so isolated are incapable or unworthy of participating in community life.[10]

Social welfare policy in the UK in relation to intellectual disability: From normalisation values to Valuing People Social, political and financial factors favoured the inception of normalisation in the UK. The concept of community care, and growing public awareness of the dreadful living conditions in long-stay mental institutions, had prepared the ground for the concept of normalisation to emerge in the UK. Normalisation was received as an ideological framework which: (1) was clearly based on basic human values, (2) took account of the social context in which people lived, (3) concentrated on the impact of services on their lives, and (4) challenged the traditional and paternalistic responses which characterised welfare services, and the professionals who ran them.[11] These goals became evident in the 1971 White Paper *Better Services for the Mentally Handicapped*.[12] The current White Paper on intellectual disability, *Valuing People*,[13] succinctly summarises the normalisation aims of the 1971 White Paper:

10 *Olmstead* v. *LC* 527 US 581.

11 S. Whitehead, 'The Social Origins of Normalisation' in H. Brown and H. Smith, eds, *Normalisation: A Reader for the Nineties* (London: Routledge, 1992) at 47.

12 Department of Health and Social Security, *Better Services for the Mentally Handicapped*, Cmnd 4683 (London: Her Majesty's Stationery Office, 1971).

13 Secretary of State for Health, *Valuing People: A New Strategy for Learning Disability for the 21st Century*, Cm 5086 (London: The Stationery Office, 2001).

> It set an agenda for the next two decades, which focused on reducing the number of places in hospitals and increasing provision in the community. It committed the Government to helping people with learning disabilities to live 'as normal a life' as possible, without unnecessary segregation from the community and emphasised the importance of close collaboration between health, social services and other local agencies.[14]

One of the key goals of the 1971 White Paper was the physical relocation of persons with intellectual disability from long-stay units to community care settings. As large mental hospitals were slowly being shut down, and persons with intellectual disability started flowing into local communities, different sets of problems and challenges started to emerge.

With the physical relocation of persons with intellectual disability in the community a tangible fact, the new challenge is the actual, rather than just the physical, inclusion of persons with intellectual disability within society. Accordingly, the new White Paper on intellectual disability, *Valuing People: A New Strategy for Learning Disability for the 21st Century*, marks the turn of the tide for normalisation in the UK, in the sense that the expressed goal of governmental policy is no longer to make normal the life of persons with intellectual disability.

As the White Paper notes:

> Very few [persons with intellectual disability] have jobs, live in their own homes or have choice over who cares for them. This needs to change: people with learning disabilities must no longer be marginalised or excluded. *Valuing People* sets out how the Government will provide new opportunities for children and adults with learning disabilities and their families to live full and independent lives as part of their local communities.[15]

In all but the name, *Valuing People* continues to endorse the goals that the normalisation movement has been advocating for. The White Paper sets down four principles that the government proposals are based on:

> social inclusion, civil rights, choice and independence. People with learning disabilities have the right to be full members of the society in which they live, to choose where they live and what they do, and to be as independent as they wish to be.[16]

These principles are then translated into tangible objectives, such as enabling people with learning disabilities to have as much choice and control as possible

14 Ibid. at 16–17.

15 Ibid. at 2.

16 Ibid. at 14.

over their lives through advocacy and a person-centred approach to planning the services they need.[17]

It is important to note that within these four principles, specific mention to human dignity is made. The White Paper stresses that: 'All public services will treat people with learning disabilities as individuals with respect for their dignity, and challenge discrimination on all grounds including disability.'[18]

Finally, the 2001 White Paper stresses the importance of advocacy in relation to the problems that persons with intellectual disability face.

Very recently, the 2001 White Paper was updated through consultation which ended in March 2008. *Valuing People Now* is a reaffirmation to the changes in social policy which were brought about by the 2001 White Paper.[19]

Importantly, however, this social policy document takes stock of what has been achieved in the seven years that followed the publication of the 2001 White Paper and describes a rather bleak picture of what remains to be done:[20]

- The Social Exclusion Task Force identified people with moderate and severe learning disabilities as one of the most excluded groups in our society.
- Only 15 per cent of people with learning disabilities have a home of their own.
- More than 30 per cent of people with learning disabilities live in residential care homes, a significant proportion of which are miles away from their place of origin and their families.
- Many people with learning disabilities are living with older family carers who have their own needs.
- Only one in ten of those known to social services has any form of paid employment, and of those only very few work more than 16 hours a week.
- People with learning disabilities report that they are often the target of hate crime, that they are dependent on very limited and expensive public transport to get around, and that being lonely is one of the things they fear the most.
- The 2008 report of the Parliamentary Joint Committee on Human Rights, *A Life Like Any Other?*, highlighted continued and extensive failure of services and society to accord people with learning disabilities their basic rights.

---

17 Ibid. at 26.

18 Ibid. at 23. Other mentions of dignity in official documents include the references made to the principle of human dignity in the context of the Joint Committee Report on the Draft Mental Health Bill. There, it was recognised that the detention of psychiatric patients should respect their dignity. See Joint Committee on the Draft Mental Health Bill, *Draft Mental Health Bill*, HL Paper 181 HC 1294, Session 2001–2002 (London: The Stationery Office, 2002) at 6. It is unfortunate, however, that such mentions of the principle do not elaborate further as to its meaning and normative content.

19 Department for Health, *Valuing People Now: A New Three-year Strategy for People with Learning Disabilities*, Gateway Reference 10531 (2009).

20 Ibid. at 28.

- *Healthcare For All*, the report of the independent inquiry into access to healthcare for people with learning disabilities, reported significant and ongoing inequalities in access to healthcare services and in the quality of services.

Valuing People Now is squarely based on the four principles that were first presented in the 2001 White Paper. Rights, independent living, control and inclusion are similarly the guiding principles of this three-year plan.[21] In addition to this, *Valuing People Now* stresses the importance of a human rights approach to issues of intellectual disability. The document notes:[22]

> This strategy promotes a human rights based approach *and the rights set out in the UN Convention on Human Rights* [emphasis added]. It confirms that adults with learning disabilities have, and should be able to enjoy on an equal basis, the same human rights as everyone else. It sets out the further steps that are needed for people with learning disabilities to achieve freedom, respect, equality, dignity and autonomy in their everyday lives. This includes action to:
>
> - promote human rights in healthcare through promoting good practice;
> - support independent advocacy to achieve a greater impact for people with learning disabilities, including people from black and minority ethnic communities and those with complex needs;
> - address the specific issues for people with learning disabilities on safeguarding in the *No Secrets* consultation;
> - reduce hate crime towards people with learning disabilities;
> - address issues around social exclusion, poverty and isolation; and
> - promote the involvement of people with learning disabilities and family carers in all aspects of local, regional and national workforce planning and delivery.

This volume shares the opinion of official policy that a human rights approach is required in the case of intellectual disability. Intellectual disability is a complex social phenomenon. A simple affirmation that persons with intellectual disability should enjoy on an equal basis the same human rights as everyone else belies this complexity. The same argument applies with equal force to the affirmation of *Valuing People Now* that it promotes the rights set out in the UN Convention on the Rights of Persons with Disabilities.

Gerard Quinn gives an excellent account of what is at stake in relation to the CRPD:[23]

---

21 Ibid. at 30.

22 Ibid. at 31.

23 G. Quinn, 'Resisting the Temptation of Elegance: Can the Convention on the Rights of Persons with Disabilities Socialise States to Right Behaviour' in O.M. Arnardóttir and G.

> the Convention itself would appear to allow windows through which States might rationalise – and even reconcile – existing exclusionary practices … For example, most of the rights of the Convention are said to be secured 'on an equal basis with others'. Much will turn on how this phrase is interpreted by the incoming treaty monitoring body … At one level it requires an acknowledgment of reckonable differences between persons with disabilities and others. And, invoking the Aristotelian conception of equality, this would furthermore require 'equals to be treated equally and unequals to be treated unequally'. It doesn't take much imagination to see how this acknowledgment about objective inequality would be used (really abused) to rationalise separate treatment and to continue as before …

UK social policy offers hardly any guidance as to how this much-desired equality shall be achieved. More importantly, it over-simplifies what equality is in the case of intellectual disability. Persons with intellectual disability are not the same as everyone else, as they lack cognitive and social skills. How, then, should the unlike be treated on a similar basis? There is real danger then that the ratification of the CRPD will resemble putting new wine into old wineskins.

Providing advocacy services, reducing hate crime and addressing the exclusion and poverty of persons with intellectual disability surely go a long way in providing them with a better quality of life.

These social policy actions, however, can achieve very little in the way of augmenting the personal freedom of choice of persons with intellectual disability. Providing advocacy services and ensuring the involvement of the person with intellectual disability does not mean that the person's choices or rights will be respected.

Depending on the psychological evaluation of the person, she may be considered as incapable of consent, and choices about the person will be made by others in her best interests. The door is open to paternalism and abuse, unless there are sound guidance and proper safeguards as to how these decisions should be made.

Advocacy and self-advocacy The previous analysis of social policy towards persons with intellectual disability has also highlighted the role of advocacy in social welfare. It is through advocacy that the involvement of the person with intellectual disability is secured in the provision of welfare services. However, the importance of advocacy lies primarily in the fact that it makes audible the voice and preferences of persons with intellectual disability.

The European normalisation movement had always emphasised the importance of more choice, of more freedom, that must be given to persons with intellectual disability. This claim for more choice has also spearheaded the campaigns of disability rights organisations in relation to persons with intellectual disability. Within this

---

Quinn, eds, *The UN Convention on the Rights of Persons with Disabilities: European and Scandinavian Perspectives* (Leiden: Martinus Nijhoff Publishers, 2009) at 216–17.

process of enabling persons with intellectual disability to acquire and make use of more choice, the concepts of advocacy and self-advocacy were developed.

Valuing People stresses the importance of advocacy for persons with intellectual disability and adopts as official policy to expand the advocacy network over the UK:

> Effective advocacy can transform the lives of people with learning disabilities by enabling them to express their wishes and aspirations and make real choices. Advocacy helps people put forward their views and play an active part in planning and designing services, which are responsive to their needs. This applies to people with severe and profound disabilities and to the less severely disabled.[24]

Advocacy also features in *Valuing People*, the update to *Valuing People Now*, where it is stressed that all people with learning disabilities can speak up and be heard about what they want from their lives – the big decisions and the everyday choices. If they need support to do this, they should be able to get it.[25] Expenditure on advocacy services by local authorities has risen since the 2001 White Paper was published, which shows that advocacy is increasingly becoming an essential part in the process of social care provision.

On the other hand, self-advocacy is very much about self-empowerment. For self-advocacy writers, only persons who cannot advocate for themselves can have an advocate appointed for them, who will make sure that the person will receive proper support to understand the decisions to be made and will be able to express her own views and wishes. Persons with intellectual disability, so self-advocacy claims, communicate, and the challenge is to develop skills in recognising people's individual styles of communication, responding to them, and offering opportunities to make meaningful choices:

> The essence of self-advocacy is being able to exert some control and influence over your life, and at a basic level this will involve indicating needs and desires, rejecting and refusing things, and making choices that matter.[26] In helping people to advocate for themselves, it is challenging to find a balance between informed choice and what is in the person's best interests. This involves achieving a balance between safety, health and freedom of choice; personal liberties and how society expects people to behave and encouragement without bullying.[27]

---

24 Secretary of State for Health, *Valuing People: A New Strategy for Learning Disability for the 21st Century*, Cm 5086 (London: The Stationery Office, 2001) at 46.

25 Department for Health, *Valuing People Now: A New Three-year Strategy for People with Learning Disabilities*, Gateway Reference 10531 (2009) at 101.

26 H. Sanderson, 'Self-advocacy and Inclusion: Supporting People with Profound and Multiple Disabilities' in T. Philpot and L. Ward, eds, *Values and Visions: Changing Ideas in Services for People with Learning Difficulties* (Oxford: Butterworth-Heinemann, 1995) at 244.

27 Ibid. at 246–7.

As social welfare services, advocacy and self-advocacy are very important to persons with intellectual disability. They provide support to the person with intellectual disability so that she can communicate and express any choices she makes in relation to the provision of social care she receives. This description of social policy responses to persons with intellectual disability belies the hard and intense struggles of persons with disabilities for the provision of better social care and welfare services.

Most importantly however, these changes in social policy would not have been possible if persons with disabilities had not been able to advance a different way of conceptualising disability and persuade as to its rightness. This novel way of thinking about disability is the social model of disability, to which the analysis now turns.

The Social Model of Disability and Intellectual Disability

A historical perspective Over the past few decades, people with disabilities worldwide became cognisant of their difference and organised in social pressure groups in order to challenge segregation and exclusion from mainstream society. These groups originated from people with physical disabilities, who were fighting against the oppression and powerlessness they were experiencing in their daily lives, either as long-term residents in welfare institutions or as mobility-impaired citizens coping with everyday life.

The paradigm example of such a group in the UK is the Union of the Physically Impaired Against Segregation (UPIAS), which was formed in 1972.[28] Discussions within the group led to an analysis of physical disability as a social relationship in which disabled people were oppressed. By making this revolutionary claim, the UPIAS was challenging the concept of disability as a biologically determined condition. The group denied altogether the traditional, medical views of their disability as a personal tragedy, which hindered them from participating meaningfully in social life.

Instead, the UPIAS stressed that disability was something that could be challenged and eliminated. The group put out a call for disabled people to take control of their own lives and emancipate themselves. The UPIAS demanded that physically disabled persons stop being separated from mainstream society. All government funding for residential institutions and special schools should also stop. This funding should be channelled instead to ensure that disabled persons were being provided with support so as to live independently within mainstream society.

In terms of the history of the disability rights movement, the group's greatest achievement was its role as an awakening call to action and emancipation. Active

---

28 J. Hunt, 'A Revolutionary Group with a Revolutionary Message' (2001) *Coalition* 22–30. Available at: <http://www.leeds.ac.uk/disability-studies/archiveuk/Hunt%20J/a%20revolutionary%20group%20with%20a%20revolutionary%20message.pdf>.

struggle against social oppression was the means by which disabled people would overcome their passivity and their dependence.

The UPIAS policy statement adopted in 1974, and amended in 1976, describes eloquently the situation of physically disabled persons at the time. It also provides an insight into the claims of the group. Some passages deserve mention in full:[29]

> The Union aims to have all segregated facilities for physically impaired people replaced by arrangements for us to participate fully in society …
>
> We find ourselves isolated and excluded by such things as flights of steps, inadequate public and personal transport, unsuitable housing, rigid work routines in factories and offices, and a lack of up-to-date aids and equipment …
>
> This society is based on the necessity for people to compete in the labour market in order to earn a living. To the employer of labour, the physically impaired are not usually as good a buy as the non-impaired. We therefore end up at or near the bottom of this society as an oppressed group …
>
> Our position is similar to that of many people who are middle-aged or elderly, who have had break-downs, who are 'mentally handicapped', black, ex-prisoners, unskilled workers, etc. We are usually among the first to lose our jobs and be cast on the scrap-heap when it suits the 'needs' of the economy …
>
> The cruelty, petty humiliation, and physical and mental deprivation suffered in residential institutions, where isolation and segregation have been carried to extremes, lays bare the essentially oppressive relations of this society with its physically impaired members …

These extracts from the UPIAS policy statement reveal the growing consciousness of physically disabled persons as an oppressed minority group within mainstream society. The reason advanced for this social oppression is the reduced productivity of physically disabled workers in relation to able-bodied ones. The policy statement also clearly targets architectural barriers, which hinder persons with physical disability from full participation in mainstream society.

These basic statements were later developed into what is now known as the social model of disability. Before examining the concept in greater detail, it is important here to note that the origins of the social model are rooted in an understanding of physical disability. Social oppression against physically disabled persons takes the form of a hostile architectural and work environment. Segregation and exclusion from mainstream society is achieved by separate housing institutions or special transport.

---

29 Union of the Physically Impaired Against Segregation, *Policy Statement* (1976). Available at: <http://www.leeds.ac.uk/disability-studies/archiveuk/UPIAS/UPIAS.pdf>.

This, however, means that the oppression and segregation of persons with intellectual disability did not form part of the novel analysis and the revolutionary claims the UPIAS was advancing. The UPIAS was, after all, a group of physically disabled persons. Moreover, at the time the UPIAS was being formed, issues of intellectual disability were being addressed through normalisation. It is not surprising, therefore, that intellectual disability is absent from its policy statement. Significantly, this absence of mention of intellectual disability was carried over to the initial theoretical development of the social model of disability.

Social models of disability? A detailed discussion of the different views and writings in relation to disability is beyond the scope of this analysis. What matters at this point is to draw a clear line between the traditional, medicalising view of disability and the social model. The different typologies of the social model of disability will only be summarised.

Views similar to those expressed by the UPIAS were based on the everyday experiences of physically disabled persons, who were forced to put up with an indifferent and segregating society. Based on their personal experiences, disabled persons came to challenge the traditional, biological and individual model of their disability.[30] This medical understanding of disability focuses on the impairment of the individual, while disregarding the context within which that impairment manifests itself.

On the contrary, the new approaches to disability asserted that social attitudes and environmental factors were crucial to understand disability. These factors contextualise disability within a particular social setting. This social environment discriminates against persons with disabilities. It follows that the social context must change in order for the discrimination to cease. Table 1.2, borrowed by Traustadóttir,[31] illustrates lucidly the differences between the two perceptions of disability.

Several patterns of thought have emerged within the social model of disability. Three different typologies of the social model may easily be identified.[32] These are the British social model of disability, the Scandinavian relational approach and the North American minority group approach.

The British social model of disability also forms the basis of the argumentation we will adopt. Throughout the volume, references to the social model of disability imply the British model. Central to this concept of disability is the distinction between impairment and disability. Impairment is the underlying biological factor, whereas disability manifests itself within a social environment

30 R. Traustadóttir, 'Disability Studies, the Social Model and Legal Developments' in O.M. Arnardóttir and G. Quinn, eds, *The UN Convention on the Rights of Persons with Disabilities: European and Scandinavian Perspectives* (Leiden: Martinus Nijhoff Publishers, 2009) at 8.

31 Ibid.

32 Ibid. at 9.

Table 1.2 Differences between the medical and social models of disability

Medical model	Social model
Focus on the impairment and the individual	Focus on the social context and environment
Emphasis on clinical and medical diagnosis	Emphasis on the relationship between the individual and society
Emphasis on individual deficits	Emphasis on social barriers
Views the person as the problem that needs to be fixed or cured	Views discrimination, exclusion and prejudice as the problem
Medical, psychological and rehabilitative services are the answer	Ending discrimination and segregation, and removing barriers is the answer

which restricts persons with impairments by placing barriers which hinder these persons from fully participating in social life. In this way, the British social model argues that the cause of the problem is not the person, but rather the society in which she lives.

This conceptualisation of disability has gained immense popularity among persons with disabilities, as well as scholars of disability studies. Yet the British model has not been without its detractors. Importantly, the social model has been criticised for placing too much emphasis on social and structural barriers, whilst overlooking the cultural and experiential dimensions of disability. Similarly, the social model has been accused of neglecting the experiences, needs and interests of persons with particular kinds of impairments, such as persons with intellectual disability or deafness.[33]

A different typology of the social model of disability is the relational approach to disability, prevalent in Scandinavian countries.[34] This approach was gradually developed on the basis of normalisation principles. The aims of normalisation were to ensure that persons with disabilities enjoyed the same quality of life as everyone else. Their patterns of living should be based on the lifestyle of persons without disability. They should also be awarded the same rights as everyone else.

This line of thought came to challenge segregation against persons with disabilities. By doing so, attention was drawn to the social environment in which persons with disabilities were living, just as the British social model was also suggesting.

This means that the relational approach is very close to the British social model of disability. The focus is placed on lifting the environmental barriers which hinder persons with disabilities from fully participating in society.

Crucially, however, the relational approach is not based on the distinction between impairment and disability. Rather, the relational approach is based on a different set of characteristics. The first of these is the mismatch between the person

33 Ibid. at 10–11.

34 Ibid. at 12.

and her social environment. Even though the person does not have capacities within the typical range, it is also the environment that is not adapted to the wide range of human diversity. Secondly, disability is contextual. For instance, a person who is blind has no disability when talking over the phone. Thirdly, disability is relative. A good example is the cut-off point used in IQ tests to diagnose a person as having an intellectual disability. Depending on the psychological definition of intellectual disability which is used, as the concept evolves, a person may be labelled quite arbitrarily as having an intellectual disability.

A different typology of the social approach to disability is the one developed in North America. This understanding of disability is rooted in the tradition of the North American civil rights movement. Persons with disabilities are viewed as a minority group. Prejudice and discrimination against persons with disabilities call for the introduction of civil rights legislation, which will lift these inequalities. This minority group approach is similarly not based on a firm distinction between impairment and disability. Emphasis is here again placed on the social environment and the different kinds of social barriers which restrict persons with disabilities.

In spite of these differences, the typologies of the social model of disability are firmly grounded in the common understanding that radical changes in the social environment are the key to providing persons with disabilities with equal rights and a chance to be included in liberal societies on the same footing as everyone else.

The present volume considers that this general remark requires further qualifications in the case of intellectual disability. It is time to examine whether the social model of disability is cognisant of the peculiarities of intellectual disability and whether these differences are adequately addressed.

The social model of disability and intellectual disability: A strained relationship At the beginning of the 1980s, the social model of disability was being developed by physically disabled persons, based on their experiences as physically disabled members of society. Most importantly, the aims of the social model at that time were addressed to physically disabled persons only. Again, a passage from the UPIAS policy statement is illuminating:

> Both inside and outside institutions, the traditional way of dealing with disabled people has been for doctors and other professionals to decide what is best for us. It is of course a fact that we sometimes require skilled medical help to treat our physical impairments – operations, drugs and nursing care. We may also need therapists to help restore or maintain physical function, and to advise us on aids to independence and mobility. But the imposition of medical authority, and of a medical definition of our problems of living in society, have to be resisted strongly. First and foremost we are people, not 'patients', 'cases', 'spastics', 'the deaf', 'the blind', 'wheelchairs' or 'the sick'. Our Union rejects entirely any idea of medical or other experts having the right to tell us how we should live, or withholding information from us, or take decisions behind our backs.

This passage shows that the revolt against medical tradition and authority has to do with autonomy. Persons with physical disability reject the imposition of medical authority, because they are people. No one has the right to tell these people how they should live, or take decisions behind their backs. These claims are worded in a vocabulary of liberal terms and ideas. Best interests, freedom of choice, the right to be left alone, informed consent are all hidden behind these statements.

Crucially, however, this liberal and liberating message was not being advanced in favour of persons with intellectual disability as well. At the time when the UPIAS and similar groups were shaping the ideas which would later inform the social model of disability, normalisation principles still held sway in relation to issues of intellectual disability. It was only after the social model of disability gained immense popularity among people with disabilities that intellectual disability came under the liberating scope of the social model.

Jan Walmsley, writing as late as 1997, notes:

> A major development of recent years has been the inclusion of people with learning difficulties in the Disability Movement. The application of ideas associated with the social model of disability to the situation of people with learning difficulties has the potential to be an empowering and energising development.

However, the simple application of the social model of disability to persons with intellectual disability begs the question whether a theoretical approach which was developed by physically disabled persons with the problems physically disabled persons faced in mind can be meaningfully applied to intellectually disabled persons, who have a distinct kind of disability. Jan Walmsley is equally sceptical when she writes:

> Unlike other groups of disabled people with different impairments, it is unclear whether they [persons with intellectual disability] will ever be able to engage on equal terms. It is not just a matter of time, resources, technology and positive attitudes. It is not just a learning difficulty, the sort we are too ready to say we share because we too have learning difficulties. It is where normalisation has not got all the answers. This is an area where oppression and exclusion take a distinct form for people with learning difficulties ...[35]

The argument here is again one of coherence. This time coherence relates to what is accepted in relation to physically disabled persons in the light of the social model of disability. Physically disabled persons demand that social barriers

35 J. Walmsley, 'Including People with Learning Difficulties: Theory and Practice', in L. Barton and Mike Oliver, eds, *Disability Studies: Past, Present and Future* (Leeds: The Disability Press, 1997) at 76. Available at: <http://www.leeds.ac.uk/disability-studies/archiveuk/walmsley/chapter4.pdf>.

which discriminate against them be lifted. In the case of persons with intellectual disability, the barrier is legal and is based on autonomy. By denying that persons with intellectual disability have autonomy, the law is effectively placing them outside its scope. This means, on the one hand, that the social model of disability points to the right direction in relation to how things must change in respect of intellectual disability. However, further thinking is required to bring about these changes in a way that will lift the legal barriers which restrict persons with intellectual disability. The question here is how to interpret the law so that persons with disabilities may be transformed to become active bearers of human rights.

Chapter 2
A Principled Approach to Human Rights Issues Raised by Intellectual Disability

The Challenge Intellectual Disability Poses to Liberalism

A recent book examining the strained connection between liberalism and intellectual disability has provided a sound theoretical background for the questions the present volume tries to answer. *The Future of the Disabled in Liberal Society* by Reinders is a thoroughgoing argument on intellectual disability within the liberal framework.[1]

The starting point for Reinders' ethical analysis is the question of whether using genetic testing for reasons of preventing a disabled life implies a negative evaluation of the lives of handicapped people. As such, the aims and content of Reinders' analysis are very different from those of the present volume. Reinders provides an ethical argumentation in favour of valuing the lives of persons with intellectual disability and against genetic screening. Reinders' main claim is:[2]

> that people with mental disability and their families have reasons to be worried about their future in liberal society. The rapid proliferation of genetic testing may have discriminatory effects, because it brings the birth of disabled children within the focus of 'reproductive choice', which makes their parents answerable to the charges of 'irresponsible behavior'.

Instead, Reinders presents moral arguments and suggests ways to think about disabled lives primarily as possible sources of meaning, rather than as the cause of deficit, in an attempt to expand the scope of moral debate on genetics, so that persons with intellectual disability can be included as full members in the liberal community.

In contrast to Reinders' line of argumentation, the present volume focuses on issues which arise from the legal position of persons with intellectual disability as bearers of human rights within a liberal legal framework, such as that of the UK or Germany. Yet the backbone of Reinders' analysis of liberalism provides much of the thinking behind the argumentation that we will rely on, and as such, needs to be described briefly here.

---

1 H. Reinders, *The Future of the Disabled in Liberal Society: An Ethical Analysis* (Notre Dame, IN: University of Notre Dame Press, 2000).

2 Ibid. at x.

Reinders' book engages in a lengthy analysis of how questions concerning intellectual disability are being framed in liberal society. Reinders claims that the context of moral debate in liberal society is provided by the convictions and beliefs that enable its members to maintain that particular society, and names these convictions and beliefs as the liberal convention.[3] Reinders sets out five constituent elements of the liberal convention that have immediate bearing on his analysis.

First, the liberal convention includes the paramount moral value of free choice, which grants individuals the freedom to act according to their own preferences as long as they do not violate the equal freedom of others to do so as well.

Second, Reinders points out that once it is accepted that people have a right to choose for themselves the kind of life they prefer, the value of their lives cannot be measured by external standards. The life one leads is valuable by the mere fact that one is capable of valuing it at all.

Third, the liberal convention holds the belief that the status of persons is of primary moral concern. Persons are taken as moral agents, that is to say, as beings capable of choosing rationally and acting upon their preference. This does not mean that nonpersons fall outside the scope of liberal morality, but that they are only indirectly included in it – for example, infants, because they will potentially become persons.

Fourth, the liberal convention attributes high value to social and political equality. People ought to be treated equally according to their status as moral agents, which is further grounded in their capacity to decide for themselves how they should live. This capacity as the ground of equality rules out unequal treatment on the basis of characteristics such as religion, class, race or sex.

Lastly, the liberal convention entails the belief that public morality should not address the issue of the relative value of different conceptions of the good. The goal of the state is not to promote particular ends in life, but to secure equal opportunities for its citizens to realise their own ends under the rule of law.

This understanding of liberalism underpins many of the arguments the present volume is advancing. But a further important point in Reinders' reasoning is his analysis of the inclusion of persons with intellectual disability in liberalism.[4] How can one try to account for the inclusion of persons with intellectual disability in liberal society as a moral community? Reinders claims that the conception of the individual presupposed in liberal theory is based on capacities of human beings as moral agents – the powers of reason and free will. Discrimination is morally objectionable in liberal theory because it fails to give due respect to other persons. To discriminate against other persons is to ignore their capacity as human agents by treating them unequally on grounds of morally irrelevant characteristics, such as race, sex, religion or age.

However, since the characteristic of intellectual disability affects one's capacity for moral agency, this theory of discrimination appears to exclude persons with

3 Ibid. at 21.

4 Ibid. at 105.

intellectual disability from its protection. Reinders therefore concludes that liberal morality does not have much strength, if any, to generate moral arguments for the protection of people who do not possess the powers of reason and free will.

Even though Reinders' ethical arguments are convincing in the context of liberal morality, the present volume looks into the legal framework supporting liberalism, to make a contrary claim: that an interpretation of a liberal legal system, based on human rights, can be found to include persons with intellectual disability on a par with the rest of the social community. In order to understand how such an interpretation is possible, a brief presentation of socio-political attitudes towards intellectual disability is required. We will present how liberal societies, such as the UK, have responded to intellectual disability, so as to re-interpret these responses in the best possible light.

The Link between Intellectual Disability and Autonomy

So far, the Introduction has roughly sketched what intellectual disability is and why it sits uneasily within the liberal framework. In spite of these difficulties, liberal societies provide care to persons with intellectual disability, and we have briefly described how this is achieved. It is now time to provide a rough outline of how we will interpret and make sense of these facts.

A good way of introducing this analysis is to distinguish the case of intellectual disability from that of physical disability. Most commonly, physically disabled persons are faced with external, physical barriers, which make it difficult for them to have full mobility and control over their lives. In certain instances, the effect of these barriers may exclude the person from social life, to such a degree that she may not be able to lead a fulfilling life. State action can therefore be required to remove these barriers.

On the contrary, a person with intellectual disability is not faced with extraneous, physical impediments which interfere with controlling her own life. In lay terms, the psychological definition of intellectual disability is low IQ, combined with limitations in adaptive skills. In legal terms, intellectual disability translates into three typologies: limited, impaired or no autonomy.

A person with intellectual disability can have *limited autonomy* if she retains autonomy for some actions, but not others – for example, she may be able to buy things from stores, because she knows how to count money, but may not understand what complicated medical surgery entails. *Impaired autonomy* here designates persons with intellectual disability with fluctuating capacity; persons with borderline intellectual disability would be an example of this. Finally, the typology of *no autonomy* describes situations such as persons with severe intellectual disability who have no ability to communicate.

In all these categories, the intellectual disability of the person may impede her from making decisions, either simple or complicated, and may even exclude her from a fulfilling life. In this sense, the question emerges of what is required to allow the person to flourish as an individual, and secure more choice and protection for her. If the person's disability consists of limited, impaired or no autonomy, and autonomy is a prerequisite for effective participation in social and professional life, it follows that the missing autonomy of the person must be upheld or fostered by state action in order for the person to be able to exercise choice.

Upholding autonomy means that the state is under a legal duty to re-create or supplement the autonomy of a person with intellectual disability in those areas where she is non-autonomous.[5] The classic example, common in civil law countries, is the legal representative, or tutor of incapacitated persons, who looks after the legal affairs of the person and represents her in legal transactions. In this way, the autonomy of the person with intellectual disability is exercised by proxy, and her voice and interests remain audible in the legal world. Rather more informally, within the context of social services provision, the advocate fulfils precisely the same role. In this line of reasoning, advocacy is not simply a social welfare service, but rather becomes an essential means for upholding the autonomy of the person with intellectual disability. Subsequently, the importance of advocacy cannot be underestimated.

Fostering autonomy, on the other hand, is a distinct issue. Having an advocate or legal representative consulting the person with intellectual disability and looking after her interests and affairs goes a long way in providing more choice and protection for her. Yet autonomy is also very much about self-determination, empowerment and individual freedom, and these are also the claims of persons with intellectual disability, who want to assume more control over their lives through self-advocacy.

Therefore, merely upholding the autonomy of persons with intellectual disability via the provision of legal representatives or advocates defeats the purpose of providing them with more choice and freedom. It follows that the state is under a legal duty to provide support to persons with intellectual disability so that they can acquire more self-determination, to the extent that their disability allows.

Physically disabled persons require the removal of physical, architectural barriers,[6] or a high level of medical care,[7] in order to make the most of their lives; persons with intellectual disability require proper education, vocational and skills training, networks of advocacy, psychological support and care so as to do exactly the same.

This line of argumentation provides the basic material which occupies much of the present volume. For now, it is important to keep in mind the claim of this

5 This point has not been lost in German academic literature relating to the system of carership of incapacitated persons under German law (Betreuungsrecht). See V. Lipp, *Freiheit und Fürsorge: Der Mensch als Rechtsperson* (Tübingen: Mohr Siebeck, 2000) at 118.

6 As in *Botta* v. *Italy*, 24 February 1998, *Reports of Judgments and Decisions* 1998-I 412.

7 As in *Sentges* v. *The Netherlands*, 8 July 2003, [2004] CCL Rep. 400.

initial analysis: persons with intellectual disability, despite being almost out of place in theories of liberalism, present liberal societies with a claim for support, so that their limited or missing autonomy is upheld and fostered. To the extent that liberal societies provide that support, persons with intellectual disability become equals with the rest of the social community. Advocacy and self-advocacy are two important ways in which liberalism can respond to the challenges of intellectual disability.

Presenting the Broader Theoretical Issue of this Volume: The Quest for a Theory of Liberal Equality to Squarely Accommodate Persons with Intellectual Disability

The initial claim of the Introduction has been that persons with intellectual disability present liberal societies with a claim for support so as to have their autonomy upheld and fostered. Persons with intellectual disability lack autonomy, to varying degrees. This value, which is one of the cornerstones of liberalism, is, however, enjoyed by all other members of society. Yet by providing proper support to persons with intellectual disability, liberal societies can achieve equality in that respect.

Such a broad-brush claim begs the question why liberal societies would want to achieve equality in relation to the value of autonomy enjoyed by the members of the social community. As Reinders has pointed out in his analysis of the matter, persons with intellectual disability do not possess the powers of reason and free will; they are out of line with conventional liberal morality. Should liberal societies support these persons?

Even though there are many different ways in which this question can be answered, we have chosen as a starting point the elements of ethical individualism developed by Ronald Dworkin, which can be modified to accommodate the differences of persons with intellectual disability in a satisfactory way.[8]

In *Sovereign Virtue*, Dworkin expounds his theory of equality. Dworkin is aware of the weaknesses of classical theories of liberal equality, and therefore seeks to find the most basic common denominator which renders members of society equal. In accordance with liberal ideals, he claims that from an objective point of view, it is important that human lives are not wasted, but rather, that they are a success. The capabilities and talents of each person should be allowed and helped to flourish, thus contributing to social progress. This is the principle of equal importance.

On the other hand, Dworkin accepts that, to a great extent, whether a human life will be a success and will not be wasted also depends on the will of the person to strive for her improvement. The person should make the most of her life, but

8 R. Dworkin, *Sovereign Virtue: The Theory and Practice of Equality* (Cambridge, MA: Harvard University Press, 2000) at 448–9.

in accordance to liberal ideals, cannot be forced to do so. This is the principle of special responsibility. We will argue that the two elements of ethical individualism that Dworkin's egalitarianism advances – the principle of equal importance and the principle of special responsibility – can be adapted accordingly to suit persons with intellectual disability.

Persons with intellectual disability are usually vulnerable, lacking in adaptive skills and intelligence; to a greater or lesser extent, they lack autonomy. In accordance with the principle of equal importance, for their lives to be a success and not to be wasted, persons with intellectual disability should be provided with appropriate support so that whatever autonomy they may exercise is upheld and fostered by society.

However, since persons with intellectual disability may, to some extent, lack autonomy, they cannot be held totally accountable under the principle of special responsibility. This does not mean that Dworkin's theory of equality excludes persons with intellectual disability from its ambit. Rather, it must be accepted that to the extent that an person with intellectual disability lacks autonomy, the special responsibility for her life to be a success falls back on society; liberal society must, in these instances, steer the potential of the person with intellectual disability in socially meaningful ways, while focusing upon the specificity and individuality of the person with intellectual disability.

With these minor adaptations of Dworkin's ethical individualism, persons with intellectual disability can be included as equals in liberal society; and their being equal theoretically justifies the provision of support that they need in order to acquire more self-determination and autonomy.

This claim then leads to the question of how liberal societies can find meaningful ways to foster the potential of persons with intellectual disability. How can arbitrariness and abuse be avoided? Since this is a legal work, these questions translate legally as the interpretive question noted at the beginning of this chapter: what does it mean for persons with intellectual disability to hold human rights at law in liberal society?

We will try to answer this question based on the principle of human dignity. In this sense, it is perhaps time to examine some of the aspects of the principle, so as to understand the meaning and use of human dignity in the text.

How Should the Autonomy of Persons with Intellectual Disability be Fostered? The Normative Content of Human Dignity in this Volume

In order to analyse the connection between liberalism and intellectual disability, one inevitably has to use concepts which are not based on autonomy, or liberal individualism, as is traditionally understood. Persons with intellectual disability and the disability rights movement have a claim to acquire more freedom, to have their wishes, their needs heard, and not remain passive recipients of social welfare.

Such a claim can best be understood in terms of a human rights analysis. Legal systems which support frameworks of human rights must accommodate the different needs of persons with intellectual disability by interpreting their human rights in ways which take into account their differences and their vulnerability. We will claim that this interpretation can best be achieved by using the principle of human dignity.

In a nutshell, human dignity focuses upon the person with intellectual disability in a holistic way. It takes into account her needs, her wishes, her potential and her deficiencies to propose ways in which the person can be enabled to exercise her human rights to acquire more freedom. The normative content of human dignity in this volume is to enable the person with intellectual disability to achieve greater freedom, which must be legally protected.

A good way of illustrating this point is to take a brief comparative look at the different interpretations of the principle of human dignity in two civil law countries, Germany and France.

Human Dignity in the German Legal Order: Introductory Remarks

The protection of human dignity by the German legal system is solemnly declared in the first article of the Basic Law, as a direct reaction to the atrocities committed by Nazi Germany. As Article 1 of the Basic Law gives no definition of the principle, German constitutional theory has developed its own theories of human dignity. One of the most important of these is the theory developed by Luhmann.[9] Luhmann regards human dignity as an achievement. Human beings have dignity because they accept different roles within society. Persons thus integrate into society by virtue of their efforts in these roles and develop their personality. By virtue of this fact, any state action that hinders the evolution of the individual's personality is a violation of the person's human dignity.

This theory has been justly criticised by other German constitutional scholars, as it leaves persons with limited or no ability to develop their personality outside the scope of human dignity. Other theories of human dignity take this point into account. Hofmann, in his inaugural lecture as professor at the Humboldt University of Berlin, voiced his own thoughts about human dignity.[10] His perception of human dignity is a communicative one. Persons have human dignity by reason of their membership in society. In this sense, their achievements or their integration are insignificant. What must be protected by this human dignity is their potential to take part in social development.

In the specific context of mental illness, another concept of human dignity was expounded in an important article by Neumann.[11] Neumann draws elements

9 B. Pieroth and B. Schlink, *Grundrechte Staatsrecht II*, 16th ed. (Heidelberg: C.F. Müller, 2000) at 80.

10 H. Hofmann, 'Die versprochene Menschenwürde' [1993] AöR 353.

11 V. Neumann, 'Menschenwürde und psychische Krankheit' [1993] Krit. Vjschr. 276.

from Luhmann's theory and combines them with the Kantian concept of human dignity. In this sense, human dignity is still regarded as an achievement. Protection of human dignity means that the state cannot obstruct the conditions necessary to this achievement. But contrary to Luhmann, Neumann stresses that persons that do not have the ability to develop their personality still have human dignity. They belong to the human race, which in the idealist conception of Kant's theory has dignity by virtue of its humanity. In this sense, protection of a mentally ill person's dignity is protection of the person's quality as a subject of law and protection of the person's individuality.

In the German legal system, human dignity plays the same enabling role which is ascribed to the principle in this volume. Human dignity is about developing one's personality, having one's individuality protected, and being able to participate in society. We will expand on these views to provide legal arguments that persons with intellectual disability must also be provided with adequate support to achieve these aims, given their vulnerability and limited skills.

Human Dignity in the French Legal Order: A Brief Analysis

In stark contrast to this enabling function of human dignity, French law has come to a diametrically opposite conclusion as to what human dignity means. The principle is quite new in the French legal order, having acquired prominence from 1994 onwards. At that time, preparatory works and voting on French laws on bioethics were under way, and Parliament felt that there were no constitutional guidelines as to how these laws should be drafted.[12] This is the reason why the President of the National Assembly deferred the matter to the Conseil Constitutionnel, asking that jurisdiction to pronounce on the constitutionality of the proposed laws and on the constitutional principles that should be applied in their case.

In its decision 94-343/344 DC,[13] the Conseil Constitutionnel effectively rewrote the Preamble to the French Constitution of 1946 and anchored human dignity as a constitutional principle in this new interpretation of the Preamble, deciding that the protection of human dignity against any form of slavery or degradation is a constitutional principle.

Following this case, many new French laws incorporated explicit references to human dignity in relevant subject matter.[14] What is perhaps more important is the way the principle of human dignity was applied by other French courts. The best-known of these cases are two judgments of the Conseil d'Etat, known

12 B. Mathieu, 'La dignité de la personne humaine: quel droit? Quel titulaire?' [1996] D. 282.

13 Cons. Constitutionnel, 27 juillet 1994, Rec. 1994.100, 94-343/344 DC.

14 For instance, in medical law, *loi n° 2002-303 du 4 mars 2002*, JO, 5 March 2002, 4118, introduces in Article 1110-2 the principle that: 'the patient has the right to respect of her dignity'. See generally P. Jourdain et al., *Le nouveau droit des malades* (Paris: Litec, 2002) at 38.

as the 'dwarf-throwing cases', Commune de Morsang-sur-Orge and Ville d'Aix-en-Provence.[15]

In these cases, the court examined the legality of the decisions of the mayors of Morsang-sur-Orge and Aix-en-Provence to ban dwarf-throwing competitions. The mayors, acting in their capacity as general police, prohibited spectacles of dwarf-throwing, which consisted of inviting spectators to throw a dwarf wearing protective clothing as far as possible on a protective floor covering.[16]

In its judgment, the Conseil d'Etat integrated human dignity in the French public order by examining the nature of these dwarf-throwing events. The court followed closely the opinion of the public prosecutor, who stressed that throwing a physically handicapped person in a contest diminishes the person to an object. The dwarf, by accepting being thrown away, becomes, in the eyes of the law, an object of sport. This is contrary to the public order, and this is why the dwarf's consent is irrelevant. The court effectively used human dignity as a constraint on the person's autonomy. By doing so, the court imposed a certain objective human dignity on the subjective and autonomous choice of the dwarf.

The French interpretation of human dignity, as an element of public order restraining individual freedom, however valid, sits uneasily within the context of the present volume. In the following analysis, arguments relating to the human dignity of persons with intellectual disability are designed to provide these persons with more freedom and equality.

The Principle of Human Dignity: Philosophical Intricacy and Legal Simplification?

So far, this chapter has shown that intellectual disability poses distinct forms of challenges to the traditional understanding of liberalism, which is based on autonomy and consent. Seen from the viewpoint of social approaches to disability, this traditional understanding of liberalism erects an almost insurmountable legal barrier. This barrier excludes persons with intellectual disability from the full enjoyment of their human rights.

For this reason, we will advance a different understanding of liberalism, which includes human dignity as an interpretive principle of the law. This section analyses the principle in some detail. The analysis begins by briefly describing the historical evolution of the principle. It becomes evident that the elaborate theorising of human dignity in philosophical theories over the centuries is fairly absent from

15 Cons. d'Etat, 27 October 1995, *Commune de Morsang-sur-Orge*, Rec. 1995.372 and Cons. d'Etat, 27 October 1995, *Ville d'Aix-en-Provence*, D. 1996.177 (Annot. G. Lebreton). For a brief commentary, see also S. Millns, 'Dwarf-throwing and Human Dignity: A French perspective' [1996] *JSWFL* 375.

16 M.-L. Pavia, 'La découverte de la dignité de la personne humaine' in M.-L. Pavia and T. Revet, eds, *La dignité de la personne humaine* (Paris: Economica, 1999) at 13.

contemporary legal thinking relating to the principle. Especially in the area of human rights, even though human dignity is presented as the normative foundation of these rights, no explicit references are made to its substantive content.

The Philosophical and Religious Development of the Principle

> In ancient times, the term dignity usually referred to respect for individuals with high social status; it was a dignity of rank. In other instances however, dignity was used to describe man in contrast to animals. Plato writes that, according to the sophist Protagoras, the essential quality of all men was based on decency and law. These were the gifts bestowed by Zeus to everyone. By virtue of these divine gifts and the relationship between the Gods and men, all men were of the same kind and differed from the animals.[17]

It was the Stoics who first coined the term 'human dignity'. It was formulated during the second and first centuries BC by Panaetius of Rhodes and Cicero in Rome, but did not become a universal term among other Stoic philosophers. The original Latin term *dignitas hominis* denotes worthiness, the external aspect of a person's social role that requires respect and embodies the charisma and the esteem presiding in office, rank or personality. It is concrete dignity inherent in the rational persona, given by nature to all human beings.[18] For the Stoics, human dignity was an inherent part of their philosophy:

> Typical of Stoic philosophy was the thought that the whole cosmos is penetrated by the reason and rationality of God, the *logos*. Nothing in the world is categorically alien to the rest of the world. Everything is interconnected with all the rest and it is steered and interpenetrated by the *logos*: nature, human beings, social communities and even God. The ethical task is to recognise the laws of *psysis* in all the realms that constitute the world and to adapt themselves to them since they represent the unchangeable will of the godhead.[19]

The dignity of man is thus based on his reason, his self-control, and his rule over beasts and the world. The word *dignitas* calls to mind the majesty of the Republic and the magistrate of the Caesar. It denotes rank, authority and splendour.[20] Man has such splendour because he has both reason and the capacity for free moral decision-making.

---

17 J. Eckert, 'Legal Roots of Human dignity in German Law' in D. Kretzmer and E. Klein, eds, *The Concept of Human Dignity in Human Rights Discourse* (The Hague: Kluwer Law International, 2002) at 43.

18 H. Cancik, 'Dignity of Man and Persona in Stoic Anthropology: Some Remarks on Cicero, De officiis I 105-107', in ibid. at 19.

19 Ibid.

20 Ibid. at 27.

In their typology, the ideas of the Stoics form a type of human dignity based on the special physical characteristics of man. The Stoic conception of dignity is based on capacity. The capacity to think and act according to the *logos* is the foundation of human dignity. It consequently follows that if a human being does not – that is, cannot – reason and act in accordance with the *logos*, then that person has no dignity.

Christianity picked up on this meaning and interpreted the dignity of all human beings theologically: man assumes a special position in the divine order of creation, because man is made in the image of God and has an immortal soul.[21] The first consequence of the image of God in human beings justifies a clear species distinction between human beings and the animal kingdom.[22] Man and woman are placed at the pinnacle of creation.

The other consequence of the idea of man as an image of God refers to the inherent quality and dignity of human beings in themselves:

> Whatever else it may mean to say the human person is in the image of God, it must mean, as Eastern Orthodoxy has insisted, that the human person, like the Deity, is in some sense a mystery … When we meet another person, however poor, lowly, diseased or dumb, we stand before something which holds the divine.[23] To be in the image of God then, is not primarily a matter of our capacity to do anything. It is a matter of the relationship to himself which God confers on us … The image of God is not a capacity we possess or lose, but rather a part of our essence. Thus essence as being's God's image, not capacity, is what gives a human being species membership and the right to life protection by the community.[24] Of course we can, and do, treat other people like 'its', as mere objects, but always to the loss of our humanity. We do this in pornography, in harmful experiments on unwitting human victims, in indiscriminate killing in war … Without God and without the sanctity of the person made in the image of God, women and men will become not gods, but mere objects to manipulate in a world of manipulable objects …[25]

In their typology, these theological interpretations form the type of human dignity based on the special place of man in divine creation. The theological idea of

21 K. Bayertz, 'Die Idee der Menschenwürde: Probleme und Paradoxien' [1995] ARSP 465.

22 S. Rae and P. Cox, *Bioethics: A Christian Approach in a Pluralistic Age* (Grand Rapids, MI: W.B. Eerdmans, 1996) at 130.

23 J. Soskice, 'Creation and Relation' in K. Fulford, G. Gillett and J. Soskice, *Medicine and Moral Reasoning* (Cambridge: Cambridge University Press, 1994) at 25.

24 S. Rae and P. Cox, *Bioethics: A Christian Approach in a Pluralistic Age* (Grand Rapids, MI: W.B. Eerdmans, 1996) at 132.

25 J. Soskice, 'Creation and Relation' in K. Fulford, G. Gillett and J. Soskice, *Medicine and Moral Reasoning* (Cambridge: Cambridge University Press, 1994) at 26.

human dignity is not based on capacity, but on the factual prerequisite of being born human. In this sense, the anthropocentrism of the Bible is less demanding or discriminating: the importance of being born human is paramount to any other consideration.

The renaissance thinkers build on these older concepts, but place them in a fundamentally different context. The following eloquent passage from Gibson's monograph on Hieronymus Bosch summarises the different intellectual trends in early Renaissance thought:

> In his *Oration on the Dignity of Man*, composed around 1486, the young Florentine humanist Pico della Mirandola celebrated the excellence and felicity of mankind. Man is unique among creatures in possessing a free will, the power to determine his nature and destiny; and through the proper exercise of this will he can attain the state of angels. 'For it is on this very account', exclaims Pico, 'that man is rightly called and judged a great miracle and a wonderful creature indeed.'
>
> Some eight years later, Sebastian Brant published the first edition of his *Ship of fools*, a series of poems satirising humanity's failings and foibles. 'The whole world lives in darksome night,' Brant complains, 'in blinded sinfulness persisting, while every street sees fools existing'. The difference between these two conceptions of man is vast but explicable. Pico reflects the optimistic faith of the Italian Renaissance in man's abilities. Brant, however, like many of his contemporaries in Northern Europe, still lived in the shadow of the Middle Ages, which took a much dimmer view of human nature: corrupted through the sin of Adam, man struggles weakly against his evil inclinations, more likely to sink to the level of the beasts than to rise with the angels.[26]

The Renaissance literature on dignity then, is a polemic against this medieval but still widely held view that life on earth is deplorable, or *miseria*, and that the Earth itself is a vale of tears.[27] On the contrary, the terrestrial life of human beings was recognised by these philosophers as valuable in itself. Humans have dignity not so much because they are created in the image of God, but because they are placed at the pinnacle of creation within the world. Christian anthropocentrism is upheld, but put to serve terrestrial aims. The concept of dignity is reshaped to give the human being a new self-awareness and confidence necessary in order to improve this world and the human fate.[28]

---

26 W. Gibson, *Hieronymus Bosch* (London: Thames and Hudson, 2000) at 33.

27 K. Bayertz, 'Die Idee der Menschenwürde: Probleme und Paradoxien' [1995] ARSP 465.

28 Ibid. at 466.

The thinkers following the Renaissance took up this concept of dignity that was necessary for scientific and artistic progress, but focused more and more on the elements of reason and the ability to think.

The evolution of thinking about human dignity as an element of the individual found its culminating point in the works of Kant. Kantian thought on dignity forms the basis of the concept of human dignity in modern times, which can be broken down to three constitutive elements.[29]

First, human beings have dignity because only they have self-consciousness and the ability to think. Human beings are conscious of their existence; and it is this characteristic mark that separates man from animal. Only man has the ability to observe nature and decode its secrets. Enlightenment philosophers conceived this process of scientific knowledge and subsequent control over nature as never-ending, so they conceived human rationality in the same terms.

The second constitutive element is the common belief that human beings were also different from the animals because humans did not have a fixed place within nature. Man was free to live where he chose, do as he chose and become what he chose. This concept parted company with older classical beliefs describing the place of man in nature as immutable and unchanging. The essence of being human was self-alteration. Coupled with the belief that human rationality, seen as scientific progress, was endless, the ability of human beings to change themselves was also conceived as never-ending. Thus, the perfectibility of human beings became another justification for their dignity and excellence.

Third, this notion of endless human perfectibility, unrestrained by any natural law conceptions, found its correlative in the rejection of older concepts about the teleology of nature. Nature was seen as something normatively neutral that had no goals or inherent value. Since nature was neutral, and man rational and able to perfect himself, man became the only source of normativity. Man, not nature, set the norms and values of human existence. It was especially Kant who stressed this: human autonomy, the ability to set and follow moral rules, became the foundation of human dignity.

Seen from this perspective, the modern concept of human dignity has undergone a drastic change. It is no longer linked with the idea of man as an image of God. Indeed, it is man that has become God through human dignity: man is capable of thinking rationally, of altering and mastering his existence, and more importantly, man can set his own moral rules and values freely. In this way, rational and autonomous persons possess human dignity.

The typology of Enlightenment and especially Kantian thought on human dignity forms the type of deontological human dignity. In Kantian thought, morality is conceived as the correlative of autonomy. Morality here means accepting and following the categorical imperative. The correlative of this morality is dignity. Since only human beings can abide by this morality, it follows that only humans have dignity. Kant's idealist concept of man as endowed with reason fails in the

29 Ibid.

empirical world. But for Kant, even human beings that do not – that is, cannot – perceive the categorical imperative have dignity, because they idealistically would be able to reason.

Through the appeal of Kantian thought, the principle of human dignity continued to play an important role in the philosophical tradition of Europe; yet it is only after World War II that a greater interest in the principle has been rekindled. This, in part, is due to the international legal reaction to the atrocities committed by Nazi Germany, and we will now turn to these legal developments.

The Legal Aspect of Human Dignity from the Aftermath of World War II Onwards: The Fountainhead of Human Rights in International Law

Recent scholarship has focused on how the idea of human dignity has played the role of a founding principle in some of the earliest declarations of liberalism and human rights.[30] Human dignity provided the normative and theoretical background against which these liberal documents were conceived. Thus, human dignity plays an important role in the interpretation of these declarations and fills gaps in their understanding.

But there is another way in which human dignity has had a greater impact in law, especially public international law and the law of human rights. In the aftermath of World War II, the first and most important documents of the new international legal order had recourse to the idea of human dignity. The UN Charter and the Universal Declaration of Human Rights (UDHR) mentioned it explicitly, only to be followed by numerous other international conventions or declarations and national constitutions.

The UN Charter is the product of public discussion, governmental planning and diplomatic exchange during the war. The Charter was created to have practical use and serve realistic aims. It is therefore not surprising that, unlike the Covenant of the League of Nations, the proposals for the Charter did not envisage a Preamble, although one was included on the insistence of Field Marshall Smuts.[31]

The reference to human dignity occurs in the second paragraph of the Preamble. Some of the national delegations in the San Francisco Conference advocated the insertion of a human rights charter in the Preamble. The idea was abandoned, but served as a precedent to the UDHR some years later. In this sense, the reference of the Preamble to 'the dignity and worth of human persons, [and] in the equal rights of men and women' is a reference to fundamental human rights that was used instead of a much wider elaboration of human rights. It can be considered as a mini-human rights charter, and has the same legal validity as the other deliberations

---

30 See M. Meyer and W. Parent, eds, *The Constitution of Rights: Human Dignity and American Values* (Ithaca, NY: Cornell University Press, 1992).

31 R. Wolfrum, 'Preamble' in B. Simma, ed., *The Charter of the UN: A Commentary*, vol. 1, 2nd ed. (Oxford: Oxford University Press, 2002) at 33.

of the Charter.[32] In practice, however, the impact of the Preamble upon UN organs' decisions has been minimal.[33]

The UDHR echoes the wording of the Preamble of the UN Charter, and can be seen as a careful elaboration of the mini-human rights charter of the Preamble. Human dignity crops up no less than five times in the context of the UDHR: twice in the Preamble, once in Article 1, and twice in the social and economic rights entrenched in Articles 22 and 23 para. 3.

The first three paragraphs of the Preamble focus on human rights and dignity and the consequences that violations of dignity and human rights have for the world. It is stressed that the 'recognition of the inherent dignity and of the equal and inalienable rights of all members of the human family is the foundation of freedom, justice and peace in the world'. The spirit and philosophy of the UDHR is focused on the individual, and on the rights necessary to the inherent dignity of the individual within society. It is not exclusive of one group or another, but aims at the protection of the human rights of every person.[34] The Preamble sets out the dignity and the equal rights of human beings as focal points. These requirements underline each article and each right in the UDHR, so that human dignity and equality can be regarded as the normative foundations of the Declaration.

Article 1 of the UDHR is the clearest expression of the importance human dignity acquired in the drafting of the Declaration. But it also provides a lucid example of how human dignity was conceived and interpreted within the context of the UDHR. First of all, the article refrains from any reference to religious or philosophical traditions. There is equally no reference to the concept of person, which would carry notions of natural law into the article. Instead, the neutral term 'human being' is preferred. Moreover, human dignity is emphatically joined to the notion of equality and freedom; Article 1 asserts that all human beings are born free and equal. Finally, the reason why human beings have dignity is implicitly founded in their reason and conscience.

In these terms, the Declaration's concept of human dignity through Article 1 is a deliberate attempt to break with the past and its bankrupt ideas:

> the Declaration is not based on a concept of man as a being that is able to produce culture by way of its technical reason, but rather refers to moral reasoning as establishing equality among human beings and thus giving the unity of mankind it ethical and moral meaning.[35]

---

32 Ibid. at 35.

33 Ibid. at 37.

34 J. Mårtenson, 'The Preamble' in A. Eide et al., eds, *The Universal Declaration of Human Rights: A Commentary* (Oslo: Scandinavian University Press, 1992) at 20.

35 K. Dicke, 'The Founding Function of Human Dignity in the Universal Declaration of Human Rights' in D. Kretzmer and E. Klein, eds, *The Concept of Human Dignity in Human Rights Discourse* (The Hague: Kluwer Law International, 2002) at 117.

But more importantly, the concept of human dignity in Article 1 of the UDHR provided the thin but crucially important normative basis on which representatives of several cultures could reach agreement.[36] It allowed a new beginning for universal human rights that was less metaphysical and more political than any of its predecessors. This political, contextual link between human dignity and human rights renders the latter sensitive to the plurality of political and cultural commitments in the modern world. Thus, it facilitates the process by which human rights can develop in the international context.

In recent years, interest in the idea of human dignity has been rekindled. For the most part, modern writers have recourse to either Kantian or theological interpretations of human dignity for their arguments.[37] But other writers, especially in bioethics and human rights, refer to human dignity in a more indiscriminate manner, without taking into account the distinctions drawn in the past. In most of these cases, the concept of human dignity applied is not clear enough.

Beyleveld and Brownsword portray the confusion about human dignity that reigns in the realm of bioethical discourse quite clearly.[38] For some, human dignity is seen as empowerment: it is the dignity inherent in all human beings that grants them autonomy, freedom of choice and absolute control over their life and body.

Others, however, rely on human dignity arguments in order to assert collective control over the exercise of individual autonomy. In this way, human dignity reframes in more radical terms the old debate of libertarianism versus communitarianism. But precisely because its ethical or normative content is either left unclear or placed on contingent facts, human dignity can be fashioned to support either side of the debate, leading the dialogue to a deadlock.

This description of human dignity as either empowerment or restraint ties in well with another description of human dignity undertaken by Feldman, in a rare discussion of human dignity in UK law.[39] Feldman points out that there are three different kinds of dignity, each pulling in a markedly different direction. There is the dignity of the individual, the collective or social dignity, which also accommodates the dignity of social sub-groups within a larger pluralist society, and then there is the human dignity of the species. Discussion on human dignity varies according to which kind of human dignity one is advocating.

---

36 T. Lindholm, 'Article 1' in A. Eide et al., eds, *The Universal Declaration of Human Rights: A Commentary* (Oslo: Scandinavian University Press, 1992) at 51.

37 See, for example, D. Beyleveld and R. Brownsword, *Human Dignity in Bioethics and Biolaw* (Oxford: Oxford University Press, 2001), for a Kantian-Gewirthian view on dignity, and K. Bayertz, ed., *Sanctity of Life and Human Dignity* (Dordrecht: Kluwer Academic, 1996), for mostly theological interpretations.

38 D. Beyleveld and R. Brownsword, *Human Dignity in Bioethics and Biolaw* (Oxford: Oxford University Press, 2001) at c. 1 and 2.

39 D. Feldman, 'Human Dignity as a Legal Value' [1999] Pub. L. 682 and [2000] Pub. L. 61.

In the context of the present volume, some of the references made to human dignity in contemporary case law acquire greater relevance. The Introduction mentioned the theory of promised human dignity, as developed by Hofmann.[40] Hofmann tries to found human dignity in the opposite direction to Kantian-deontological theories, which place paramount importance on the moral capacity of the individual. For Hofmann, an individual can have human dignity only within a political community that has been founded on the promise of a mutual recognition of the dignity of every individual within that political community.

The promise of the political community to recognise human dignity in every member of the community does not depend on a threshold of subjective capacities that the members must have. On the contrary, this political community acknowledges in everyone a more or less accomplished social partner, to whom the community grants the same human dignity as to everyone else. This attitude is again translated into a language of dignity. This time, however, it refers to the dignity of the political community itself. In other words, it would be undignified of a liberal political community to condition the intensity of its promise of human dignity on the subjective qualities of each member of the community.

Within the German constitutional framework outlined earlier in the discussion of German law, Hofmann offers a much more plausible and attractive foundation of human dignity, which is not based on some ideal moral capacity of the individual, but rather on a mutual promise of all the members of the German political community to protect and uphold human dignity, regardless of the subjective capacities of each member.

Ronald Dworkin has referred to the principle of human dignity, in the context of dementia. Dworkin's perception of human dignity will be analysed at length later in this chapter; what must be noted here is that, for Dworkin, the right to dignity is the right of everyone to be recognised by society as the bearer of critical interests – as a person whose life is intrinsically important to be allowed to flourish. Interestingly, Dworkin perceives dignity as having a social side as well: it would be undignified of a society to withhold the recognition of any of its members as a bearer of critical interests.[41]

The previous historical presentation of how the principle of human dignity has evolved in both philosophy and case law has shown the richness of concepts that the principle carries with it. However, it has also shown that, after World War II, human dignity has been used in an indiscriminate manner, which is more political and less philosophical, especially in the law of human rights. This poses problems in the interpretation of human rights in difficult cases, such as intellectual disability. In order to adequately protect the human rights of non-autonomous persons, a substantively rich reading of human dignity as the fountainhead of these rights

40 H. Hofmann, 'Die versprochene Menschenwürde' [1993] AöR 353.

41 R. Dworkin, *Life's Dominion: An Argument about Abortion and Euthanasia* (London: HarperCollins, 1993) at 233.

must guide the process. Yet very little guidance can be found in the law as to how human dignity is to be perceived.

This argument is also valid in relation to the ECHR. In Chapter 4, we will present the case law of the ECtHR with regard to disabled applicants. This analysis will show that the vagueness surrounding the normative content of human dignity has caused the ECtHR neither to apply the principle in a coherent way nor to adequately address violations of the human rights of intellectually disabled applicants.

Applying the Principle of Human Dignity in an Interpretive Way to the HRA 1998 to Legally Accommodate the Needs of Persons with Intellectual Disability in English Law

The previous sections of this chapter have given a short account of the principle of human dignity as a powerful idea which has been put to many uses at different times. Whereas the philosophical concept of human dignity has usually turned on man's free will and his ability to reason, the legal expression of human dignity has, as the normative ground of human rights, been more general; it encompasses all human beings, without making any distinction as to moral or other characteristics.

In Chapter 4, we will explore the importance of human dignity in relation to the ECHR and the ECtHR, arguing that the principle of human dignity forms an inherent, even though hidden, part of the ECHR. Given the fact that the principle of human dignity has not been given any substantive definition in the ECHR, we will claim that a coherent application of the principle requires the ECtHR to develop a theoretical framework of what human dignity is and how it is to be protected by the ECHR. The absence of such theoretical reasoning is why, we claim, the ECtHR has failed to address issues of disability and human rights protection in a satisfactory way.

What is more, the arguments that we have put forward in relation to the interpretation of human dignity as part of the ECHR apply with equal force to English law, since the ECHR was incorporated in English law by means of the HRA 1998. As such, the principle of human dignity also forms part of the interpretive concepts that the HRA 1998 has incorporated into English law. This section attempts to define how the human rights of persons with intellectual disability can be understood, or interpreted, in English law, in a way which respects their human dignity, and therefore accommodates their differences and needs.

The Legal Link between Human Dignity and Autonomy

It was noted in the Introduction that persons with intellectual disability are different from other members of society or the political community in liberal societies, in that they lack, to a greater or lesser degree, the individual characteristic on which liberalism is based – autonomy. Liberal theory presupposes that all members of society are autonomous. Liberalism protects, and places great emphasis on, the protection of autonomy, since it allows the individual to be responsible for making important choices about her life; to be true to her character, her convictions and beliefs, and act in accordance with these. Moreover, autonomy in liberalism is protected independently of the subjective fact of whether the individual is actually making these important choices out of personal conviction, a deeper sense of responsibility, or because of sheer impulse and irrationality.

Persons with intellectual disability, to the extent that their disability allows, may or may not have that sense of self. They may or may not feel they are acting out of conviction, or of a deeper sense of what their life plan is. In many instances, persons with intellectual disability may not have much control over their daily lives, as they may lack the skills for even simple, menial tasks.

In the Introduction, a distinction was drawn between several different typologies of intellectual disability.[42] A person with intellectual disability can have limited autonomy if she retains autonomy for some actions but not others – for instance, she may be able to find her way around a city but be unable to count money, so she cannot use public means of transportation. A person with intellectual disability may have impaired autonomy if she displays fluctuating capacity for decision-making; persons with borderline intellectual disability would be an example of this category. Finally, there are also persons with intellectual disability who cannot be considered to have any autonomy; this typology of no autonomy basically includes persons with congenital, severe intellectual disability who lack the ability to communicate. It is especially this third category of persons with intellectual disability that poses the greatest problems to liberal theory.

These typologies of intellectual disability show that the greater the extent of intellectual disability, the weaker the claim to autonomy is. In this sense, persons with intellectual disability are disadvantaged in relation to other members of society, in that they do not have the necessary skills to make important decisions which would define their own lives for themselves. To the extent that persons with intellectual disability have and communicate wishes, their decisions may even endanger their own safety or health. For instance, a person with intellectual disability may refuse to take medication for epileptic seizures, thus risking severe harm. These decisions may also be erratic, and in certain instances may stem from pathological reasons, such as phobias; in the above example, the person may be in mortal fear of doctors. Moreover, the lack of adaptive skills and intelligence that persons with intellectual disability usually display makes them vulnerable to abuse.

On the other hand, liberal societies and liberal legal systems such as English law naturally accord human rights to persons with intellectual disability. For the reasons described, persons with intellectual disability may only have a limited ability to make use of these rights, and may have a limited ability to protect, or have these rights protected. These does not mean that persons with intellectual disability are in fact waiving the protection or the exercise of their rights; their failure to make use of their human rights is due to their lack of autonomy, and is not a product of informed choice.

42 See p. 29.

This is where the principle of human dignity must apply, to cover both for this diminished autonomy and for the missing autonomous exercise or protection of human rights.

In the case of autonomous persons, human dignity accords human rights to the members of liberal political communities. Human rights in liberalism, in their basic, negative form, demarcate areas of freedom for the benefit of the individual. It is in these areas of freedom that the individual can make her own choices, fulfil her potential and develop her own personality, out of a deeper sense of her self, if she so chooses. As persons usually are autonomous, the state usually does not interfere with the exercise and protection of their rights.

In the case of persons with intellectual disability, the element of autonomy which is necessary for the effective use of human rights may be, to a greater or lesser extent, missing. To the extent that persons with intellectual disability do not have the capacity for autonomous agency and the ability for self-empowerment, the areas of liberty that the state is not supposed to interfere with remain sterile and unused. In these instances, human dignity is legally required to be applied in relation to human rights protection, so that human rights in the case of persons with intellectual disability can acquire legal and actual effectiveness. Otherwise, if persons with intellectual disability were left to their own devices in relation to the protection and use they make of their human rights, their rights would remain, to a greater or lesser degree, ineffective. On the contrary, however, this volume has supported the claim that persons with intellectual disability can, if they receive proper support, achieve this aim of self-empowerment and make more decisions for themselves, to the extent that their disability allows.

The legal framework of support to persons with intellectual disability which can be derived from the previous argumentation has already been alluded to in the Introduction.[43] The disability of persons with intellectual disability entails to some degree a certain loss of autonomy. For this reason, the basic concern inherent in such a legal framework of support is to ensure that the autonomy of the person with intellectual disability is upheld by the placement of a legal representative for the person. This legal representative may be empowered to make decisions on behalf of the person with intellectual disability and represent her in her legal affairs. In this sense, the missing autonomy of the person is being exercised by proxy.

However, this basic form of guardianship is not satisfactory any more, as the claims of the disability rights movement are gaining ground internationally. As Herr has succinctly written: ‘Guardianship intrudes on fundamental liberties and privacy rights, employs vague criteria, fails to tailor the scope of the guardian’s authority, denies procedural safeguards, and lacks adequate monitoring and review.’[44]

---

43 See p. 30–31.

44 S. Herr, ‘Self-determination, Autonomy, and Alternatives for Guardianship’ in S. Herr, L. Gostin and H. Koh, eds, *The Human Rights of Persons with Intellectual Disabilities* (Oxford: Oxford University Press, 2005) at 430.

Drawing elements from the earlier comparative analysis of English and German law, it becomes clear that this form of guardianship has to be replaced by a legal framework of both protection and support, which will be offered non-coercively and will be tailored to the needs of each person with intellectual disability.

In contrast to the way English law has conceptualised the application of the best interests test by virtually any person who has a duty of care towards the person with intellectual disability, the legal framework of support we are advancing recognises the importance of having one person appointed as the legal representative of the person with intellectual disability, with sharply demarcated powers of decision-making authority, whereas, under the current provisions of the Mental Capacity Act 2005, the number of court-appointed deputies is to be kept to a minimum. However, it is only under such conditions that the formation of a personal relationship between the person providing care and the person with intellectual disability may be enabled.

On the other hand, this volume goes beyond the requirement of German law that a personal relationship of care has to be formed between the person with intellectual disability and the carer. We will claim that the support and care the person with intellectual disability has to receive must also enable her, to the extent that her disability allows, to acquire more self-empowerment and enjoy more of her human rights. As Herr again forcefully puts forward: 'It is the task of humane twenty-first century societies to recognize that the capacities of persons with disabilities are not static, that they may learn and grow and, if offered support commensurate with their needs and aspirations, live autonomously.'[45] However, this is a claim whose content has not been fully explored in disability rights literature.

In this sense, the question that we now try to answer is how the provision of support to persons with intellectual disability should be conceptualised. As noted above, the legal framework advanced in this volume is based on the principle of human dignity. Within this proposed framework, the principle applies in two different ways.

First, human dignity has an enabling function: it provides a sound legal basis for guardianship regimes or similar legal institutions of support. Since guardianship helps persons with intellectual disability to exercise their autonomy by proxy, they thus become equal to autonomous members of the social or political community. It must be noted that, to the extent that human dignity is used to cover for the missing autonomy of persons with intellectual disability and justify the provision of support so that these persons may have their autonomy upheld, the principle of human dignity does not have a specific moral orientation or content.

Second, human dignity also guides the actual provision of support to persons with intellectual disability, so that they may have their lacking or missing autonomy protected and fostered. The principle is here used to propose ways in which the autonomy of persons with intellectual disability may best be fostered and also

45 Ibid. at 430–31.

explain how this support can best be given. For this reason, a substantively rich concept of human dignity is required in order to trigger an interpretive process as to how persons with intellectual disability can be supported.

As the historical presentation of the principle of human dignity in the previous section has shown, it is conceivable to conceptualise human dignity as a moral benchmark, with specific normative content. This benchmark may be philosophical, such as the Kantian formula not to treat persons as a means to end, but rather as an end in themselves; it may also have legal content, as the French dwarf-throwing judgments have clearly shown.[46] In those cases, it was decided that a dwarf, by agreeing to be tossed about by other people in contest, becomes an object of sport. This was held to be contrary to human dignity, and by implication, to French public order.

The next section seeks to give an account of how human dignity can guide the provision of support to persons with intellectual disability, so that they can acquire greater self-empowerment.

In a nutshell, this section began with the claim that the principle of human dignity in human rights law gives effect to human rights. As far as autonomous persons are concerned, human dignity accords these areas of liberty. Liberal legal systems protecting human rights then allow autonomous individuals to make use, or not make use, of these freedoms. To the extent that persons with intellectual disability do not have autonomy and thereby lack the ability to benefit from their rights, human dignity extends its normative scope, to the effect that persons with intellectual disability are provided with adequate support so that they can be helped to make use of their rights, and thereby flourish, in the way that liberalism allows other, autonomous, members to do. The next section investigates the substantive content of the principle of human dignity, which points to how this support can best be provided to persons with intellectual disability.

Human Dignity, Human Rights, Intellectual Disability and Autonomy

In relation to human rights, the principle of human dignity is the normative reason why people are accorded these rights. We have claimed that the simple fact of according human rights to non-autonomous persons, or persons with problematic autonomy, amounts to mere lip-service to human rights, and the principle of human dignity behind them, unless proper support is given to persons with intellectual disability so that they can make use of these rights. However, human dignity as securing the effectiveness of human rights is only part of how the issue must be conceptualised.

In order to understand this other side of human dignity as guiding the provision of support to persons with intellectual disability to have their autonomy fostered and supported in order for their human rights to become effective, we must turn to important aspects of how human dignity has been conceptualised in academic writing.

46 See p. 35.

Even though Dworkin's *Life's Dominion* relates to a very different set of problems from those we analyse, some points of Dworkin's thought, especially his reference to dignity, are crucial to this section. In the last chapter of *Life's Dominion*, Dworkin examines issues relating to life past reason.[47] He takes the example of Margo, a demented elderly woman who had in her past life been an autonomous person. With the onset of dementia, Margo lost the ability to make decisions for herself. She could neither relate to her past nor accumulate new memories, yet she was apparently very happy being cared for in her apartment.

Dworkin accepts that demented persons are not autonomous. He argues that to the extent that the choices and wishes of demented persons do not reflect a coherent sense of self and do not set out even short term-aims, recognising a right to autonomous action for them would be pointless.[48] On the other hand, Dworkin claims that demented persons entrusted to the care of others have a right to beneficence – the right that the carer will make decisions on behalf of the demented person which will serve her best interests.[49]

For Dworkin, demented persons have both experiential and critical interests. Demented persons naturally have experiential interests, as they are sensate human beings. And even though they cannot voice an opinion as to their critical interests, they none the less hold such interests, as they retained autonomy before becoming demented. Their previous autonomous choices, and the way that they had set up their life plan according to their individual personality, continue to influence their lives after the onset of dementia, and define how their critical interests may be conceived. According to Dworkin, 'a person who has become demented retains his critical interests because what happens to him then affects the value or success of his life as a whole.'[50]

Dworkin strengthens his argument by making a reference to human dignity. He conceives the principle in the sense that 'people have a right not to suffer *indignity*, not to be treated in ways that in their culture or community are understood as showing disrespect'.[51] He then argues that the greatest indignity for an individual is not to have her critical interests acknowledged by society; this also causes indignity to the same society which denies critical interests to its members. Dworkin concludes that since demented persons retain critical interests after the onset of dementia, they also have a right to dignity.

The analytical distinctions made in this presentation of dementia by Dworkin pave the way for a modified argument in the case of persons with intellectual disability. The claim of the previous section has been that human dignity dictates that proper support must be given to persons with intellectual disability so that

47 R. Dworkin, *Life's Dominion: An Argument about Abortion and Euthanasia* (London: HarperCollins, 1993) at 218–41.

48 Ibid. at 225.

49 Ibid. at 229.

50 Ibid. at 237.

51 Ibid. at 233.

they can get the most of the human rights accorded to every individual in society. The question is how this support is to be provided while respecting their dignity and rights.

The analysis of human dignity as the right not to suffer indignity brings the focus of attention to the distinction that Dworkin draws between experiential and critical interests.[52] Experiential interests are easy to grasp. They relate to the feeling of well-being of each person and secure her existence – for instance, the interest not to feel pain or be a victim of abuse. However, critical interests are much deeper. They relate to the worth of each individual life, and secure that every life has equal worth. Critical interests are the parameters that each person sets out according to which her life can be a success. Moreover, to the extent that a liberal political community protects the critical interests of each member of that society, equal worth and importance is accorded to each individual life.

In relation to autonomous persons, these critical interests are defined by the autonomous action of each individual, according to the liberal standard that each individual is free to make her own choices and decide for herself what is important in her life. But what happens in the case of persons with intellectual disability, where that autonomy may be contested or even missing? Persons with intellectual disability do not only have experiential interests, but critical interests as well, even though their lack of autonomy may be so great that they may not be aware of their critical interests. These critical interests may be defined by previous autonomous choices that the person has made – for instance, an autonomous person may have had a road accident, and her severe head injuries may have caused her to become intellectually disabled. The previous life of that person, as an autonomous individual, can indicate with sufficient accuracy how the critical interests of that person may be perceived even though the person is now non-autonomous.

In the case of persons with congenital intellectual disability, defining their critical interests becomes a matter of interpretation. Persons with intellectual disability may or may not lack to a certain degree an acute sense of the self. On the other hand, they may have preferences and wishes, and sometimes very strong ones, about what they wish to do with their lives. To the extent that these persons with intellectual disability have wishes and are able to communicate these wishes, these have to be taken into account when the critical interests of the person are defined. In the case of intellectual disability, critical interests are something that have to emerge interpretively by assessing the person holistically, taking into account firm or erratic wishes, healthy or unhealthy preferences, fears, needs, developmental possibilities, special skills and talents, in order to allow the individual characteristics of the person to shine through. The aim is to shape

52 See also R. Dworkin, *Sovereign Virtue: The Theory and Practice of Equality* (Cambridge, MA: Harvard University Press, 2000) at 242, about volitional and critical interests. Volitional interests are being satisfied when the person achieves what she in fact wants; critical interests consist of having or achieving what makes a person's life a better life to have or achieve.

these critical interests based on the individual characteristics of the person with intellectual disability in a coherent way so that the person can enjoy more self-empowerment, achieve greater control over her life, and exercise her human rights more fully. This aim goes beyond the right to beneficence, as Dworkin perceives it, which only serves to protect the best interests of the person.

An example illustrating this point would be the hypothetical life of Margaret. She is 20 years old, she is moderately intellectually disabled, and has finished attending a special school for persons with intellectual disability. She lives in a care home in the community, but is not pleased with her housing and she is bored staying there. She is good with numbers and can read. A job at the till of an office canteen would suit her perfectly. Since she is good with numbers, there is no reason not to pay her salary to her directly while providing her with counselling as to how to organise her finances. Then Margaret could be helped to find a place of her own where she would feel happy. At the same time, it is known that she has a family history of heart problems. For this reason, even though she is not a physical person, she is taken to the community swimming pool to have a swim twice a week together with other persons with intellectual disability whose company she enjoys.

This example shows how framing the critical interests of a person with intellectual disability as respecting their human dignity and rights is different from the utilitarian calculations made in the context of the common law best interests, where everything is reduced to a problem-solving exercise when and if problems arise:

> The best interest principle instructs us to determine the net benefit for the patient of each option, assigning different weights to the options to reflect the relative importance of the various interests they further or thwart, then subtracting costs or 'disbenefits' from the benefits for each option. The course of action to be followed, then, is the one with the greatest net benefit to the patient. The mere fact that a treatment would benefit the patient is not sufficient to show that it would be in the individual's best interests, since other options may have greater net benefits, or the costs of the option to the patient – in suffering and disability – may exceed the benefit.[53]

In relation to demented persons, Dworkin eloquently points out that 'Value cannot be poured into a life from the outside; it must be generated by the person whose life it is ...'[54] To the extent that a person with intellectual disability has individual characteristics, the value of her life can only be realised fully when her critical

53 A. Buchanan and D. Brock, *Deciding for Others: The Ethics of Surrogate Decision-making* (Cambridge: Cambridge University Press, 1989) at 123.

54 R. Dworkin, *Sovereign Virtue: The Theory and Practice of Equality* (Cambridge, MA: Harvard University Press, 2000) at 230.

interests are shaped by a coherent interpretation of those characteristics, since she cannot set out these critical interests for herself in full.

Moreover, Dworkin's analysis of experiential and critical interests in relation to human dignity as the right not to suffer indignity also points to the fact that it would cause persons with intellectual disability great indignity not to recognise that these persons have critical as well as experiential interests. Given the previous argument, it becomes clear that the lives of persons with intellectual disability have equal worth in liberal society, and that it is objectively important that these lives will be a success, that they will be allowed to flourish, to the extent that their disability allows, rather than be wasted. Human dignity requires that liberal political communities acknowledge the existence of critical interests in relation to persons with intellectual disability, and that these are interpretively defined in a way which takes into account their lives as a whole.

In this sense, the analysis of Dworkin at this point strengthens the claim in the previous section, as it would also cause the liberal political community great indignity to fail to provide persons with intellectual disability with effective human rights whose protection is guaranteed to other, autonomous, members of society. It causes indignity to liberal societies that persons with intellectual disability can easily become victims of abuse and may not have the ability to protect themselves legally against their abusers. For this reason, liberal political communities must also provide support to persons with intellectual disability to help them make the most of human rights which are guaranteed to everyone, without exception.

A Theory of Liberal Equality Accommodating the Difference of Intellectual Disability

The previous section made the claim that persons with intellectual disability who are in the care of other persons and are not autonomous do not just have a right to beneficence, but a right to dignity as well. Legally speaking, the principle of human dignity as the normative reason why they are accorded human rights also requires that persons with intellectual disability are provided with support so that they can enjoy these human rights more fully.

Using the Dworkinian concepts of experiential and critical interests, we have refined how this support must be given and what its content is: assessing the individual as a whole, and making a coherent interpretation of what her critical interests are, based on her individual characteristics, so that proper support can be given to allow her to enjoy as much of her human rights as possible. This support flows from the right of persons with intellectual disability to dignity, rather than their right to beneficence.

The disability rights movement quite rightly presents the lives of persons with intellectual disability as meaningful and worth living, and in this sense, we have been reformulating the claims of the disability rights movement and of persons with intellectual disability for more freedom and self-empowerment, in an interpretive framework based on the legal validity of human rights.

However, the interpretation of human dignity and human rights which we have proposed so far has been based on the individual characteristics of the person with intellectual disability. As was noted in a previous section, the features of intellectual disability that each person may display can vary greatly. In some cases of persons with profound and multiple congenital disabilities, the task of unearthing their individual characteristics may be almost impossible, as they may be unable to communicate. The example of the applicant in the case of *HL* v. *UK* is instructive.[55] HL was autistic, was unable to communicate, and was usually passive in relation to the care or treatment he received. Can it be said that such a person holds critical interests? How are the dignity and human rights of persons so profoundly disabled to be understood?

In order to answer this question, we have to turn to the more general issue of equality, which the Introduction noted as the broader theoretical inquiry of this analysis.

In *Sovereign Virtue*, Dworkin explores the principle of equality in liberal theory, and bases his own concept of liberal equality on what he calls the critical morality of ethical individualism. The relevant passages merit citation:

> My own critical morality rests on a pair of humanist ethical ideals that I call ethical individualism and that define the value associated with human life. The first principle holds that it is objectively important that any human life, once begun, succeed rather than fail – that the potential of that life be realized rather than wasted – and that this is equally objectively important in the case of each human life … The second principle acknowledges this objective importance, but insists nevertheless that one person – the person whose life it is – has a special responsibility for each life, and that in virtue of that special responsibility he or she has the right to make the fundamental decisions that define, for him, what a successful life would be.[56]

Dworkin then goes on to explain briefly where the principles of ethical individualism point to as the basis of a theory of political morality:

> If we take these two principles of ethical individualism as fundamental guides in constructing a theory of political morality, it will be an egalitarian theory, because it will insist that government must treat the life of each person it governs as having great and equal importance, and construct its economic and other structures and policies with that egalitarian principle in mind, and it will also be a liberal theory, because it will insist that government must leave people finally free to make decisions that set the parameters of success for their own lives for themselves.[57]

55 For an extensive discussion of the judgment, see pp. 96–98.

56 R. Dworkin, *Sovereign Virtue: The Theory and Practice of Equality* (Cambridge, MA: Harvard University Press, 2000) at 448–9.

57 Ibid. at 449.

Dworkin's thoughts have acquired great prominence in the present volume because he gives an account of liberalism and liberal equality in a vocabulary of concepts and moral ideas which is broad enough not to omit persons with intellectual disability from their scope. As noted in the Introduction, traditional accounts of liberalism and the liberal convention have been criticised by academic scholars in the field of intellectual disability as exclusionary, since they are based on man's moral ability for reason and free will, moral characteristics which may be more or less absent in the case of persons with intellectual disability.[58]

In contrast to such theories of liberalism and equality, the first principle of Dworkin's ethical individualism, the principle of objective importance, encompasses from the start all human life and considers each human life to have equal worth, instead of basing liberal theory on reference to autonomous agents. The principle of special responsibility then attractively reformulates the importance of autonomy and autonomous action in liberal theory. Autonomy is highly valued in liberalism because it is through autonomous action that members of society can best be allowed to flourish. Without denying this fundamental tenet of liberalism, Dworkin interprets it as a right of each person to make the fundamental decisions that define for herself what a successful life would look like.

Importantly, such a formulation makes room to examine what happens, or should happen, to members of liberal societies who are unable, to a greater or lesser extent, to make such fundamental decisions fully for themselves, such as persons with intellectual disability.

On the one hand, it must again be repeated here that people with intellectual disability need more help to succeed in life; but given the proper support, they can fulfil their potential and give meaning to their life. In egalitarian terms, therefore, the principle of objective importance requires liberal societies to provide that extra help and support that persons with intellectual disability need, so that the potential of their lives can be realised rather than wasted.

On the other hand, persons with intellectual disability may lack the intelligence, the experience and the social skills required to make informed choices about their critical interests; they may not be able to perceive their critical interests fully. In these cases, the previous section claimed that the critical interests of each person with intellectual disability must be found interpretively, based on the individual characteristics of the person. To the extent that persons with intellectual disability are be provided with such a framework of support which enables them to have more freedom of choice, more self-empowerment, without losing sight of their critical interests, it can be said that they stand up to the special responsibility that they have to make their life a success.

In this sense, the special responsibility that persons with intellectual disability have is not diminished, but different from that of autonomous persons, who are in an exclusive position to make informed decisions about their life. For persons with intellectual disability, their critical interests are set down with the help of the

58 For Reinders' account of the liberal convention, see p. 28.

liberal society, in a way which respects their individual characteristics and needs, and serves their human rights. Within that framework, persons with intellectual disability are free to make their own choices, which add worth to their life and improve their life experience.

This means that for those persons with intellectual disability who have severe and multiple disabilities, who can neither communicate their wishes nor allow their critical interests to be determined easily based on their individual characteristics, the special responsibility to make their life a success has to fall back entirely on the liberal social community. Even if the person with intellectual disability cannot understand and make any decisions on her own, she cannot be excluded from the application of the principle of objective worth: her life must, in some way, be made to succeed; her life cannot be wasted.

This claim of the present volume can best be understood in the light of Hofmann's theory of the promised human dignity referred to in the Introduction.[59] Hofmann perceives liberal social communities as contract-based. All members of society pledge to respect human dignity and base social, legal and political structures on the respect of human dignity. This is the reason, we add, why liberal communities set out bills of constitutional or human rights. In such a contractarian theory, human dignity guarantees that everyone, without exception, will be allowed to make a contribution to society; no member of the social community will be left out, but will be allowed to flourish. And, if needed, we add, the person will be supported to do so.

Even in the difficult case of severe intellectual disability, such as that of persons like HL, the liberal social community cannot afford to deviate from the principle of equal and objective worth. The life of even the most severely disabled person has to be allowed, and helped, to succeed. As noted above, even though the provision of such support is commensurate to available resources, a bare minimum is obligatory. Since it is very hard for the social community to find subjective elements which could trigger an interpretation of how that life could be shaped critically, a liberal society which respects human dignity and human rights should set out ways in which the person can enjoy the most she can from her human rights and/or make a substantial contribution to society. For instance, this reasoning may give a radically different justification as to why severely persons with intellectual disability who are incapable of consent should none the less be allowed to participate in medical research into the causes of and possible therapies for their disability. By allowing these persons to participate in research, society allows them to make a contribution to medical and social progress.

In this sense, Dworkin's contention that value cannot be poured from the outside into the life of a person may be meaningful in the context of demented persons, but cannot apply rigidly in the field of intellectual disability. Unless the liberal social community accepts the special responsibility to find ways in which even the most profoundly disabled person can participate in society, that person's

59 See p. 33.

life is in fact denied its intrinsic worth, and therefore that person's human dignity is violated. Even though the person's critical interests cannot be based subjectively or understood by the person that holds them, the success of the person's life will be felt, perceived and acknowledged by the social community, which allows the person to enjoy her human rights and/or make a contribution to society. In the face of an alternative which inevitably reduces persons with intellectual disability to passive recipients of care, with a prime concern to protect their experiential interests under utilitarian calculations, we prefer to advance an argument as to how their lives can be conceived of as a success, rather than as a failure.

We will furnish two arguments to strengthen this interpretation of the principle of special responsibility, in relation to severely persons with intellectual disability. The first flows from Dworkin's analysis of the principle of human dignity as the right not to suffer indignity, discussed in the previous section. There, it was mentioned that dignity not only refers to the individual and her right to dignity, as the right to have her critical interests acknowledged by society, but also refers to the dignity of the social community. According to this line of thought, it would cause indignity to society to fail to acknowledge the existence of critical interests in relation to even the person with the most severe intellectual disability. Since a plausible interpretation of how these persons can contribute meaningfully to society can be put forward, the dignity of the liberal social community dictates that an effort be made so that all persons with intellectual disability be allowed to flourish.

The second argument we will put forward relates to the remarks made in relation to intellectual disability in the Introduction. There, it was noted that without denying the medical issues relating to intellectual disability, the concept of who counts as intellectually disabled is also socially constructed, and has to do with social norms governing how a particular society views the attribute of being born human.[60] This section sets out a more detailed presentation of this issue.

In *The Future of the Disabled in Liberal Society*, Reinders makes some illuminating remarks about the terminology concerning disability, handicap, disease and illness.[61] Reinders claims that 'whereas disease refers to physiological, psychological or anatomical dysfunction, disability or handicap refer to the social consequences of such dysfunction,'[62] and stresses that 'without the suggestion that physical or psychological reality be ignored, it has been established that in many instances the social response to certain mental conditions caused more harm than these conditions themselves'.[63]

60 See also T. Stainton, 'Identity and Ethical Politics of Prenatal Testing' [2003] JIDR 533.

61 H. Reinders, *The Future of the Disabled in Liberal Society: An Ethical Analysis* (Notre Dame, IN: University of Notre Dame Press, 2000) at 42.

62 Ibid. at 43.

63 Ibid. at 42.

In this sense, Reinders' argument is that disabilities caused by different kinds of genetic diseases raise different moral issues, because some can be regarded as illnesses, while others cannot:

> Given the fact that illness is necessarily a pathology, the appropriate response is medical care. But in cases of limited capabilities the problem resulting need not be stated in medical terms at all. Limited capabilities are a source of human suffering depending on the social and cultural environment ... Given this distinction, one can say, for example, that children with Down syndrome seem to be capable of living reasonably happy lives provided that their lives are not assessed in terms of normality.[64]

The social and cultural contingency of disability is more readily visible in cases of physical disability. For instance, if the built environment of a particular society consisted of only ground-floor buildings, then wheelchair users would not really be considered as mobility-impaired. Therefore, to the extent that social perception plays an important role in defining disability, it would be unfair of the same society which regards some people as intellectually disabled not to allow these persons to contribute to social progress by accepting an interpretation of liberal equality based on the principles of ethical individualism, properly modified to better accommodate the difference of persons with intellectual disability from other members of the social community.

In this sense, the theoretical argument of this section has been to show that a plausible interpretation of liberal equality can be found so as to fully accommodate the different needs of persons with intellectual disability. The principles of ethical individualism that Dworkin has advanced can be modified successfully to show that even the person with the most severe intellectual disability should be provided with support to pursue her critical interests and enjoy her human rights more fully.

On the one hand, the principle of equal importance becomes the egalitarian foundation for why persons with intellectual disability cannot be excluded from liberal societies. On the other hand, the principle of special responsibility reveals that in some difficult cases of persons with severe intellectual disability, the responsibility for rendering their lives a success becomes a matter of social concern and an issue of collective responsibility. Showing that persons with intellectual disability can fit within the framework of ethical individualism demonstrates that they are equal to other members of the social community, and a fair account of equality in the case of intellectual disability would thus justify the budgetary provision of extra support to persons with intellectual disability so that they may be helped to exercise and protect their human rights more fully.

To the extent that the critical interests of persons with intellectual disability have to be shaped by interpreting their individual characteristics, or by setting

---

64 Ibid. at 45.

out socially meaningful ways of contributing to society, the question arises how these vulnerable persons can be protected from abuse. For instance, it is decided that persons with intellectual disability incapable of consent will donate blood regularly, as it is considered that their becoming blood donors critically improves their lives. Is that in fact so, or are they perhaps treated as cans of blood?

We believe that the proper answer to this question and similar ones has to come from the safeguards with which human rights are being protected. For instance, it can be said that, in general, persons with intellectual disability can become regular blood donors, unless they have needle phobias or giving blood is medically contra-indicated in their case. In true Dworkinian fashion, the issue here has to be decided in a manner which best coheres with the basic principles of the political community and respects the safeguards of the human right at stake.

In order to elucidate this issue more carefully and also sharpen the theoretical discussion of equality, human dignity and human rights of the previous sections, it is time to turn to a description of what the substantive provisions of a legal framework accommodating the difference of persons with intellectual disability might actually look like.

The Legal Framework of the Duty of Care Owed to Persons with Intellectual Disability Informed by Human Rights Considerations

The purpose of this section is to illustrate, in a general manner, how any legal framework respecting the dignity and rights of persons with intellectual disability should be structured. In this sense, detailed guidance to a fictional legislator will be avoided.

The legal framework we are advancing is, as already mentioned, based on the human rights and the human dignity of the person with intellectual disability. As far as human dignity is concerned, it must be repeated that, on the one hand, we are referring to the human dignity of the individual, and on the other hand, to the dignity of the political community. The dignity of the individual means assessing her needs holistically, as a person, and identifying areas of potential which must be supported in order for the person to have a critically successful life. The core of the human dignity of the person with intellectual disability is a claim for support to achieve this.

What, then, is the dignity of the political community? The dignity of the political community cannot be defined in the abstract. At best, the dignity of the political community can be described as an answer to the question that the political community is asking itself: how can this particular society treat with dignity persons with intellectual disability? Does it allow research? Does the social community allow that they are locked up in huge asylums? How many loopholes does the law allow to people who abuse persons with intellectual disability? Yet again, the absolute minimum that the political community has to agree upon is the provision of support for the person to become as autonomous as possible and for the person's potential to flourish. This can be subject to considerations of social welfare policy and allocation of scarce resources, but a minimum of support must be provided.

As far as human rights are concerned, the irreducible core of any legal framework which respects the rights of persons with intellectual disability is based on the general, or specific, safeguards of each human right. It goes without saying that the decisions of the political community as to how to treat with dignity persons with intellectual disability have to follow the safeguards set down for each human right. This is much easier to grasp in the case of the human rights enshrined in the ECHR, most of which specify safeguards for protection.

This human dignity reasoning affects the legal position of persons with intellectual disability, and correlatively, the duty of care owed to them, in a two-tiered process. Firstly, questions of policy are raised relating to the extent of the claim for support, so that the autonomy of the person with intellectual disability will be fostered. This is not something that this volume can answer conclusively, other than say that an absolute minimum is obligatory.

Secondly, the duty of care has to be examined in relation to the human dignity of the individual. A guide to the normative content of the duty of care would enumerate the following:

1. a personal relationship between the carer and the person, which also should be sustained;
2. assessment of the person's needs, potential, living and social conditions – in short, a holistic view of the person;
3. provision of support which fosters the development of the person's autonomy, to the extent that this is possible and enables the person to develop her potential; again, here normalisation aims and ideals are important; what is aimed at is to help the person, within the constraints of available funds, to get as much out of life as possible;
4. striking a balance between the need for protection and the claim of the person for more free choice, in favour of free choice; as the analysis of German law will show,[65] this has to be achieved by providing the person with veto rights in relation to medical interventions, but also to other aspects of private life, such as housing;
5. enable all the above considerations within an interpretive context; this volume claims that the support given to the person can be seen both as an interference and as an enabling factor for the person to exercise her rights; an epileptic, person with intellectual disability may have seizures, following which she is disoriented and confused; this means that she cannot be taken out for a walk at the park; but this means that at the next opportune moment when such a walk at the park will not endanger her welfare – for example, the weather should be warm if she is frail and she should have had no epileptic fit that day, it would constitute a breach of her human right to personal liberty, according to Article 5 of the ECHR, not to take her out to the park.

---

65 See pp. 33–34 and Chapter 6.

An Application of the Human Dignity Reasoning Based on a Recent Judgment

The judgment of the national courts In *R. (on the application of Collins)* v. *Lincolnshire Health Authority*,[66] the applicant, Katie Collins, was a 35-year-old woman with severe learning disabilities caused by cerebral palsy, then living at Long Leys Court in Lincoln, a purpose-built complex of five bungalows and communal facilities for severely disabled adults where she had her own bedroom. Long Leys was a separate unit within the grounds of St George's Hospital. The bungalows were staffed jointly by the Health Authority and by Lincolnshire Social Services. Prior to living at Long Leys, the applicant was a patient at Harmston Hall Hospital, elegantly termed an old-style hospital for those with learning difficulties.

The applicant ineffectively challenged the decision of Lincolnshire Health Authority that it would cease to provide long-stay care for her at Long Leys. The authority proposed that the applicant and 14 other long-term patients residing there should be relocated in the community, so that Long Leys would be used as an assessment and treatment centre. The care plans that set the health and social care needs of each patient, including the applicant, were impressive: in the case of Katie, 24-hour social care support would be given, and also access to her GP and other community healthcare services.

In this case, two distinct policies were in effect: first, the policy of Lincolnshire Health Authority to shut down Long Leys as a residential unit and use the facilities for other purposes, and second, the policy of normalisation, which dictated that persons with intellectual disability should live in the community, and not in institutional settings. These two policies, either taken together or each on its own, infringed on Katie's right to private life, as Katie objected to being moved out of the facility it.

How can one be sure that these policy decisions did justice to Katie's rights? The fact that persons with intellectual disability receive health and social care certainly does not place them at the mercy of any decision that the Health Authorities make concerning them.

Another way to look at the problem is to examine a variation of the case. Suppose Katie had already been relocated and living in the community, in a small group home in some urban residential area within Lincolnshire, and again the Health Authority was to decide that Katie should be relocated in some other group home which was better funded. Katie again objected, because she had made friends in the area were she was living and there was a nice small café around the corner where she could be taken by her carer, accompanied by her peers, to eat blueberry muffins and have tea with friends. Should Katie again be relocated?

One can see now how the circumstances of the case have changed. Katie was enjoying some good quality of life and lived in the community, all in the interests

66 *R. (on the application of Collins)* v. *Lincolnshire Health Authority* [2001] EWHC Admin. 685.

of normalisation. The Health Authority, in all its wisdom, decided again to relocate her, so that she could have better care, or better living conditions. However, Katie was happy as she was.

In the light of the analysis in the previous sections, it becomes evident that the question here is transformed from a utilitarian calculus of what is in Katie's best interests – whether to be relocated or not – to an interpretive argument about what Katie's critical interests were. Suppose that Katie was extremely sensitive to, or frightened by, visits from persons she did not know; relocating her to community settings where she would be in frequent contact with the outside world would cause her continuous fear and distress. This would not only cause harm to Katie's experiential interests, but to her critical interests as well; if she would be better off in a more segregated setting, it would deny her dignity, her life having equal worth, to relocate her to the community. The ruling in *Olmstead* v. *LC* is instructive in the caveats it incorporates in that respect, while affirming the right of persons with intellectual disability to be physically present in the community:

> Institutional placement of persons who can handle and benefit from community settings perpetuates unwarranted assumptions that persons so isolated are incapable or unworthy of participating in community life.[67]

By virtue of such a line of reasoning, the focus of attention in welfare issues concerning the care of persons with intellectual disability moves away from the tried and tested model of common law courts to rely on medical expertise. The relevant passage from the judgment, where medical expert opinion is carefully cited, is instructive of just how much this medical model continues to influence judicial decision-making in common law:

> Dr Sidahmed then explained in the next paragraph that in his opinion: '... Katie would be much better off, with opportunities to help her develop her potential, in an ordinary home. She, like us all, will go into a Hospital bed, get treated and leave to go home.'
>
> Dr Sidahmed is, as I say, the consultant psychiatrist. His task is to assess whether Katie would be better off at Long Leys or elsewhere and to advise the authority accordingly. He is not responsible for the formulation of the authority's policy.[68]

In contrast to this mentality, we have been advocating a more principled approach which moves away from the individual circumstances of each case and asks more general questions about how the lives of persons with intellectual disability are to

67 *Olmstead* v. *LC* 527 US 581.

68 *R. (on the application of Collins)* v. *Lincolnshire Health Authority* [2001] EWHC Admin. 685 at [27–8].

be shaped critically by society. The elements of the safety net are, according to our analysis, the self-advocacy and normalisation criteria: more choice, same rights and equal quality of life. Within two or more options that serve normalisation purposes in more or less the same ways, the choice is in the hands of the person with intellectual disability if the person can have wishes and/or communicate them. In this sense, any options that fall within the aims of normalisation policy are a matter for the person with intellectual disability to decide, and her decision should trump broader policy considerations.

For instance, if Long Leys was a group home within the community in some quiet residential area and the Health Authorities decided to relocate because the rent for the particular house used was too high and there were financial cut-backs in service provision but Katie objected, her objection should trump the decision of the authority.

In this sense, we here advocate for a power to object. The person with intellectual disability has the power to object to a human rights infringement or improvement when normalisation goals can also, even less adequately, be achieved without them. According our argument, this can be a workable legal criterion against which the provision of social care may be measured.

Ultimately, recognising a power to object will provide further protection to the person with intellectual disability. And since this veto right will only have effect between normalisation options, the basic objection that the person with intellectual disability will be able to harm her own welfare is removed. We argue that recognising such a power to object is ultimately coherent with the prevailing individualism of liberal society.

The decision of the ECtHR The case of Katie was eventually brought before the ECtHR, as Katie's parents made an application to the ECtHR alleging that the right for respect of her private life had been violated by the fact that she had been relocated, despite her wishes and the apparent promise of Lincolnshire Health Authority assuring her and her parents that she would have a home for life in Long Leys.[69]

The ECtHR was satisfied, first of all, that the applicant, who had lived in Long Leys under the care of the authority and under a promise of a home for life, could claim that her right to respect for her home guaranteed under Article 8 § 1 of the ECHR had been interfered with by the decision of the authority to move her elsewhere.

Then the ECtHR continued to examine whether this interference complied with the restrictions of the right for respect for private life inherent in Article 8. The ECtHR held that since judicial review of the case in the High Court upheld the decision for relocation, the relocation of Katie was lawful.

Moreover, the ECtHR held that the assurance that the applicant would be granted a home for life was not, in the event, found to amount to a legally

69 *Collins* v. *United Kingdom*, 15 October 2002, [2003] EHRR CD 6.

binding obligation on the Health Authority to comply with the applicant's personal preferences. The ECtHR did not consider this to be unreasonable. Given the vagaries of future circumstances, a statement made in 1990 could not realistically have been expected to guarantee the continued suitability of Long Leys as a placement for the applicant, whether for practical, medical or other reasons.

For these reasons, the ECtHR accepted that the decision to move the applicant from Long Leys into alternative social care was not disproportionate, gave proper consideration to her interests, and was supported by relevant and sufficient reasons relating to her welfare. Katie's application was therefore rejected as manifestly ill-founded.

The deficiencies of the approach of common law courts to issues of intellectual disability which have already been noted in the earlier discussion of English law are also evident in the present reasoning of the ECtHR. As in other judgments, the ECtHR relies heavily on medical expertise and the judgments made in the national courts; moreover, the margin of appreciation which the ECtHR grants to national authorities as being better placed to make substantive decisions of policy and of provision of healthcare, makes it all the more difficult for the ECtHR to take a more engaged position in relation to allegations made by intellectually disabled applicants.

Subsequently, the ECtHR, just like national authorities, can be criticised for not having developed a substantive, principled approach concerning how human rights issues relating to persons with intellectual disability are to be resolved.

In closing, the first part of this volume has demonstrated the differences between intellectual disability and other kinds of disability. By translating the issue of intellectual disability into the language of the social model, it becomes evident that the barriers which hinder the full participation of persons with intellectual disability in society are predominantly legal. In order to lift these barriers, a different concept of autonomy must be advanced in the case of persons with intellectual disability. The principle of human dignity may provide far greater protection to the human rights of persons with intellectual disability.

PART II
The Protection of Human Rights for Persons with Intellectual Disability in Practice: The Marginalisation of Disability in International and National Law

Chapter 3

The UN Convention on the Rights of Persons with Disabilities

The first part of this volume was devoted to a theoretical analysis of how intellectual disability may fit within liberal theory and human rights. We presented the argument that persons with intellectual disability are faced with the legal barrier of autonomy, which excludes them from full participation in society and full enjoyment of their human rights. In the context of a broader theory of equality, the principle of human dignity may provide a coherent framework of human rights protection for persons with intellectual disability.

In contrast to the previous theoretical approach, the second part aims to show that current legal frameworks of human rights do not provide adequate protection to persons with intellectual disability. This deficiency in human rights protection is caused by the fact that no coherent answer to the different characteristics of intellectual disability has been offered by these legal frameworks of human rights.

Chapter 3 begins the analysis by presenting the United Nations Convention on the Rights of Persons with Disabilities (CRPD). We argue that the CRPD constitutes an immense leap forward in the human rights protection of persons with disabilities. However, the CRPD is a human rights document which aims to encompass all kinds of disability. It was not drafted with intellectual disability exclusively in mind. Certainly, many of the specific issues that intellectual disability raises have been addressed by the CRPD. None the less, we argue that difficult interpretive questions in the application of the CRPD arise in relation to persons with intellectual disability.

Chapter 4 continues the analysis of international law by presenting the case law of the European Court of Human Rights (ECtHR) in respect of persons with intellectual disability. In the context of the European Convention on Human Rights (ECHR), human rights issues raised by intellectual disability have been marginalised by the ECtHR. The analysis of the case law shows convincingly that the ECtHR cannot address the human rights issues that intellectual disability raises unless it develops a basic understanding of human dignity as an interpretive principle which is applicable to all ECHR rights.

Turning to national law and practice, Chapter 5 offers an analysis of English law in relation to persons with intellectual disability, criticising in particular the sterilisation case law. The best interests test, which has evolved through the sterilisation case law, is considered to offer very poor safeguards against paternalism and abuse.

Strikingly, the enactment of the Human Rights Act (HRA) has changed remarkably little in relation to the legal position of persons with intellectual disability in English law. This is also due to the fact that there is no significant case law of the ECtHR relating to intellectual disability. More importantly, the Mental Capacity Act (MCA), which was enacted several years after the HRA, does not alter the larger picture. The MCA is based on the best interests test, rather than incorporating a more sophisticated and principled approach to issues of intellectual disability.

Chapter 6 conducts a comparative analysis of German law in relation to intellectual disability. In German law, the principle of human dignity has been used as an interpretive tool. Human dignity has been a guiding principle to both legislators and the judiciary. This has led to a coherent legal approach towards persons with intellectual disability, which respects their human rights. Despite this, there are several German judgments which interpret the law in a far more restrictive manner. This, we argue, does not diminish the importance of having a clear legal benchmark based on human dignity, against which current legal practices may be measured and perhaps found wanting.

The Evolution of International Law towards a Disability-specific Human Rights Document

The 1970s witnessed the growing consciousness of persons with disabilities, evident in their forming disability pressure groups, such as the Union of the Physically Impaired Against Segregation. These groups of persons with disabilities are collectively referred to as the disability rights movement. At the same time, the evolution of the social model of disability buttressed the efforts of the disability rights movement to claim more rights and more freedom for persons with disabilities.

On an international level, these efforts were gradually recognised by the United Nations. In 1971, the Declaration on the Rights of Mentally Retarded Persons was adopted by the General Assembly of the UN.[1] Four years later, the Declaration on the Rights of Disabled Persons was also adopted.[2] During the 1980s, further progress was made, as 1982 marked the beginning of the International Decade of Disabled Persons.

These international documents and World Programmes were of fundamental importance in terms of awareness-raising. Disability was gradually becoming a more visible issue in international human rights law. However, the Declarations soon came under attack by the disability rights movement. Firstly, these

1 *Declaration on the Rights of Mentally Retarded Persons*, GA Res. 2856(XXVI), UN GAOR, Supp. No. 29 at 93, UN Doc. A/8429 (1971).

2 *Declaration on the Rights of Disabled Persons*, GA Res. 3447(XXX), UN GAOR, Supp. No. 34 at 88, UN Doc. A/10034 (1975).

Declarations were not binding legal instruments. Secondly, the spirit of the Declarations reflected the traditional, medical model of disability and was tainted by paternalism.[3]

At the risk of belabouring the point, these criticisms could not ring truer than in the case of the 1971 Declaration on the Rights of the Mentally Handicapped.

Article 1 of the Declaration affirms that 'the mentally retarded person has, to the maximum degree of feasibility, the same rights as other human beings'. This affirmation of the human rights of persons with intellectual disability is conditional upon the factor of feasibility. However, a conditional affirmation of human rights runs contrary to the established practice of other UN human rights documents. For example, the Universal Declaration of Human Rights solemnly proclaims in Article 1 that 'all human beings are born free and equal in dignity and rights'. Ensuring a conditional protection of human rights for persons with intellectual disability begs the question whether this protection is equal. To make matters worse, feasibility is also a vague concept. Thus, it immediately becomes apparent that the 1971 Declaration takes with the one hand what it gives with the other.

Article 7 continues in much the same vein by declaring that:

> whenever mentally retarded persons are unable, because of the severity of their handicap, to exercise all their rights in a meaningful way or it should become necessary to restrict or deny some or all of these rights, the procedure used … must contain proper legal safeguards against every form of abuse …

A final mention should be made of the issue of guardianship in the Declaration. Article 5 states that 'the mentally retarded person has a right to a qualified guardian when this is required to protect his personal well-being and interests'. Part I of this volume has explained how guardianship has lost favour among persons with disabilities. New ways of respecting the views and wishes of persons with disabilities, such as advocacy and self-advocacy, have been developed instead. It is worth repeating the gist of such criticism: 'Guardianship intrudes on fundamental liberties and privacy rights, employs vague criteria, fails to tailor the scope of the guardian's authority, denies procedural safeguards, and lacks adequate monitoring and review.'[4] In this sense, securing a right to guardianship only serves as a further abrogation of the human rights of persons with intellectual disabilities.

A different way of addressing the issue of disability was needed.

---

3 M.A. Stein and J. Lord, 'Future Prospects for the United Nations Convention on the Rights of Persons with Disabilities' in O.M. Arnardóttir and G. Quinn, eds, *The UN Convention on the Rights of Persons with Disabilities: European and Scandinavian Perspectives* (Leiden: Martinus Nijhoff Publishers, 2009) at 21.

4 S. Herr, 'Self-determination, Autonomy, and Alternatives for Guardianship' in S. Herr, L. Gostin and H. Koh, eds, *The Human Rights of Persons with Intellectual Disabilities* (Oxford: Oxford University Press, 2005) at 430.

However, at that time, many states were reluctant about the need to negotiate a new comprehensive human rights convention.[5] Economic considerations regarding the cost of drafting a disability-specific convention were put forward. A further argument was that there was no need for a new convention because the existing human rights instruments were universal in character.[6] In theory, all UN human rights documents apply to persons with disabilities in the same way as they do to everyone else.

It was only in 2001 that the situation changed radically, after intense lobbying from disability rights organisations. Lawson summarises the arguments which were presented in favour of drafting a new human rights instrument.[7] First, it was argued that in spite of the universality of human rights documents, these conventions were simply not applied to persons with disabilities. Disability had remained an invisible human rights issue. Persons with disabilities were not perceived as subjects of human rights, who deserved equal protection of their rights. In this sense, adopting a disability-specific convention would flag disability as an important human rights issue and raise the visibility of persons with disabilities.

Second, it was argued that a new convention would provide the opportunity to render human rights more specific in relation to disability. The general formulation of human rights would be replaced by detailed provisions of human rights. These provisions would address the specific issues that disability raises in respect of human rights protection, much in the same way as, for example, the UN Convention on the Rights of the Child does in respect of children's rights.

A third and final argument in favour of adopting a new convention concerned data collection. Adopting a human rights convention on disability would mean that its implementation would be bolstered by a monitoring body. National reports regarding the convention would have to be submitted to this monitoring body on a regular basis. The obligation to furnish these reports would in turn force national authorities to establish national monitoring bodies which would collect data. These data would become an invaluable source in order to ascertain the protection accorded to the rights of persons with disabilities on a global scale.

These arguments slowly gained ground, and in December 2001 the General Assembly of the UN finally established an Ad Hoc Committee to consider drafting a disability-specific human rights treaty. The drafting process ended in December 2006, when the Convention on the Rights of Persons with Disabilities was adopted by the General Assembly.

---

5 D. MacKay, 'The United Nations Convention on the Rights of Persons with Disabilities' [2007] *Syracuse Journal of International Law and Commerce* at 323.

6 A. Lawson, 'The United Nations Convention on the Rights of Persons with Disabilities: New Era or False Dawn?' [2007] *Syracuse Journal of International Law and Commerce* at 586.

7 Ibid. at 583.

Substantive Provisions of the CRPD which are of Particular Relevance to Intellectual Disability

The short presentation of the CRPD above has given the general background in international law against which it was adopted. A detailed analysis of all the provisions of the CRPD is beyond the scope of this chapter. What is important, however, is to examine the place accorded to intellectual disability within the CRPD.

As mentioned, the CRPD is a disability-specific human rights instrument. It was drafted with the active participation of disability groups and organisations worldwide. The CRPD represents the international recognition of the struggle of the disability rights movement for more rights and more freedom of choice. As such, the CRPD presents a universal view of the human rights of persons with disabilities. However, many of the provisions of the CRPD are relevant to issues of intellectual disability. These are scattered throughout the CRPD.

Article 1, which states the purpose of the CRPD, mentions that the CRPD aims to promote respect for the inherent dignity of persons with disabilities. Respect for inherent dignity also features in Article 3, which proclaims the principles of the CRPD.

Article 9 sets down in great detail the right to accessibility. The wording of the provision is more geared towards persons with physical disability: 'access, on an equal basis with others, to the physical environment, to transportation, to information and communications, including information and communications technologies and systems, and to other facilities and services open or provided to the public …'.

In spite of this, access to information and communications is of vital importance to persons with intellectual disability. Persons with intellectual disability may have problems understanding difficult words or complex sentences. This in turn makes it even more difficult for them to assess the information and reach an informed decision. The same applies to communication. Persons with intellectual disability may have difficulty in expressing themselves verbally. For instance, it may be easier for them to understand information through images. This degree of detail is absent from paragraph 2 of Article 9, which gives a expansive list of appropriate measures that states have to take in respect of accessibility. Sentence (f) merely sets down the obligation for states to 'promote other appropriate forms of assistance and support to persons with disabilities to ensure their access to information'. In a similar way, Article 21 of the CRPD is also broadly defined. Article 21 guarantees the right to freedom of expression and opinion, and access to information. Sentence (b) sets down an obligation to states to facilitate 'the use of sign languages, Braille, augmentative and alternative communication, and all other accessible means, modes and formats of communication of their choice by persons with disabilities in official interactions'.

Article 10 of the CRPD guarantees the right to life. This provision is very important for persons with intellectual disability, in two ways. The first concerns the unborn child with intellectual disability; the Introduction mentioned Reinders' moral argument against genetic screening as essentially discriminatory.[8] The second concerns children with intellectual disability, who by reason of their ill-health are placed under a Do Not Resuscitate (DNR) order, as in the case of *Glass* v. *UK*.[9] In that case, the parents contested the medical treatment their child was receiving, as they feared it would lead to a premature death. Could it be said that Article 10 of the CRPD applies in these difficult cases to provide persons with intellectual disability with greater protection for their right to life?

The wording of the Article does not provide any argument to support this claim: 'States Parties reaffirm that every human being has the inherent right to life and shall take all necessary measures to ensure its effective enjoyment by persons with disabilities on an equal basis with others.' For this reason, much will depend on how the Committee on the Rights of Persons with Disabilities interprets Article 10 in respect of genetic screening and other forms of pre-natal testing aimed at reducing the birth rate of persons with intellectual disability.

On the contrary, situations similar to the facts of *Glass* are dealt with under sentence (f) of Article 25 of the CRPD. Article 25 protects the right to health of persons with disabilities. Sentence (f) in particular prohibits the 'discriminatory denial of health care or health services or food and fluids on the basis of disability'.

Article 12 of the CRPD is of crucial importance to persons with intellectual disability, as it guarantees the right to equal recognition before the law. Paragraph 1 is a reaffirmation that 'persons with disabilities have the right to recognition everywhere as persons before the law'. In the case of persons with intellectual disability, this provision translates into an affirmation that they are active subjects of rights, and not passive objects of social care.

Paragraph 2 declares that 'persons with disabilities enjoy legal capacity on an equal basis with others in all aspects of life'. Paragraph 3 imposes an obligation on states to 'take appropriate measures to provide access by persons with disabilities to the support they may require in exercising their legal capacity'. These two provisions are very important for persons with intellectual disability. Negative stereotypes and paternalistic attitudes continue to persist in the everyday lives of persons with intellectual disability. The Report of the Joint Committee on Human Rights, *A Life Like Any Other: Human Rights of Adults with Learning Disabilities*, warrants citation in this respect:[10]

---

8 See p. 27.

9 *Glass* v. *UK*, 9 March 2004, [2004] EHRR 15. For an analysis of the case, see p. 95.

10 Joint Committee on Human Rights, *A Life Like Any Other: Human Rights of Adults with Learning Disabilities*, vol. 1, HL Paper 40-I HC 73-I, Session 2007–2008 (London: The Stationery Office, 2008) at 34.

> Other witnesses told us that far from being enabled to make complaints about their treatment, people with learning disabilities could be excluded from day to day decisions and choices about how they lived their lives: Most people with learning disabilities are still being told where to live. Most people with learning disabilities are told what to do during the day.

Importantly, as late as the 1980s, issues of discrimination in legal capacity were also evident in national legislation. The well-known case of *X and Y* v. *The Netherlands* is a classic example of this.[11] In that case, an adult woman with intellectual disability did not have the capacity, under Dutch law, to institute proceedings against the man who had raped her. To make matters worse, her father also did not have the capacity to institute criminal proceedings on her behalf. The father was the legal guardian of the incapacitated daughter for as long as she was a minor. In other words, the gap in Dutch law effectively meant that the young woman was denied legal capacity on the ground of her intellectual disability.

Paragraph 4 of Article 12 of the CRPD essentially regulates any restrictions imposed on the legal capacity of persons with disabilities:

> States Parties shall ensure that all measures that relate to the exercise of legal capacity provide for appropriate and effective safeguards to prevent abuse in accordance with international human rights law. Such safeguards shall ensure that measures relating to the exercise of legal capacity respect the rights, will and preferences of the person, are free of conflict of interest and undue influence, are proportional and tailored to the person's circumstances, apply for the shortest time possible and are subject to regular review by a competent, independent and impartial authority or judicial body. The safeguards shall be proportional to the degree to which such measures affect the person's rights and interests.

Again, the relevance of this provision for persons with intellectual disability cannot be stressed enough. Paragraph 4 of Article 12 represents an enlightened update of the similar provision in the 1971 Declaration on the Rights of the Mentally Handicapped. Article 7 of that Declaration states:

> whenever mentally retarded persons are unable, because of the severity of their handicap, to exercise all their rights in a meaningful way or it should become necessary to restrict or deny some or all of these rights, the procedure used … must contain proper legal safeguards against every form of abuse …

Here, it immediately becomes apparent that vague, paternalistic concepts such as the 'exercise of rights in a meaningful way' have become unacceptable in the context of the CRPD. Instead, pride of place has been accorded to the rights, wills

11 *X and Y* v. *The Netherlands*, 26 March 1985, Ser. A No. 91. For an analysis of the case, see pp. 90–91.

and preferences of the person. The proportionality of the interference is also an important consideration. Paragraph 4 of Article 12 brings the regulation of legal capacity for persons with disabilities in line with established doctrine and practices of mainstream human rights instruments.

The final paragraph of Article 12 deals specifically with property. Paragraph 5 guarantees 'the equal right of persons with disabilities to own or inherit property, to control their own financial affairs … and … that persons with disabilities are not arbitrarily deprived of their property'.

Article 13 guarantees the right to access to justice. Paragraph 2 is especially important in relation to intellectual disability: 'In order to help to ensure effective access to justice for persons with disabilities, States Parties shall promote appropriate training for those working in the field of administration of justice, including police and prison staff.' Persons with intellectual disability are frequent victims of crime, not only on account of their vulnerability, but also because of hate crime.[12] However, in their dealing with the criminal justice system, persons with intellectual disability are frequently met with distrust, as they are considered unreliable witnesses.[13] In addition to this, a judgment of the ECtHR, *Perks et al.* v. *UK*, highlights the difficulties persons with intellectual disability face during trial.[14] In that case, Perks was sentenced to several days in prison for wilful refusal or culpable neglect to pay the Community Charge, as the magistrate did not notice any of Perks' disabilities.

On the other hand, paragraph 1 of Article 15 raises an important issue with regard to consent. This provision states: 'No one shall be subjected to torture or to cruel, inhuman or degrading treatment or punishment. In particular, no one shall be subjected without his or her free consent to medical or scientific experimentation.' The issue here is whether persons with intellectual disability are capable of consenting freely to medical or scientific experimentation. In the case of persons who have severe intellectual disability, or difficulties in communication, the requirement of free consent may be overly restrictive. In our view, the term 'consent' must be interpreted in a broad way, so as not to exclude persons with intellectual disability from participating, if they so wish, in medical experiments, especially if these may be of benefit to them. It is regrettable that the CRPD has not given a definition of consent in Article 2, which would reflect the difference of intellectual disability in this respect.

Article 16 is another important provision of the CRPD for persons with intellectual disability. Paragraph 1 declares that: 'States Parties shall take all appropriate legislative, administrative, social, educational and other measures to

---

12 Joint Committee on Human Rights, *A Life Like Any Other: Human Rights of Adults with Learning Disabilities*, vol. 1, HL Paper 40-I HC 73-I, Session 2007–2008 (London: The Stationery Office, 2008) at 68–9.

13 Ibid. at 71–2.

14 *Perks et al.* v. *UK*, 12 October 1999, [2000] EHRR 33. For an analysis of the case, see pp. 92–94.

protect persons with disabilities, both within and outside the home, from all forms of exploitation, violence and abuse, including their gender-based aspects.' The Report of the Joint Committee on Human Rights highlights this need in a very eloquent way:

> adults with learning disabilities undergo degrading experiences in health and residential care settings … This implies that poor treatment and neglect of some of the most vulnerable people in our society, at the times when they are ill, in need of care and support, and most dependent on others to secure their most basic and fundamental rights, is endemic.[15]

Article 19 guarantees the 'equal right of all persons with disabilities to live in the community, with choices equal to others'. This right acquires special importance in the case of persons with intellectual disability, as they are a group with very diverse needs. For instance, many persons with intellectual disability would prefer to live independently. Others are best cared for in residential settings. In this sense, providing a range of housing options and living accommodations which reflects their preferences and needs is essential for their well-being. In order to achieve full inclusion and participation in the community, Article 19 imposes an indicative list of obligations on states to provide choice of place of residence, personal assistance and access to community support services.

Article 20, on the other hand, is another example of a provision of the CRPD which is geared towards persons with physical disability, by guaranteeing the right to personal mobility.

Article 22 guarantees the right to privacy. In the case of persons with intellectual disability, the right to privacy is of fundamental importance. Persons with intellectual disability living in residential accommodation are particularly susceptible to intrusions in their private life. Paragraph 1 of Article 22 states: 'No person with disabilities, regardless of place of residence or living arrangements, shall be subjected to arbitrary or unlawful interference with his or her privacy, family, home or correspondence or other types of communication …'.

Article 23 is another crucially important provision of the CRPD for persons with intellectual disability. This provision follows as a logical progression of the right to privacy and guarantees the right to respect for home and the family.

Paragraph 1 proclaims that states 'shall take effective and appropriate measures to eliminate discrimination against persons with disabilities in all matters relating to marriage, family, parenthood and relationships, on an equal basis with others'. The normative content of the right to respect for the home and the family is made more tangible by providing specific aims. Under sentence (a) of paragraph 1, states are under the obligation to ensure 'the right of all persons with disabilities

15 Joint Committee on Human Rights, *A Life Like Any Other: Human Rights of Adults with Learning Disabilities*, vol. 1, HL Paper 40-I HC 73-I, Session 2007–2008 (London: The Stationery Office, 2008) at 52.

who are of marriageable age to marry and to found a family on the basis of free and full consent of the intending spouses is recognized'. Here, the concept of free and full consent may impose a high threshold for the capacity of persons with intellectual disability to marry. Consent must be understood here in a broad way, so as to enable persons with intellectual disability who may only have a loose understanding of marriage and family to claim protection under Article 23.

Sentence (c) touches upon one of the most controversial issues which affect persons with intellectual disability. This is the issue of non-consensual sterilisations, which are carried out for non-medical reasons. Sentence (c) unequivocally declares that 'persons with disabilities, including children, retain their fertility on an equal basis with others'. This provision is expected to make it increasingly difficult for national jurisdictions to authorise non-consensual sterilisations when these are not indicated by medical necessity. Again, much will depend on how the Committee on the Rights of Persons with Disabilities will interpret this provision of the CRPD in order to provide adequate protection from arbitrary interferences to the fertility of persons with disabilities.

Paragraph 2 of Article 23 regulates family affairs. It imposes an obligation on states to 'render appropriate assistance to persons with disabilities in the performance of their child-rearing responsibilities'. The evidence given before the Joint Committee on Human Rights which is cited in its subsequent report reveals just how unfairly the social care system treats parents with intellectual disability:

> Sue phoned our office a few months ago informing us that her child had been taken away from her and she was not being given any rights to visit. The reason given for taking her child away was that she was not able to look after the child. When asked what support and training she had had to look after her child she said that she did not have any support. She was told it would be very expensive to provide this support.[16]

Paragraph 4 of Article 23 regulates one of the most frustrating issues which persons with intellectual disability are especially confronted with: the removal of the parental care of their children. Paragraph 4 strikes a fair balance between the right of the parents to respect for their family life and the best interests of their children. The provision states:

> a child shall not be separated from his or her parents against their will, except when competent authorities subject to judicial review determine, in accordance with applicable law and procedures, that such separation is necessary for the best interests of the child. In no case shall a child be separated from parents on the basis of a disability of either the child or one or both of the parents.

16 Ibid. at 61.

However, the evidence presented before the Joint Committee on Human Rights, reveals a bleak picture with regard to the frequency of removal of parental care in the case of parents with intellectual disability:

> We received evidence that the children of people with learning disabilities are more likely to be removed from their parents' care than the children of people who don't have learning disabilities. Research suggests that this happens in around 50% of cases involving a parent with a learning disability. The National Survey reported that 7% of the people that took part in the survey were parents, but only 52% of those people were looking after their children.

Given the very limited or non-existent support which parents with intellectual disability receive in respect of their parenting skills, a significant addition to paragraph 4 would be that no care proceedings may be instituted unless adequate parenting support has been given to the parents, but this support has failed. In other words, removal of parental care should be a step of last resort, and only when the perceived failure of the parents is not due to external difficulties, negative perceptions as to their parenting skills and the inadequate provision of social care.[17]

Article 24 guarantees the right to education, which is essential for providing persons with intellectual disability with the necessary skills and knowledge so that they develop to their full potential. Paragraph 1 of Article 24 reflects this by imposing an obligation on states to 'ensure an inclusive education system at all levels and lifelong learning directed to: (a) The full development of human potential and sense of dignity and self-worth, and the strengthening of respect for human rights, fundamental freedoms and human diversity …'.

Article 26 guarantees the right to habilitation and rehabilitation. Paragraph 1 imposes an obligation on states to 'take effective and appropriate measures, including through peer support, to enable persons with disabilities to attain and maintain maximum independence, full physical, mental, social and vocational ability, and full inclusion and participation in all aspects of life'.

Developing vocational ability is important for persons with intellectual disability, as this ensures a smoother passage in the labour market. Article 27 of the CRPD, which guarantees the right to work and employment, reflects this in sentence (d) of paragraph 1: 'Enable persons with disabilities to have effective access to general technical and vocational guidance programmes, placement services and vocational and continuing training.'

A final mention should be made of Article 29, which guarantees the right to participate in political and public life. This provision of the CRPD is important in relation to intellectual disability. Traditionally, persons with intellectual disability have been given a limited right to vote and be elected. The CRPD sets a new human rights standard by declaring that 'persons with disabilities can effectively

17 A. Dimopoulos, 'Intellectually Disabled Parents before the European Court of Human Rights and English Courts' [2009] EHRLR 82.

and fully participate in political and public life on an equal basis with others, directly or through freely chosen representatives'. Some of the means to achieve this aim include accessible and easy to understand voting procedures, or assistance in voting by a person of their choice. Given the importance attached to advocacy and self-advocacy by the disability rights movement, stressing the importance of providing advocacy in the political process may have been an important addition to the protective measures of Article 29.

The Interpretive Problems of Applying CRPD Rights in Respect of Persons with Intellectual Disability

The previous analysis of a great many of the provisions of the CRPD makes it clear that intellectual disability is not left out from the scope of the CRPD. In this respect, the CRPD operates as a universal declaration on the rights of persons with disabilities. It was drafted with the significant contribution of non-governmental organisations (NGOs) which specifically represented persons with intellectual disability. For these reasons, persons with intellectual disability may claim protection under the provisions of the CRPD. However, as pointed out earlier, intellectual disability poses a distinct set of human rights challenges. Here, the barriers which preclude persons with intellectual disability from participating fully in society are predominantly legal. The question, therefore, is whether this difference is taken into account and is addressed by the CRPD.

The starting point for an answer to this question is that the CRPD represents a vindication of the social model of disability in international human rights law. The history of the social model, especially the British one, reveals that issues of physical disability provided the initial impetus for its development. It was at a later stage that the scope of the social model was expanded to cover issues of intellectual disability as well. As a result, we claimed that the social model has not yet explained how the (legal) factors that disable persons with intellectual impairments may change. This underlying ambiguity is carried over to the CRPD.

For instance, the term 'disability' is not given any definition in the CRPD. On the contrary, only the term 'persons with disabilities' is defined in Article 1. There, it is used as a generic term which, broadly defined, includes 'those who have long-term physical, mental, intellectual or sensory impairments which in interaction with various barriers may hinder their full and effective participation in society on an equal basis with others'.

In addition to this, other uncertainties persist. How is one to structure the requirement of consent in Articles 23 (concerning marriage) and 15 (concerning medical and scientific experimentation)? Here, a fair balance has to be struck between the need to protect persons with intellectual disability from abuse, and their meaningful participation in society. Setting too high a threshold of capacity to consent would signal a return to paternalistic attitudes in what is an immensely forward-looking human rights convention.

The same ambiguity is evident in the principles which underpin the CRPD. These are enumerated in Article 3. Sentence (a) states: 'Respect for inherent dignity, individual autonomy including the freedom to make one's own choices, and independence of persons'. This loosely connected inventory of concepts serves well as a declaration of principles. However, the application of these principles to the human rights of persons with intellectual disability requires far more work. Chapter 2 was dedicated to an analysis of human dignity which reveals how complex and malleable a concept it is. Importantly, human dignity may also be conceived as a restraint on autonomy. Autonomy itself is a disabling factor for persons with intellectual disability.

Clearly, the CRPD is an international human rights document. As such, it is the product of many deliberations, hesitations, contributions and compromises between sovereign states. These ambiguities cannot, and should not, tarnish the huge importance of the CRPD for the lives and rights of persons with disabilities. It is particularly important to stress here the integral character of the CRPD, which is invoked in the concluding sentence of the Preamble: 'a comprehensive and integral international convention to promote and protect the rights and dignity of persons with disabilities will make a significant contribution to redressing the profound social disadvantage of persons with disabilities ...'. Even though the CRPD upholds a formal distinction between so-called civil-political rights and social-economic rights, the rights guaranteed by the CRPD are bolstered by positive action and a monitoring body, which renders justiciability to socio-economic rights.[18] This is especially important in the case of persons with intellectual disability, because both positive action and socio-economic rights are extremely important in order to ensure the full protection of their human rights.

On the other hand, it is clear that the protection of the rights of persons with intellectual disability is fraught with problems of interpretation, even under the enlightened and disability-specific provisions of the CRPD. Even so, the adoption of the CRPD is a major leap forward in international human rights law. It represents the first serious effort to discontinue the marginalisation of disability within human rights. As such, the legal effects of the CRPD are still in process. It remains to be seen whether the CRPD may make a significant difference in the human rights protection of persons with intellectual disability.

However, ample evidence exists as to how the issue of disability has been so far marginalised in existing human rights law. As mentioned previously, existing human rights documents fail to provide adequate protection to persons with disabilities, even though human rights are unequivocally applicable to them as well. This claim has been one of the most important reasons for adopting a disability-specific convention.

18 I.E. Koch, 'From Invisibility to Indivisibility: The International Convention on the Rights of Persons with Disabilities' in O.M. Arnardóttir and G. Quinn, eds, *The UN Convention on the Rights of Persons with Disabilities: European and Scandinavian Perspectives* (Leiden: Martinus Nijhoff Publishers, 2009) at 67–77.

The next chapter goes analyses the framework established by the European Convention on Human Rights and the European Court of Human Rights in relation to intellectual disability. This analysis throws into sharp relief the interpretative problems of applying human rights in the case of persons with intellectual disability.

Chapter 4

The European Convention on Human Rights and the Case Law of the European Court of Human Rights in Respect of Applicants with Intellectual Disability

The previous chapter has provided an analysis of current developments in international human rights law which improve the legal protection afforded to persons with disabilities. However, we have also claimed that the CRPD requires further thinking and interpretive effort with regard to persons with intellectual disability. Ambiguities concerning principles such as dignity must be resolved so as to provide this group of persons with adequate human rights protection.

These ambiguities are made clearer if one examines current human rights law and practices. A good example is the ECHR, because it is a general human rights document, which has a unique monitoring framework in the form of an international court. By examining how intellectual disability has been marginalised under the ECHR, finding ways to change this situation becomes easier.

Human Dignity in the ECHR

The legal and social reorganisation of post World War II Europe followed the examples set by international law after the war. As often as not, the similarities are striking: European states had recourse to a new inter-state organisation, the Council of Europe. The aim of the Council was and is to achieve greater unity between its member states. It was also acknowledged that this aim of unity and co-operation was to be pursued through the maintenance and further realisation of human rights and fundamental freedoms through the Council's initiatives, such as Conventions. That is why a European Convention of Human Rights was adopted under the auspices of the Council of Europe and ratified by the member states of the Council. These institutions are reminiscent of the UN and the UDHR.

But this is where the similarities with international developments end, and the distinct, European character of this new legal-political framework emerges. The Council of Europe is not modelled on the UN Security Council; military action is outside its scope. More importantly, the ECHR is a legally binding treaty between mutually contracting parties, not a declaration. Moreover, the enforcement of this treaty is not left to the customary devices of international law or to political pressure. An enforcement mechanism, in the form of an international court, the European Court of Human Rights, was set up for this purpose. The ECtHR was empowered not only to adjudicate in inter-state disputes about the ECHR, but also to examine complaints lodged by private individuals about alleged breaches of the ECHR by member states.

As with the developments in international law, human dignity played an important role in the drafting of the ECHR. Equally, however, no clear definition of human dignity arises from the *travaux préparatoires* or the wording of the ECHR. In fact, the term 'human dignity' does not even feature in the final text of the ECHR. Gradually, though, the influence of human dignity has been asserted through the case law of the ECtHR, but the elusive references made to dignity by the ECtHR meticulously refrain from analysing the concept.

The origins of the ECHR go back to a time before the Council of Europe was created.[1] The Congress of Europe, convened by the International Committee of Movements for European Unity, was held in May 1948. Its aim was to demonstrate wide support for the cause of European unity and provide practical recommendations for the accomplishment of this objective. The final plenary session of the Congress addressed a Message to Europeans, where, among others, the desire of a Charter of Human Rights guaranteeing liberty of thought, assembly and expression, as well as the right to form a political opposition, was expressed.

This idea was taken up by the Juridical Section of the European Movement, which produced a draft of a human rights convention in which the contracting parties would undertake to uphold the fundamental liberties of their citizens and establish a European Court to adjudicate in cases of alleged violation. This draft was then submitted in July 1949 to the Committee of Ministers of the Council of Europe.

Parallel to these European developments, the Universal Declaration of Human Rights was being adopted by the General Assembly of the UN in December 1948. Moreover, once the UDHR had been passed, the General Assembly instructed the UN Commission on Human Rights to produce drafts of what were later to become the International Covenant on Economic, Social and Cultural Rights and the International Covenant on Civil and Political Rights. As a result of this early interest at the UN in the subject of human rights, when the Council of Europe took up the matter in 1949 it was able to refer to the statement of the rights contained in the UDHR, together with the first draft of the projected UN covenant.

As work on the draft of the ECHR slowly progressed, many opposing views had to be reconciled. At first, after the submission of the draft convention at the Committee of Ministers in July 1949, the Committee did not agree to pass the human rights convention issue on its agenda. However, the Assembly of the

1 J. Merrills and A. Robertson, *Human Rights in Europe*, 4th ed. (Manchester: Manchester University Press, 2001) at 5. For a much more detailed account of the diplomatic and political antagonisms underpinning the development of the ECHR, see A. Simpson, *Human Rights and the End of Empire* (Oxford: Oxford University Press, 2001) at c. 13.

Council insisted, and finally the Committee gave way. In September 1949, the Assembly's Committee on Legal and Administrative Questions presented its report, which was adopted with some modifications as Recommendation 38 of the Assembly. The Committee's report listed 12 basic civil and political rights, all of which had already been included in the UDHR.

Recommendation 38 was scrutinised by numerous other committees and went through many stages of evolution before developing into the final draft of the ECHR. Importantly, in June 1950, the Conference of Senior Officials, which in its turn looked into previous reports of other committees on the recommendation, accepted the view that the rights to be protected should be defined in detail, and not merely enumerated in the Convention. As might have been expected, in the majority of cases the definitions closely followed those already worked out by the UN Commission when preparing the early drafts of the Covenants.

This subtle connection between the various UN human rights documents and the drafting of the ECHR provides a first proof of how considerations of human dignity were also taken into account in the European human rights movement. The influence of the UDHR and of the deliberations preceding both the Declaration and the draft of the first Covenant were very strong. The list of the 12 rights enumerated in Recommendation 38 was taken from the UDHR. The definition of these rights followed closely the wording of the draft covenant, which, just like the UDHR, was linked to human dignity. Therefore, it is only natural to suggest that the idea of human dignity passed on from the UN deliberations to the drafting of the ECHR and influenced its content.

A closer look at the documents of the *travaux préparatoires* clearly shows that human dignity was on the minds of many delegates discussing the framework of the ECHR in the various meetings of the Assembly of the Council. Time and time again, sporadic references to human dignity were made – each, however, giving the concept of dignity a different twist. A summary of some of these references is quite illuminating.

At the first session of the Council's Consultative Assembly, one of the Greek representatives, Antonopoulos, referred to human dignity as an element of the common European heritage:

> Man is an end in himself! The city and the State are so many organs constituting the means of preserving his dignity, of ensuring the pacific development of his personality and of guaranteeing for him humane living conditions. This, it seems to me, is the common ideology of free Europe … We must, therefore, fortify the structure and widen the bases of these fundamental freedoms, which form the veritable ramparts of human dignity.[2]

2 Council of Europe, *Collected Edition of the Travaux Préparatoires*, vol. 1 (The Hague: Martinus Nijhoff, 1976) at 32.

This reference to human dignity was not lost on the Italian representative Cingolani, who equally mentioned human dignity, but in a very different context that also involved the doctrines of the Catholic faith. Cingolani mentioned the Declaration of Philadelphia that was adopted by the International Conference of Work in 1944:

> In this Declaration there is a true and appropriate definition of human personality, which puts freedom and human dignity in the first place, and defines labour as an expression of man's sovereignty over the riches of the earth … in his capacity as a real collaborator in the divine work of preserving creation.[3]

In the specific circumstances of a European Convention on Human Rights, the Italian representative also linked the ECtHR with human dignity. He stressed 'the necessity for such a body, and also the principle of the joint responsibility of the democratic states and the Council of Europe for the defence of mankind's most precious possession – freedom and the dignity of the human person'.[4]

Equally, the Belgian delegate, de la Vallée-Poussin, summarised the essence of European civilisation as opposed to other forms of social organisation by referring to human dignity. He remarked:

> What is it that we defend in this Assembly, when we speak of Human Rights? … Quite simply, it is the dignity of the human being, the conviction shared by us all that every man is worthy of respect, that every man has the right to live in safety and dignity, that no man can be a subject of indifference to us however weak or however near to death he may be.[5]

The very influential Sir David Maxwell-Fyfe from Great Britain also mentioned human dignity. According to him, the work of the Council's Assembly and the normative framework of the Convention that the Assembly should develop must have one aim: 'to delimit the conditions in which alone the dignity of the human spirit will stand free, firm and unassailed'.[6]

A final mention should be made to the opinion expressed by the Irish delegate Norton in the Assembly. According to him:

> Our democratic philosophy induces in all of us general concepts of Human Rights and human dignity … this Council of Europe could usefully employ its energies in the task of recreating the old time respect for Human Rights and human dignity … We must make it clear that our concepts of human dignity and Human Rights are something different from what we see in Eastern Europe.[7]

---

3 Ibid. at 33.
4 Ibid. at 34.
5 Ibid. at 44.
6 Ibid. at 50.
7 Ibid. at 51–2.

It is clear that for some representatives, human dignity originated in ancient Greek philosophy and found its culmination in the Judeo-Christian tradition; in this sense, human dignity is presented as an important part of a common European heritage that the Convention seeks to protect. For other delegates, human dignity is an essential democratic principle that is constantly linked to the notion of liberty, as opposed to the servitude of man under the yoke of Nazism and communism. There is no question, therefore, that human dignity was an important consideration within the deliberations of the Assembly.

Why, then, is the term 'human dignity' blatantly excluded from the final wording of the ECHR? Could this mean that, after all, the Assembly and the subsequent committees conscientiously rejected the notion of human dignity? Is human dignity alien to the historical interpretation of the ECHR?

The *travaux préparatoires* are not particularly helpful on these points. However, the question of whether human dignity is indeed a factor that shaped the ECHR must be distinguished from the question of why human dignity does not appear in the text of the ECHR.

First of all, the ECHR and the movements that brought about the drafting of the ECHR were all part of the general international human rights movement that began just before the end of the war, when it became obvious to the liberal international community that established political institutions and social forms would not deal adequately with the new requirements of the post-war era.

This consciousness led to the establishment of the United Nations and the drafting of numerous declarations and covenants on human rights, one of which was the ECHR. Human dignity as an idea, as an ideal inspiring the protection of human rights, was explicitly acknowledged by most of these international documents.

It would therefore be difficult to imagine that the ECHR would form part of this human rights awareness without sharing the essential element of this awareness: the importance of human dignity in human rights protection.

The second link between human dignity and the ECHR can be found in the *travaux préparatoires*, where there are constant references to human dignity. But perhaps this diversity of opinions on human dignity was the very reason why the term does not feature in the text of the ECHR. Admittedly, such an open-ended term could cause problems of interpretation in a convention that was conceived to be fully functional and capable of being implemented not only between states, but also between states and individuals.

A further explanation regarding the absence of the term from the ECHR can only be guessed at from the *travaux préparatoires*. The deliberations of the Assembly, in which European state representatives made references to human dignity, such as those presented above, were summed up in a draft convention by the Commission on Legal and Administrative questions in its report in September 1949. The Assembly's discussion of this report did not make any reference to human dignity. Instead, the debate focused on whether a reference to natural law should be made in the Preamble of the Convention. It is possible, then, that this debate either monopolised the interest of the representatives, or made them reluctant to open up the debate once again by referring to human dignity, on which subject so many different opinions had been expressed previously. The deliberations of the Assembly on this report led to the adoption of Recommendation 38, which formed the basis of the ECHR. In this sense, the term 'human dignity' could have fallen through the cracks somewhere between the report of the Commission on Legal and Administrative questions and Recommendation 38.

It is, however, important to note that the notion of human dignity as well as the notion of natural law are latent in the catch-all phrase of the Preamble: 'have a common heritage of political traditions, ideas, freedom and the rule of law …'. Human dignity is an inherent part of the ECHR.

Recent scholarly work has attempted successfully to show the importance of the concept of human dignity within the framework of the ECHR.[8] Maurer claims that human dignity is an inherent part of the ECHR. It is an interpretive concept that guides the ECtHR in its decisions on human rights violations. 'Human dignity' is an open-ended term; no clear definition of this notion can be given. At best, it can be seen at work: the function of human dignity is to protect human rights from violations; it sets the limits of any permissible state action.

Human dignity in this sense has a dual existence within the ECHR. The absolute aspect of human dignity is the foundation of ECHR rights; this human dignity cannot be interfered with. The applied aspect of human dignity is the concrete application of ECHR rights in specific instances. At this point, infringement of ECHR rights is measured against the circumstances of the case, in the light of human dignity and the provisions of the ECHR. The Strasbourg judges are then to decide the case through this mechanism of adjudication.

In a nutshell, it is beyond doubt, even beyond the previous analysis of the *travaux préparatoires*, that human dignity is an inherent part of the ECHR, especially as the ECHR mirrors the UDHR in many respects.

However, since the ECHR was meant to be applied by an international court as enforceable law, issues of interpretation arise as to how the principle should be understood. This is all the more so in difficult cases, such as that of intellectual disability. The previous comparative analysis of English and German law has revealed that German law has responded more adequately to the challenge of intellectual disability, because carership law is interpreted there through a substantively rich principle of human dignity.

On the other hand, it was made evident from the presentation of the *travaux préparatoires* that very little guidance and no historical consensus can be found as to what the substantive meaning of the principle in the context of the ECHR is. It is time to examine the case law of the ECtHR in relation to human dignity and intellectual disability, and to a lesser extent, physical disability, in order to highlight the difficulties which arise from the vagueness of the principle and stress the need for a coherent interpretation of human dignity in relation to the human rights of persons with intellectual disability.

---

8 B. Maurer, *Le principe de respect de la dignité humaine et la Convention Européenne des droits de l'homme* (Paris: Documentation française, 1999).

Human Dignity and the Case Law of the European Court of Human Rights: The Hidden Issue of Disability

The Case Law of the ECtHR in Relation to Human Dignity

The judgments delivered by the ECtHR refer sporadically to human dignity. The ECtHR usually interprets the principle in relation to Article 3, which is considered to be the legal anchoring of human dignity in the ECHR. A complete review of the ECtHR's case law on Article 3 is beyond the scope of this volume. A brief mention is made here of the reasoning of the ECtHR in prisoner's cases, who alleged that the conditions of their confinement amounted to degrading treatment, as one of these, *Price* v. *UK*,[9] involved a severely physically disabled applicant.

In this strand of case law, the ECtHR and the Commission of the ECtHR had initially taken a cautious approach and were reluctant to find member states in violation of Article 3 unless there had been deliberate ill-treatment on behalf of national authorities. For instance, in *Keenan* v. *UK*,[10] no violation of human dignity was found, even though the ECtHR stressed once again the importance of human dignity in the context of Article 3:

> treatment of a mentally ill person may be incompatible with the standards imposed by Article 3 in the protection of fundamental human dignity, even though that person may not be able to, or capable of, pointing to any specific ill effects.[11]

More recently, however, the ECtHR has taken a more robust approach and has declared certain conditions to be in violation of the standards laid down by Article 3, particularly where the prison authorities are deemed to have special responsibility due to the prisoner's physical or mental state. In *Price* v. *UK*, the ECtHR held that Article 3 had been violated when a severely disabled prisoner had suffered intense physical difficulties while in prison.

The applicant, who was a four-limb-deficient thalidomide victim with kidney problems, was committed to prison for seven days for contempt of court after failing to answer questions regarding her financial position in proceedings for the recovery of a judgment debt. After she was sentenced, she was detained overnight in a police cell containing a wooden bed and mattress which were not adapted for a disabled person. As a result, she had to sleep in her wheelchair; the cell toilet was inaccessible, and the cell was cold and caused her kidney problems to recur. Despite the fact she was visited by a doctor who noted her complaints, she remained in that cell after being given a blanket and painkillers. She was then moved to prison and detained in the prison healthcare centre for

9 *Price* v. *UK*, 10 July 2001, [2002] EHRR 53.

10 *Keenan* v. *UK*, 3 April 2001, [2001] EHRR 38.

11 Ibid. at para. 113.

two days. Although the cell had disabled facilities, she had problems sleeping and complained that male officers had to assist her in using the toilet because of the inability of the duty nurse to lift her.

The ECtHR held that in the circumstances there had been a violation of Article 3. The ECtHR noted that the evidence submitted by the respondent state indicated that the prison and police authorities were unable to cope adequately with the applicant's special needs. The ECtHR concluded that although there was no evidence of any positive intention to humiliate or debase the applicant, the detention of a severely disabled person in conditions where she was dangerously cold, risked developing sores because her bed was too hard or unreachable, and was unable to get to the toilet or keep clean without the greatest of difficulty constituted degrading treatment within Article 3.

Price v. *UK* is one of the rare examples in the case law of the ECtHR where the ECtHR explicitly takes into account the disability of the applicant in finding a violation of an ECHR right. Given the sensitivity that the ECtHR shows in all matters relating to the deprivation of liberty, the ECtHR made a careful examination of all the aspects of the case in finding a violation. However, in several other cases brought before the ECtHR by disabled applicants who alleged the violation of ECHR rights other than Article 3, the ECtHR has been more cautious in its approach and reluctant to even find that the application of the disabled person is admissible. It is to these cases that we now turn.

The Case Law Relating to Physically Disabled Applicants

As with the case law of the ECtHR in relation to Article 3, the purpose of this volume is not to provide an exhaustive account of physical disability cases before the ECtHR, as physical disability touches upon a different set of legal problems from intellectual disability.[12] Yet the case law of the ECtHR in relation to physically disabled applicants is important in revealing the cautious judicial attitude of the ECtHR towards issues of disability. A later section in this chapter claims that this cautious approach stems in part from the underdeveloped reasoning of the ECtHR in relation to the principle of human dignity.

The first case to be brought before the ECtHR by a physically disabled applicant was *Botta* v. *Italy*.[13] A physically disabled person complained against the non-implementation of enacted statutory provisions of Italian law requiring public authorities to construct facilities for the physically disabled so that they could have

---

12 For a complete short account of the case law of the ECtHR in relation to physical disability, see O. De Schutter, 'Reasonable Accommodations and Positive Obligations in the European Convention on Human Rights' in A. Lawson and C. Gooding, eds, *Disability Rights in Europe* (Oxford: Hart, 2005) at 35. A more detailed examination of disability issues in relation to the ECHR, and the relevant case law, can be found in L. Clements and J. Read, *Disabled People and European Human Rights* (Bristol: Policy Press, 2003).

13 *Botta* v. *Italy*, 24 February 1998, *Reports of Judgments and Decisions* 1998-I 412.

access to beaches. Because local authorities in his holiday location had failed to comply with relevant legislation, Botta was subject to a number of inconveniences in accessing the beach and the sea.

In deciding the case, the ECtHR repeated that the state has positive obligations only in cases where there is a direct and immediate link between the measures sought by the applicant and his private and family life, and concluded that:

> … the right asserted by Mr Botta, namely the right to gain access to the beach and the sea at a place distant from his normal place of residence during his holidays, concerns interpersonal relations of such broad and indeterminate scope that there can be no conceivable direct link between the measures the State was urged to take in order to make good the omissions of the private bathing establishments and the applicant's private life.[14]

Given the social character of the applicant's complaint, the ECtHR found no violation of Article 8.

Another case law decision that needs to be mentioned is *Sentges* v. *the Netherlands*.[15] Sentges was suffering from Duchenne muscular dystrophy, and as a result was dependent on his carers for even the simplest menial tasks such as scratching himself. A robotic arm was considered as a solution, which would enable the applicant to acquire more freedom of movement. However, as the national health authorities declined to cover the expense of the robotic arm and national courts upheld that decision, Sentges lodged an application to the ECtHR alleging that his right to respect of his private life was being violated by the denial of national authorities to provide the robotic arm, as this would reduce his dependency from his carers, and thus would enable him to establish and develop social relationships with other human beings of his choice.

The ECtHR refrained from even examining whether a direct link existed between the denial of national authorities to fund the provision of the robotic arm and the applicant's private life. Instead, the ECtHR preferred to rely on the doctrine of margin of appreciation, and held that national authorities were in a far better position than an international court to allocate scarce health resources.

These two cases illustrate very clearly the predicament of the ECtHR as an international court, adjudicating on the basis of an international ECHR to which sovereign states have adhered; unless it can be shown conclusively, and persuasively, that the human rights of the applicant have been violated by national authorities, the ECtHR is obliged to respect the sovereignty of the respondent state.

On the other hand, in the light of the analysis this volume has offered of the disability rights movement and of the problems disabled persons face, it cannot be said that these judgments are satisfactory. In the case of *Botta*, the Italian state had

14 Ibid. at para. 35.

15 *Sentges* v. *The Netherlands*, 8 July 2003, [2004] 7 CCL Rep. 400.

already enacted legislation which required positive action towards disabled persons so that they could acquire access to the beachside. And in the case of *Sentges*, the alternative of not providing the applicant with a robotic arm, however expensive, simply denied him the opportunity to acquire a meaningful private life.

Unless a persuasive and coherent interpretation of ECHR rights can be offered in relation to the claims of disabled persons, the ECtHR does not feel empowered to brush aside the sovereignty of member states and decide differently than national authorities. This argument applies with equal force to the case law of the ECtHR in relation to intellectual disability. In fact, in the reasoning of its judgments the ECtHR has preferred to rely as little as possible to the intellectual disability of the applicant in finding or not finding a violation of an ECHR right. It is time to examine this case law in greater detail.

The Case Law Relating to Applicants with Intellectual Disability

Thirty-five years had to lapse since the ECHR was signed in Rome in 1950 for a person with intellectual disability to bring a case before the ECtHR. In this respect, *X and Y* v. *the Netherlands* represents a milestone in the case law of the ECtHR.[16]

The facts of the case are simple. Y, the second applicant, was a person with intellectual disability, and was living in a home for persons with intellectual disability. The night after Y's sixteenth birthday, B, the son-in-law of the person who ran this care home, took Y to his room and raped her. This understandably had traumatic consequences for Y, causing her major mental disturbance. X, the father of Y, went to the police and denounced B. When he tried to institute criminal proceedings against B, the police informed X that this was not possible, as Y was over the age of 16, and according to Dutch criminal law she had to institute these proceedings herself. However, as she was a person with intellectual disability, she was legally incompetent to do so.

Before the ECtHR, the applicants alleged that the legal impossibility of instituting criminal proceedings against B violated Article 8 of the ECHR in relation to Y, which protected her right to respect for her private life.

In deciding the case, the ECtHR followed previous case law concerning positive obligations inherent in Article 8:

> The Court recalls that although the object of Article 8 (art. 8) is essentially that of protecting the individual against arbitrary interference by the public authorities, it does not merely compel the State to abstain from such interference: in addition to this primarily negative undertaking, there may be positive obligations inherent in an effective respect for private or family life.[17]

16 *X and Y* v. *The Netherlands*, 26 March 1985, Ser. A No. 91.

17 Ibid. at para. 23.

The ECtHR then expanded this previous dictum by adding that these obligations may involve the adoption of measures designed to secure respect for private life even in the sphere of relations between individuals.

Given the intensity of the violation of Y's right to private life, namely rape, the ECtHR held that only criminal law sanctions were sufficient to provide adequate protection from such violations. The ECtHR therefore concluded that there was a violation of Article 8 in respect of Y. Having established a violation, the ECtHR refrained from examining the remaining allegations of the applicants.[18]

The case has received adequate attention as an example of the ECtHR protecting vulnerable persons. What has not been sufficiently aired, however, is the fact that the careful formulation of the ECtHR's reasoning does not, at any point in the judgment, specifically point out the vulnerability of persons with intellectual disability and their increased need of protection.

In other words, the finding of violation is based less on the dependence and vulnerability of persons with intellectual disability than on a blatant gap in the law 'as regards persons in the situation of Miss Y'.[19] Legally speaking, this general formulation is intended to apply to all incapacitated persons over the age of 16 who are deemed incapable of instituting criminal proceedings themselves, such as the mentally ill. The intricacies of intellectual disability are obfuscated by abstract and general formulations; the ECtHR does not champion the protection of intellectual disability as such. The relevant passage of the judgment, where the violation of Article 8 is based, is instructive:

> The Court finds that the protection afforded by the civil law in the case of wrongdoing of the kind inflicted on Miss Y is insufficient. This is a case where fundamental values and essential aspects of private life are at stake. Effective deterrence is indispensable in this area and it can be achieved only by criminal-law provisions ...[20]

The ECtHR fails to recognise that it is not only fundamental values and essential aspects of private life that are at stake, but also the horrible wrongdoing and sexual abuse of an adolescent with intellectual disability.

In a nutshell, then, the status of the applicant as a person with intellectual disability went unnoticed by the ECtHR. The vulnerability and increased need for protection of persons with intellectual disability were not highlighted in the judgment. Even though a violation of the right of Y to respect of her private life was found, intellectual disability was not singled out by the ECtHR as a sensitive area of human rights protection.

---

18 This is a typical feature of the ECtHR's case law, dictated by reasons of procedural economy.

19 *X and Y* v. *The Netherlands*, 26 March 1985, Ser. A No. 91, at para. 27.

20 Ibid.

The next case before the ECtHR to involve a person with intellectual disability was adjudicated some fourteen years later. In *Perks et al.* v. *UK*, the ECtHR joined together eight separate applications of persons who had been imprisoned for failing to pay the community charge (poll tax).[21] Of these eight applicants, it was only Perks who had intellectual disability.

The facts in the case of *Perks* involve a series of court proceedings during which he did not benefit from legal representation. Having failed to pay the community charge, the applicant was summoned in January before a magistrate, but was not legally represented at that hearing. The magistrate did not notice any of Perks' disabilities, and therefore concluded that the applicant's failure to pay the community charge was due to his wilful refusal or culpable neglect. He fixed a term of imprisonment of 30 days, but postponed its operation against weekly payments of the debt.

In May, the applicant was summoned before the Magistrates' Court as he had only paid two instalments, and was again not legally represented at the hearing. Even though he informed the court that he had been unwell and spent a week in hospital in February, the magistrates issued a warrant for his imprisonment for 28 days. Perks spent six days in custody before being released on bail.

Before the ECtHR, *Perks* alleged a violation of Article 5 para 1(b) of the ECHR. The applicant claimed that his detention was unlawful under English law because the magistrates at the second hearing did not enquire in the factual circumstances that precluded him from paying the community charge, even though he submitted to the court that he had been in hospital. By five votes to two, the ECtHR did not find a violation of Article 5 para. 1, following previous case law.[22]

The minority opinion deserves specific mention, as it held that the detention of the applicant was arbitrary. The judges of the minority stressed that Perks could only have been imprisoned if his failure to pay the community charge was due to his wilful refusal or culpable neglect. As Perks was a person with intellectual disability, he was not culpable. The mental element of the crime was absent, and the magistrates should have ascertained the mental faculties of the applicant before sentencing him to prison. Using strong language, the minority opinion concluded that there was a violation of Article 5 para. 1:

> the detention of a man in Mr Perks' situation for six days for not having paid a tax of some GBP 150 is, in itself, notwithstanding technical arguments, a flagrant violation of the right to liberty of person protected by the Convention.[23]

It must be noted that the argument put forward by the judges of the minority is correct: the applicant was imprisoned for six days for a crime he could not have committed; being a person with intellectual disability, he lacked the prerequisite mental element of culpable neglect.

---

21 *Perks et al.* v. *UK*, 12 October 1999, [2000] EHRR 33.

22 *Benham* v. *UK*, 10 June 1996, *Reports of Judgments and Decisions* 1996-III 738.

23 Joint partly dissenting opinion of judges Tulkens and Greve.

This opinion of the minority of the ECtHR is quite exceptional, in that it advances a legal argument which was not submitted in the proceedings. The procedure before the ECtHR is essentially retroactive in nature; the ECtHR only examines allegations made before it. Therefore, if a legal argument is not put before the ECtHR, the ECtHR will rarely acknowledge it of its own motion.[24] This may explain why the majority of the ECtHR did not take this otherwise correct argument into account, since, unfortunately, it was not submitted by Perks' counsel.

In general terms, the judicial odyssey which Perks suffered before the English courts reveals how defenceless persons with intellectual disability can be, faced on their own with impersonal official legal proceedings. Because of his intellectual disability, and because he was unaided by legal counsel, the applicant was unable to properly defend his right to liberty before the magistrates.

The case of *Perks* would have been a great opportunity for the ECtHR to stress that the judiciary within each national legal system should show greater alertness in ascertaining and acknowledging the possible intellectual or physical disabilities of persons presented before national courts. The majority of the ECtHR, however, refrained from distinguishing the case of *Perks* from that of the other applicants who did not have any intellectual disability. Once again, the intricacies of intellectual disability are not highlighted in the judgment of the ECtHR. It is only the minority opinion which sets aside technical arguments and goes in the heart of the issue: the false imprisonment of a person with intellectual disability who was unable to defend himself.

The other important allegation which Perks brought before the ECtHR involved a breach of Article 6 paras 1 and 3(c) in relation to the right to a fair trial. Since the applicant was not represented by legal counsel at the magistrates' hearings and did not have a right to Legal Aid, he was unable to defend himself properly, and therefore his trial was not fair. The respondent state did not contest this allegation, neither in the case of *Perks* nor indeed in the case of the other seven applicants. Accordingly, the ECtHR unanimously found a violation of the right to a fair trial in the case of all eight applicants, repeating previous case law:

> Having regard to the severity of the penalty risked by the applicants and the complexity of the applicable law, the interests of justice demanded that, in order to receive a fair hearing, the applicants ought to have benefited from free legal representation before the magistrates.[25]

Once again, the ECtHR lumped together the special case of applicants with intellectual disability with that of other applicants who were not disabled. In this way, the ECtHR refrained from expounding what constituted a fair trial in the case of a person with intellectual disability.

---

24 Again, this is a feature of the ECtHR's case law, which is dictated by reasons of procedural economy.

25 *Perks et al.* v. *UK*, 12 October 1999, [2000] EHRR 33, at para. 76.

In the case of *Perks*, the interests of justice demanded that he receive legal representation, not only because of the severity of the penalty or the complexity of the applicable law, but also because of the inherent limited understanding that he had of the proceedings, as he was a severely illiterate person with intellectual disability, unable to engage in higher-level conversation.

By failing to take into account these different aspects of the case which relate to intellectual disability, the ECtHR does not provide a complete and accurate legal reasoning as to why the right of Perks to receive a fair hearing was violated. Even though a violation of Article 6 was found, the issue of intellectual disability, was, as in *X and Y* v. *The Netherlands*, played down by the ECtHR.

The next case to be brought before the ECtHR by a person with intellectual disability was *Brennan* v. *UK*.[26]

The facts of the case can be summarised as follows: Brennan was arrested during an investigation of an IRA murder. He was transported to a holding centre for terrorist investigations, and was interviewed for 35 hours over the course of four days. The doctors who examined the applicant at this centre did not find any evidence of ill-treatment nor intellectual disability.[27] In accordance with criminal law legislation, Brennan was denied access to a solicitor for 24 hours. A police officer was present at the first meeting of the applicant with his counsel. Before seeing his solicitor, and on subsequent occasions, Brennan made several admissions about his involvement in the murder being investigated.

Before the ECtHR, the applicant claimed that the restrictions placed on his consultations with his solicitor after his arrest by the police, his allegedly oppressive interviews and the use of the admissions he made during these interviews deprived him of a fair trial, in violation of Article 6 paras 1 and 3(c) of the ECHR. The ECtHR examined these allegations in turn, holding that it was only the presence of a police officer at the first meeting of the applicant with his solicitor which violated his right to an effective exercise of his defence rights, as the applicant would not be able to discuss frankly with his counsel.

What matters in the judgment of *Brennan* v. *UK* is not so much the technical analysis of the procedural safeguards required by Article 6, so that the accused may receive a fair trial. The ECtHR again did not see the case as an opportunity to broach the issue of intellectual disability on a grand scale, and therefore did not tease out general rules which would apply to persons with intellectual disability who are arrested and interviewed for serious criminal offences. Such an approach did not take place, even though the applicant reminded the ECtHR, with respect to many of the allegations he made before national authorities, that he was 'a pliable young man of compliant personality, possessed of limited intelligence …'.[28] The

26 *Brennan* v. *UK*, 16 October 2001, *Reports of Judgments and Decisions* 2001-X 211.

27 Before the national criminal courts, Brennan was assessed to be on the borderline of intellectual disability, having an average level of suggestibility and a high level of compliance.

28 For example, para. 49.

ECtHR could have taken a sensitive stance on the issue, and held that, as a general rule, persons with intellectual disability, for instance, may require psychological support during police interviews.

Only three years after *Brennan* was decided, *Glass* v. *UK*[29] was brought before the ECtHR. A brief mention of this judgment has already been made in Chapter 3 relating to the UNCRPD.[30] Here follows a detailed analysis of the judgment in relation to Article 8 of the ECHR.

The facts of the case are lengthy and complicated. David Glass was a severely disabled child, both physically and intellectually. Following surgery, he was admitted to hospital on several occasions because of respiratory infections. In order to alleviate David's distress, the doctors decided to administer diamorphine; this was opposed by Carol, David's mother, as she believed that diamorphine would shorten his life.

Believing that David was in the terminal stage, the doctors also placed a 'do not resuscitate' (DNR) order in his medical notes without consulting his mother. Then they went ahead with administering diamorphine. The next day, David's family demanded that the diamorphine be stopped, feeling that David was being euthanased and was actually dying. David's mother tried to revive her son, and a serious fight broke out between several members of David's family and the doctors. David recovered in a few days after the fight and was discharged from hospital.

The case was eventually brought before the ECtHR, with David as the first and his mother as the second applicant. The ECtHR narrowed down the scope of the case and examined only a few of the claims relating to Article 8 in respect of David. The ECtHR noted that David's mother was his proxy in English law, and that she firmly opposed the administration of diamorphine to her son. Therefore, the administration of the medicine, contrary to the mother's objection, was sufficient to amount to an interference with David's right to respect for his private life, and in particular with his right to physical integrity.

Such an interference with the right to respect for private life can be justified, according to Article 8 para. 2, if it is prescribed by law and is necessary in a democratic society. However, the ECtHR held that the interference was not necessary; given the opposition of David's mother to the administration of diamorphine to her son, the hospital should have made an application to the High Court to have the treatment authorised. The interference was therefore not justified, and accordingly, a violation of Article 8 was found.

In a nutshell, the judgment of *Glass* v. *UK* held that medical treatment administered to a child with intellectual disability against the wishes of the child's proxy amounted to a violation of the child's right to physical integrity, as the doctors administering the treatment should have brought the issue before the High Court.

---

29 *Glass* v. *UK*, 9 March 2004, [2004] EHRR 15.

30 See p. 72.

In the context of English law, *Glass* is a very important case in asserting parental rights of consent in the face of opposing medical opinion. The judgment sends a clear message that, notwithstanding medical expertise and the authority of medical opinion, decisions relating to treatment cannot be unilaterally imposed by doctors. This remark acquires greater significance in relation to persons with intellectual disability, as their family or carers sometimes have very strong feelings as to what sort of treatment can be administered to them. Their voice must therefore be audible in the process of medical decision-making.

However, this recapitulation of the ruling in *Glass* also shows how narrow and legally technical the finding of violation is. A very significant issue, among the other claims of the applicants, was the fact that a DNR order was placed in David's medical notes without any consultation with his mother. David was medically assessed to be at the terminal stage, and end-of-life medical issues are very delicate. Moreover, David had severe physical and intellectual disabilities. Whereas the good faith of David's doctors cannot be disputed, the fact that they did not consult with David's mother before imposing the order was insensitive and paternalistic. Quite rightly, therefore, the minority opinion of the ECtHR accepted that this complaint deserved further examination.[31]

By narrowing the scope of the case, the judgment of the ECtHR in *Glass* v. *UK* followed the pattern of the previous cases involving applicants with intellectual disability. The ECtHR continued to take a narrow view of the legal issues at hand. The broader issues relating to intellectual disability which underpinned the case, such as a plausible claim for medical sensitivity to the rights of persons with intellectual disability who are assessed to be at a terminal stage of illness, were not reflected in the judgment. Again, the element of intellectual disability was played down by the ECtHR.

HL v. *UK* is, to this date, the most recent important case decided by the ECtHR involving a person with intellectual disability.[32] Before beginning the analysis of the case, *HL* must be put in context. The judgment forms part of a large body of case law on the right to liberty of persons of unsound mind, enshrined in Article 5 of the ECHR. In this series of cases, applicants who had been detained in psychiatric hospitals for treatment of their mental illness complained to the ECtHR that their detention had not been lawful. Typically, in these cases the ECtHR stressed the importance of the right to liberty in democratic society and engaged in lengthy and exhaustive examination of the legal framework and the factual circumstances of the applicant's detention.

The facts in the case of *HL* v. *UK* cannot be separated from the legal issue which underpinned the arguments of the applicant. In current English mental health law, there exist two parallel but separate legal frameworks which regulate the admission and treatment of mentally ill persons – a category which includes persons with intellectual disability – in psychiatric hospitals.

31 Separate opinion of Judge Casadevall.

32 *HL* v. *UK*, 5 October 2004, [2005] EHRR 32.

The first framework, formal admission, is set down in the Mental Health Act (MHA) 1983. Formal admission is a detailed procedure of detention which provides several important safeguards to the person formally detained. For example, in order for someone to be formally admitted, there must be written medical recommendation by two doctors. And once the person has been detained, the continuation of her detention is subject to review by the Mental Health Review Tribunal.

On the other hand, the second framework, informal admission, is not based on the MHA, but on the common law doctrine of necessity. English courts have accepted that the detention of those who are a danger, or potential danger, to themselves or others is lawful in so far as this is shown to be necessary. As it derives from the common law courts, this framework of detention does not incorporate any of the statutory safeguards of formal admission. The MHA states that informal admission is to be preferred if the person to be admitted is compliant and does not object to being admitted.

HL was an autistic person, unable to speak and with limited understanding. Following an incident of self-harming behaviour at the day care centre he was attending, he was admitted to hospital. The doctors, noting that HL did not make any attempt to leave, admitted him informally, retaining him in hospital for several months. However, HL's carers disputed the legality of his admission before the English courts. In the end, the dispute was referred to the ECtHR.

Before the ECtHR, the applicant alleged that his informal admission to hospital amounted to detention which violated Article 5 para. 1(e) of the ECHR, and that the procedures available to him for a review of the legality of his detention did not satisfy the requirements of Article 5 para. 4. The applicant also alleged that his detention as an informal patient was discriminatory, in violation of Article 5 taken in conjunction with Article 14 of the ECHR.

The ECtHR examined in depth the factual and legal circumstances under which the applicant was admitted and medically treated, and held that he was detained, as he was under constant supervision and was not free to leave the hospital. The ECtHR then went on to examine the lawfulness of the detention, and held that the absence of safeguards and procedural rules regulating informal admission failed to protect against arbitrary deprivations of liberty, and consequently violated Article 5 para. 1 of the ECHR. The relevant passage of the judgment is worth quoting here:

> As a result of the lack of procedural regulation and limits, the Court observes that the hospital's health care professionals assumed full control of the liberty and treatment of a vulnerable incapacitated individual solely on the basis of their own clinical assessments completed as and when they considered fit ...[33]

33 Ibid. at para. 124.

Here, at last, the ECtHR drew attention to the vulnerability of persons like the applicant in finding a violation of the ECHR. The formulation of the ECtHR's reasoning was by no means accidental; given the importance that the ECtHR traditionally attaches in its case law to the right to liberty, enshrined in Article 5, the ECtHR perhaps felt at ease to enrich this protective stance by stressing the vulnerability of the applicant whose right to liberty was violated.

In the context of English law, the judgment in *HL* reinforces the reasoning of the ECtHR in the case of *Glass* v. *UK*: medical authority is certainly to be respected, yet proper safeguards must be in place, and must be followed, to ensure the protection of ECHR rights in cases of possible medical misjudgements.

To turn back to the judgment, however, the ECtHR also found a violation of Article 5 para. 4 in respect of the applicant's allegation that English law did not provide adequate means of review of his detention. Technical analysis of the ECtHR's reasoning is not important here; rather, attention must be drawn to the final allegation that the applicant made before the ECtHR – that his detention as an informal patient was discriminatory. The ECtHR, having found a violation of both Article 5 para. 1 and para. 4, refrained from examining the complaint.

However, it can be shown that the framework of informal admission is discriminatory against persons with intellectual disability, such as the applicant in *HL* v. *UK*. The current basis of informal admission as opposed to formal admission is compliance. If the person does not object to the admission and remains passive, she will be admitted informally.

However, there are several medical conditions which may require the admission of a person to a psychiatric hospital. Further, some of these medical conditions can be related to a high level of compliance or passivity, such as depression, severe intellectual disability, autism an so on. This was precisely the case of HL, who was autistic, unable to speak, and of limited understanding. He remained passive to his admission in hospital, and was therefore admitted informally, which meant that none of the procedural safeguards of the MHA were available to him.

This means that the criterion of compliance on which the differentiating treatment is based cannot be shown to be objective and reasonable. There will always be some persons who are by reason of their medical condition compliant and passive; these persons will inevitably be admitted informally, and a lower degree of protection of their rights will be accorded to them. For these persons, such as HL, informal admission is discriminatory.

It is unfortunate that the ECtHR, again for reasons of procedural economy, did not examine the allegation of discrimination by the applicant. This would have forced the ECtHR to confront the different aspects of intellectual disability, such as compliance, and in finding a violation, the ECtHR would have corrected the discrimination that persons such as the applicant in *HL* v. *UK*, suffer in respect of the protection afforded to their right to liberty.

This analysis of the handful of cases brought before the ECtHR by persons with intellectual disability illustrates how much the ECtHR has failed to respond in a sensitive manner to the different, and greater, need of persons with intellectual disability to have their ECHR rights adequately protected. It becomes evident that the case law of the ECtHR is very far from taking cognisance of the intricacies of intellectual disability and applying a rigorous analysis of what it means for persons with intellectual disability to effectively hold rights under the ECHR.

On the contrary, the ECtHR has adjudicated these applications on a case-by-case basis, based on the particular circumstances of each case. In this way, the ECtHR has failed to adopt a principled approach in relation to issues of intellectual disability. This failure becomes all the more distressing in the light of the ECtHR's other judgments, which relate to positive obligations, under Article 8, in respect of physically disabled applicants. As in those judgments, it can be said that the ECtHR is very much concerned to avoid interfering with national welfare policy issues and is wary of setting down a precedent in relation to intellectual disability.[34]

A principled approach is demanded, however, so that the issues and problems that persons with intellectual disability face can be put in perspective and addressed correctly. We believe that the principle of human dignity inherent in the ECHR can provide a coherent interpretive framework as to how the human rights of persons with intellectual disability are to be understood and protected. The case law of the ECtHR, as already presented, has made little use of the principle, even in the context of Article 3. However, we claim that a human dignity reasoning would shift the focus of attention from arguments relating to the margin of appreciation which national authorities enjoy, to a persuasive legal interpretation of the human rights of persons with intellectual disability, thus enabling the ECtHR to take a more doctrinally rigorous stance on the protection of their human rights.

In terms of international human rights law, the CRPD and the ECHR represent two very different types of human rights documents. The CRPD is a very recent convention which deals with a specific class of persons, those with disabilities. In contrast, the ECHR is a universal convention, which was adopted almost half a century ago. Yet both these conventions show some weakness in accommodating the legal difference of intellectual disability, unless a coherent interpretation is given to principles such as dignity or autonomy. It is now time to turn to national legal systems and examine how the issues of intellectual disability and human rights protection have been addressed in the national laws of England and Germany.

34 As in *Sentges* v. *The Netherlands*, 8 July 2003, [2004] CCL Rep. 400.

Chapter 5
English Law in Relation to Welfare, Intellectual Disability and Human Rights

Chapters 3 and 4 have provided an analysis of international human rights law in relation to intellectual disability. The CRPD heralds a new dawn in human rights protection for persons with disabilities. However, for persons with intellectual disability, the protection afforded by the CRPD is less straightforward. The provisions of the CRPD raise difficult questions of interpretation with regard to persons with intellectual disability.

Similarly, the case law of the ECtHR highlights these interpretive difficulties. Of course, the ECHR is not disability-specific and it is not underpinned by any notion of the social model of disability. Yet the ECtHR has notably failed to update its case law and adequately protect persons with intellectual disability.

The following chapters conclude the second part of this volume by providing a comparative analysis of national law with regards to the human rights of persons with intellectual disability. This chapter examines English law, whereas Chapter 6 focuses on the German legal system.

The comparison reveals that English law is based on a more pragmatic, case-by-case approach. This approach does not favour the development of a coherent interpretation of the human rights issues which arise in the case of persons with intellectual disability. This results in inadequate human rights protection.

On the other hand, German law has adopted a principled approach. Based on the principle of human dignity, the German legal system provides a coherent benchmark against which the solutions given to human rights issues concerning intellectual disability may be measured. As it will become obvious, considerable room for improvement is left in both legal systems.

This chapter is devoted to an analysis of the current legal framework of English law in relation to persons with intellectual disability. Its aim is to illustrate how much different from our claims the normative orientation of English law is in relation to intellectual disability. The deficiencies of English law in relation to the protection of the human rights of persons with intellectual disability are criticised, and through this analysis it becomes evident that changes in the legal regulation of the issue of intellectual disability must be considered.

Traditionally, English law has used the concept of best interests as a legal mechanism through which it has handled many of the issues concerning the special needs of persons with intellectual disability. A careful analysis of best interests asserts that English law has responded in an unsatisfactory way to the increased need of persons with intellectual disability for the protection of their human rights.

These deficiencies of English law are exemplified in the approach and provisions of the Mental Capacity Act 2005 in relation to intellectual disability.

The MCA forms the latest development in English law which relates directly to persons with intellectual disability, and incapacitated persons more generally. In order to be able to evaluate the provisions of the Act, the MCA must be placed firmly in its historical context; it is only when one understands the historical accidents or influences behind the Act that one begins to realise both the importance of the Act in terms of rendering persons with intellectual disability more audible in the English legal system and its shortcomings in the legal protection of the rights of vulnerable persons.

The first section of this chapter therefore provides with an overview of the early history of best interests; it is this early period, we argue, which sets the tone for developments in the actual law. The next section provides an analysis of current law in relation to best interests; the main point of interest here is that the legal regulation of the welfare of incapacitated adults has been based on solutions, which had been given earlier to similar issues relating to the welfare of children. The third section criticises this reasoning by way of analogy, and argues that the welfare issues of adults are far more complicated than those of children; however, as the section on the MCA will show, this is a point which has been lost in the provisions of the Act. The fourth section provides a short overview of the legislative and policy context of disability to which the MCA relates closely, and the fifth analyses the Act, both in terms of legislative history, and substantive content. The argument of this section is that, although the MCA does contain certain important provisions which improve the legal position of incapacitated persons, further thinking is necessary in order to provide persons with intellectual disability with adequate protection of their human rights. The final section rounds up the analysis of the law by providing a summary of the regulation of sterilisation and organ donation in English law; this section shows that the best interests of the person with intellectual disability are being too broadly defined, allowing space for the consideration of the interests of third parties; this is, however, untenable when the human rights of the person are at stake.

The Historical Evolution of the Best Interests Test and the Provision of Welfare for Adults with Intellectual Disability

The Origins: Early, Loose Associations between Several Strands of English Law

The early history of best interests in English law is unclear. Several social institutions, such as feudalism, or legal mechanisms of judicial enforcement, such as the Court of Wards and Liveries, played a role in shaping the concept, sometimes in contradictory ways. The important point, however, in this slow evolution of best interests through the centuries is that by the early 1900s, a substantial judicial practice had been established relating primarily to the welfare of minors. This body of case law would set the tone for later developments in relation to the welfare of incapacitated adults.

Wardship In the evolution of English law, two early systems of wardship can be identified, both originating from feudal law.

The first is wardship in chivalry.[1] English feudal rights in military wardship can be traced as far back as 1100, and they are likely to have been introduced during the Conquest. Wardship arose when the feudal vassal died, leaving a minor heir, who because of minority could not perform the necessary feudal obligations. Until the heir came of age and swore fealty and took up his duties, the feudal lord held custody over the heir's land and body as an extension of his relationship with the heir's father. The rights of military wardship were purely pecuniary in character; they were saleable, and they were intended for the benefit of the feudal lord, not his ward.

The second system of wardship also stemmed from feudal rights, and was known as wardship in socage.[2] When the tenant of such land died, the heir was placed under the wardship of the nearest relation to whom the land could not descend. The wardship applied to both person and property until the age of 14. By the late thirteenth century, it was recognised that guardians in socage could not take the profits for themselves and had an obligation to protect the ward's interests and account to him. This wardship was protective in nature, and was intended to benefit the ward, rather than the person entrusted with wardship.

Until Magna Carta, the king had an absolute right to the wardship of any of his fatherless subjects. This right was known as prerogative wardship, although it only applied within the limits of military tenure. Tenants under military fealty commonly sought to avoid the burdens imposed by wardship, marriage and relief, by holding land in use. This deprived lords, and particularly the king, of feudal revenues. In an attempt to resist the encroachment of uses, the Crown took counter-measures, the most important of which was the Statute of Uses of 1536. The effect of this Act was that any use was executed and the legal ownership of the property vested in the beneficiary. Thus, infant heirs came into possession of their lands and the king could again claim the rights of wardship, marriage and relief. In order to ensure the enforcement of the Crown's revived feudal prerogatives, a special court, the Court of Wards, later known as the Court of Wards and Liveries, was established in 1540.[3]

When military tenures and the Court of Wards and Liveries were abolished by the Military Tenures Abolition Act of 1660, the concept of military wardship

1 N. Menuge, *Medieval English Wardship in Romance and Law* (Woodbridge: D.S. Brewer, 2001) at 1–2.

2 J. Seymour, 'Parens Patriae and Wardship Powers: Their Nature and Origins' [1994] OJLS 159 at 163–4.

3 Ibid. at 164.

disappeared and socage tenure, and wardship, became the dominant form of land holding. The Court of Chancery however kept alive the institution of wardship, by justifying it as an aspect of the *parens patriae* jurisdiction which had developed in parallel to wardship. In time, wardship as exercised by the Court of Chancery became purely protective in nature, resembling wardship in socage, and was substantively and procedurally assimilated to the *parens patriae* jurisdiction of the court.

Thereafter, the way was clear for the law to build on a notion of wardship which involved a fiduciary relationship. This evolution was accentuated by gradual changes in the law, prompted by the struggle of women for equality. In 1886, the Guardianship of Infants Act was passed, which gave the mother the right to be guardian of the infant children after the death of the husband, jointly with any guardian the deceased husband had appointed. The real innovation of the Act, however, was that in section 5 the courts were required to have regard to the welfare of the child when deciding the application of the mother for custody. As a result, the Court of Chancery would attach weight to the welfare of the child in the exercise of its wardship jurisdiction.[4] Indeed, as early as 1891, the Chancery Division of the Court of Appeal stresses the 'beneficial influence which the guardian ought to exercise in the child's best interests'[5] and holds that the judge should 'consult the best interests of the child'.[6]

Wardship therefore became a legal device by means of which the Chancery exercised its *parens patriae* jurisdiction over children, and it seems plausible that the criterion of best interests as the basis of the child's welfare originates from the court. Finally, it should be noted that in the case of children, the Chancery also enjoyed custodial jurisdiction, and thus had inherent jurisdiction to make children its wards.

Parens patriae jurisdiction As far as adult persons are concerned, the first certain traces of similar regulations are to be found much later. From Anglo-Saxon times, it was recognised that, as the fountain of justice, the king had the power to mitigate and supplement the law. By the fourteenth century, this power was recognised as a form of equity, which allowed the king to provide special remedial justice. In the reign of Edward I, the statute De Prerogativa Regis placed the care of persons of unsound mind solely under the Crown.

This statute thus codified what has been termed the *parens patriae* jurisdiction of the Crown. One aspect of the monarch's role was an obligation to protect the poor and weak and those who, because of their position, were unable to obtain redress from the ordinary courts. It was accepted that this obligation was owed to

4 S. Cretney, *Law, Law Reform and the Family* (Oxford: Clarendon Press, 1998) at 158 note 21.

5 *In Re Violet Nevin (An Infant)* [1891] 2 Ch. 299 at 305.

6 Ibid. at 308.

infants and idiots.[7] Later, the *parens patriae* jurisdiction was transferred from the Crown to the Court of Wards and Liveries, where it remained until the court was wound up in 1660.[8] Thereafter, the Crown exercised the *parens patriae* jurisdiction through the Lord Chancellor, to whom it was conferred by letters patent under the Sign Manual, and from him to the Court of Chancery.

By the nineteenth century, the power allowed the Lord Chancellor to empanel a jury to try whether an individual was a lunatic or an idiot. If such a finding was made, the property and/or the person were placed in the care of the Crown, which was usually delegated to a member of the insane person's family.[9] However, the *parens patriae* jurisdiction seems to have been appealed only where significant property was at stake, and it was not until the beginning of the eighteenth century that statutes began to address the insane more generally.[10]

Poor Law, lunacy and idiocy The wardship and *parens patriae* jurisdiction evolved in the Middle Ages, with limited impact, as these jurisdictions would only practically be exercised when a fair amount of estate was involved. The care of the vast majority of persons with intellectual disability was entrusted to their families, and was regarded a responsibility or burden of the family.[11]

The creation of the Poor Law in Elizabethan times[12] changed this picture slightly; families could receive relief for their disabled members, or a disabled person could be entrusted in an almshouse or workhouse.[13]

Although the distinction between lunacy and idiocy was important in law, it seems that Poor Law officials were not using these classifications consistently.[14] This means that 'idiots' were commonly lumped together with 'lunatics'.

Under the Old Poor Law, the insane would be kept with their families unless they were dangerous. Outdoor relief could be provided to assist the purchase of necessaries for the insane person, or sometimes to hire a nurse to provide supervision so that the healthy members of the family could continue to work.

---

7 J. Seymour, 'Parens Patriae and Wardship Powers: Their Nature and Origins' [1994] OJLS 159 at 167.

8 *E. (MRS.)* v. *Eve* [1986] 2 SCR 388 at 407–9.

9 P. Bartlett, *The Poor Law of Lunacy* (London: Leicester University Press, 1999) at 9.

10 Ibid. at 34.

11 P. Rushton, 'Idiocy, the Family and the Community in Early Modern Northeast England' in D. Wright and A. Digby, eds, *From Idiocy to Mental Deficiency* (London: Routledge, 1996) at 44.

12 *For the Relief of the Poor*, 1601, 43 Eliz. I c. 2.

13 *For the Punishment of Rogues, Vagabonds and Sturdy Beggars*, 1598, 39 Eliz. I c. 5.

14 P. Rushton, 'Idiocy, the Family and the Community in Early Modern Northeast England' in D. Wright and A. Digby, eds, *From Idiocy to Mental Deficiency* (London: Routledge, 1996) at 55–8.

In 1808, legislation was passed[15] enabling counties to build lunatic asylums for their pauper lunatics. Several Acts followed, providing the legal authority for the mass incarceration of pauper lunatics, and the advent of the New Poor Law in 1834 provided an extensive administrative machinery to accomplish this.

On the other hand, official policy was beginning to view the issue of idiocy as separate from the issue of lunacy. This was not only due to progress in medical science, but also to the greater visibility of persons with intellectual disability within society. In 1870, universal elementary education was introduced; pupils with learning difficulties were failing at school. In 1886, the Idiots Act was passed, which made it possible to certify idiots separately from lunatics without the approval of a magistrate, and the 1891 Lunacy Act enabled poor law authorities to establish asylums for idiots alone.[16]

Until the Lunacy Act 1891, the ideology, if any, surrounding issues of intellectual disability was paternalism.[17] It was accepted that the person could not take care of herself and that, by necessity, someone else had to make decisions on her behalf. Moreover, from the 1800s onwards, idiocy was commonly being linked to immorality.[18] The restriction of idiots in asylums was being justified as an attempt to control public morality. Idiocy was regarded as a social problem, just as lunacy was. However, under the influence of eugenics and other factors, idiocy started to be viewed as a threat to British society.

This slow evolution of legislation and social ideology, until the reception of eugenics and social Darwinism ideas which occurred around 1900, had four major consequences. Firstly, no body of law developed in relation to the care of incapacitated persons, as it would had the Court of Chancery been presented with a bulk of cases brought under the *parens patriae* jurisdiction. Secondly, as lunacy and idiocy were both regulated by the Poor Law, the changes in the Poor Law which enabled the mass restriction of pauper lunatics in asylums also facilitated the restriction of idiots in the same institutions. Thirdly, the ill treatment, abuse and neglect present in the asylums have been sufficiently well documented to understand that this class of vulnerable persons suffered a great deal during that time. Finally, just as idiocy was beginning to be viewed as a distinct issue requiring different means of care, the wide reception of eugenics eventually caused idiocy to be viewed as a social threat, and legislation to this effect to be passed.

---

15 *For the Better Care and Maintenance of Lunatics, being Paupers or Criminals in England*, 1808, 48 Geo. III c. 96 s. 19.

16 M. Thomson, *The Problem of Mental Deficiency* (Oxford: Clarendon Press, 1998) at 12.

17 G. Finlayson, *Citizen, State, and Social Welfare in Britain 1830–1990* (Oxford: Clarendon Press, 1994) at 45–80.

18 This view led to the enactment of the legal classification of 'moral imbecile' in s. 1(d) of the 1913 Mental Deficiency Act.

Best Interests until the Mental Health Act 1959

This period in the slow evolution of best interests affirms and consolidates judicial intervention in matters of welfare decisions relating to minors. A further important issue is the growing reliance of the judiciary on expert medical opinions when deciding issues of welfare.

The Mental Deficiency Act 1913: A change of ideology towards intellectual disability The heightened awareness of intellectual disability is reflected in the fact that the 1901 census included for the first time the category of the feeble-minded, who were estimated to number 133,000. This awareness, coupled with a growing anxiety concerning the fitness, both physical and moral, of the poor and the feared racial decline of British society, eventually led the government to appoint in 1904 the Royal Commission on the Care and Control of the Feeble-Minded.

The work of the Commission and its subsequent report[19] in 1908 have been described as 'championing unmitigated eugenic ideas. Even though eugenics underpin the tone and several of the proposals of the report, it is fairer to suggest that the problem of intellectual disability was being addressed in an effort to reorganise the provision of mental health care. The gist of the report was that specialised care should be provided to the feeble-minded, and that they should be removed from lunatic asylums so that these institutions could then focus on providing curative care to the insane.[20]

The report brought the issue of intellectual disability and eugenics to the forefront of public life. As early as 1909, the Eugenic Society started lobbying the government to pass legislation, which was enacted in the summer of 1913, passed by a majority of 358 to just 15.

The spirit of the Mental Deficiency Act 1913 follows the pattern of previous Lunacy Acts; these provided the authority for the mass incarceration of lunatics, to whom persons with intellectual disability were, as often as not, likened. With persons with intellectual disability crowding asylums and workhouses, it was imperative that special care be provided for these persons, if only to relieve lunatic asylums. Eugenics and other moral concerns over the perceived threat of intellectual disability further justified the segregation of mental defectives.

The Mental Deficiency Act provided the apparatus for the compulsory and permanent segregation of the feeble-minded. As such, it was viewed as an administrative solution of a social problem, and a humanitarian thing to do, as the feeble-minded were inefficiently and inhumanely cared for in asylums.[21]

---

19 *Royal Commission on the Care and Control of the Feeble-Minded*, Cd 4202 (London: His Majesty's Stationery Office, 1908).

20 M. Thomson, *The Problem of Mental Deficiency* (Oxford: Clarendon Press, 1998) at 32–3.

21 Ibid. at 40.

The Mental Deficiency Act 1913 was passed at the height of both eugenic ideas and the asylum movement. Slowly, however, the importance of eugenics began to wane, indicated by the failure to pass a Sterilisation Bill in the 1930s, and the administrative system supporting asylums to weaken. As a large part of the implementation of the Act was entrusted to local authorities by means of voluntary help, the 1913 Act initiated the concept of community care, which would dominate the provision of welfare for persons with intellectual disability after World War II.

The struggle of women for power within the family in the early twentieth century: The Guardianship of Infants Act 1925 The long campaign of women for voting rights and legal equality prompted a flow of legislation around 1900 which gradually acceded to these claims. The fight for suffrage rights was partially vindicated in 1918 when the Representation of the People Act conceded the right to vote to women who were householders and aged 30 or over.

Yet, within the family, the common law still denied a married woman any legal right to the custody and care of her children; the Guardianship of Infants Act 1886 authorised the court to grant such a right to women only after the death of their husbands, and only if this would serve the welfare of the children.

Women's groups started pressuring for changes in the law; however, their proposals were strenuously opposed by the Home Office, and it was only in 1925 that a Guardianship of Infants Act was passed. Section 1 of the 1925 Act required the court deciding any question relating to a child's custody or upbringing to regard the child's welfare as the first and paramount consideration, and directed the court not to take into consideration whether from any other point of view the claim of the father was superior to that of the mother, and vice versa.[22]

The drafting of the Act's provisions was the product of a political compromise. The Act did not make any direct statements as to the equality of husband and wife in the care of the children; but in theory, as far as court intervention in these matters was concerned, the courts only had to decide what was best for the children of the family, thus rendering the claims of both parties equal before the law. In fact, the interpretation of this provision by the courts continued to imply that the claim of the father for custody was in the best interests of his children. Yet the important point is that the judicial involvement in determining the welfare of minors which began at the time the Guardianship of Infants Act 1886 was passed was strengthened by the provisions of the 1925 Act. The welfare of minors thus became a central preoccupation of the courts, paving the way for similar regulation of adult welfare.

---

22 S. Cretney, *Law, Law Reform and the Family* (Oxford: Clarendon Press, 1998) at 175.

The period after World War II: Bolam and the Mental Health Act 1959 The end of World War II saw a radical change of public opinion over mental deficiency, which was also prompted by a revival of libertarianism reflected in the legislation of 1944–1948. A public campaign was orchestrated by the National Council for Civil Liberties in 1947, castigating the exploitation and the undue restriction of the liberty of patients in mental deficiency institutions.[23] The campaign proved successful with both the public and the press, and in 1953 the government was forced to set up the Royal Commission on the Law Relating to Mental Illness and Mental Deficiency, better known as the Percy Commission.

The administration and control of mental deficiency institutions had stagnated during the war. Another serious issue was the discrepancy in the law governing the admission to mental deficiency hospitals. Whereas the Mental Treatment Act 1930 made possible the voluntary admission of the insane, its regulations did not cover mental deficiency. The stigma of certification and incarceration still defined the law relating to mental deficiency.

The abolition of the Poor Law by the National Health System Act 1946 and the National Assistance Act 1948 were half-hearted attempts to modernise mental health law by administratively attaching mental deficiency hospitals as part of the National Health Service. Yet the substantive law remained unchanged, and this task was entrusted to the Percy Commission, on whose proposals the Mental Health Act 1959 (MHA 1959) was passed. An important point in the Percy Report was the emphasis placed on community care, in an effort to decarcerate large numbers of mental patients.[24]

Just as the 1890s Lunacy Acts have been hailed as the triumph of legalism, in that certification was to be approved by a magistrate, so has the Mental Health Act 1959 been described as the victory of psychiatry over legalism, in that the control of the mentally ill was handed over to the medical profession. At roughly the same time, in 1957, the trust placed in the medical profession reached its zenith with the ruling in the *Bolam* case.[25] The judgment stated that a doctor was not negligent if she was following a medical treatment which a responsible body of medical opinion adopted at that time. *Bolam* is important in the context of adult welfare decisions, as its underlying mentality led the judiciary to place emphasis on expert medical opinions, thus losing sight of the social context within which decisions for incapacitated adults were being made.

The MHA 1959 was primarily concerned with effacing the stigma of certification and incarceration, which were associated with the old asylum movement. However, the Act lumped together mental illness and mental deficiency under the same legal regulations. These regulations did away with many of the legal safeguards that

23 M. Thomson, *The Problem of Mental Deficiency* (Oxford: Clarendon Press, 1998) at 279–80.

24 P. Bartlett and R. Sandland, *Mental Health Law*, 2nd ed. (Oxford: Oxford University Press, 2003) at 96–100.

25 *Bolam* v. *Friern Hospital Management Committee* [1957] 1 WLR 582.

the previous legislative framework had provided, and this adversely affected the legal protection afforded to persons with intellectual disability. At that time, the intricacies of intellectual disability were not well researched; in time, it is becoming clearer that in certain cases different allowances have to be made for persons with intellectual disability.

The Act also set down a legalistic regime of guardianship which gave the guardian extensive powers, effectively the same as those of a parent of a child under 14. The process was cumbersome, and fell into disuse. On the other hand, the Act provided statutory authorisation of proxy consent only in relation to treatment relating to mental illness. This was to prove significant because in 1960, the warrant which authorised the Lord Chancellor to exercise the *parens patriae* jurisdiction was revoked. This had the effect that no one could consent on behalf of a mentally ill person or an adult with intellectual disability for treatment not related to the person's intellectual disability or mental illness.

The Themes Running Through the Development of the Law: The Hidden Issue of Equality

The passing of the MHA 1959 represents the point of no return for the *parens patriae* jurisdiction. Until that time, the evolution of the law on best interests had developed a great deal, reflecting social and political changes. Certain patterns and problem areas are discernible throughout this period, which will become even more important in the analysis of the current law which is to follow this section.

The first of these issues is the voice of persons with intellectual disability, or lunatics, within the common law. Once it was accepted that a person was an idiot or a lunatic, she became more or less isolated from legal transactions and was excluded from the legal world. This is reflected in the certification process, where the incapacitated person did not hold the position of a legal subject within the certification process, but rather was the passive object of it. The same can be said in relation to the application and evolution of the *parens patriae* jurisdiction, which is scant; in those few cases where it was applied, it involved the nomination of a person as carer for persons with intellectual disability, and little else.[26]

Given the historical and intellectual period during which the evolution of best interests began, the exclusion of idiots and lunatics from the legal world is hardly surprising. On the other hand, in order to counterbalance the absence of any influence these persons might have in legal procedures, the notion of paternalism became firmly established. It was accepted that every decision was being made on their behalf, and in this way the common law took their needs into account. This culture of paternalism, however, meant that the incapacitated were to be forever excluded from decision-making processes. As time progressed, and mental illness

26 P. Rushton, 'Idiocy, the Family and the Community in Early Modern Northeast England' in D. Wright and A. Digby, eds, *From Idiocy to Mental Deficiency* (London: Routledge, 1996) at 55–8.

or intellectual disability started being perceived as primarily medical issues, paternalism evolved into paternalism dictated by doctors, or medicalisation. Medicalisation as a paternalistic attitude also meant that the voice of persons with intellectual disability would remain unheard, but with the further justification that the specialist knew best and was to be trusted.

Yet incapacitated persons were not the only ones whose voice was stifled by the common law; another very important category of persons with extremely limited rights were women. Women were entirely subordinate to their husbands, and this was reflected in the terminology of the common law, which was known as coverture. Women, and their property, were subject to the almost absolute control of their husbands.[27] In this sense, the failure of the common law to provide adequate notions of equality between sexes also serves to explain why the voice of persons with intellectual disability was so much ignored by the legal system of the time. The gradual expansion of rights granted to women, and later to children, forms the second important area of the law on best interests.

The evolution of the wardship jurisdiction as part of the *parens patriae* powers of the Court of Chancery becomes very significant in this context; it is accepted that the court's decisions were guided by a concern for the welfare of the ward. In this sense, even though the child is neither a participant in legal proceedings nor an autonomous agent, the concern for her welfare gradually extended from just appointing a person or parent as guardian to the material examination of whether the appointment of this or the other person would be in the child's best interests.

The struggle of women for equality in the late nineteenth century stepped on this concept of welfare, making it a vehicle for feminist claims for equality within the family. As a first step, the Guardianship of Infants Act 1886 authorised the court to appoint the wife of a deceased husband as guardian of his children if it was in the children's interests to do so. The next step was the Guardianship of Infants Act 1925, where the welfare of the children was declared to be the court's paramount consideration when deciding matters of custody or care.[28] Moreover, after 1950, when Legal Aid under the Legal Aid Act 1949 became available for wardship proceedings, the courts became increasingly involved in questions of children welfare; they were routinely presented with wardship cases which called on them to decide what was in the best interests of a child.

In this sense, the claim of women for equality proved to have four major consequences in the English legal system. The first one relates to the concept of best interests. Since, by more or less historical accident, the claim of women for equality within the family found legal recognition through the guise of best

---

27 See S. Fredman, *Discrimination Law* (Oxford: Oxford University Press, 2002) at 27–8.

28 The final step, which ensured actual equality within the family, came as late as 1973, when the Guardianship of Infants Act passed the same year stated in s. 1(1) that a mother has the same rights and authority as the law allowed to the father, and that the rights and authority of mother and father were equal.

interests, the concept was destined to become a central part of family law as the women's movement gathered more and more momentum. Subsequently, best interests as such became a basic preoccupation of the courts, and courts had to make judgments as to which decision would be in the interests of the child. Based on best interests, the law and the courts granted more and more rights to women, rendering both parents equal in family law.

The second major consequence therefore relates to equality as such. After a long and hard struggle, the voice of women became audible in both the legal system and the family. When this process ended successfully in the 1970s, a certain language of rights and equality claims had been created, and many changes had occurred in society. This created a precedent for the expansion of rights by legislation or the common law; both society and the law became much more open in making the voices of other groups of people more audible. In the case of children, this happened most notably in the case of *Gillick*. In the case of adult persons with intellectual disability, this was achieved through the Mental Capacity Act 2005.

The third important area of the law relating to best interests is the issue of community care. In a sense, community care had always been provided to persons with intellectual disability, since they would normally live in the community and be cared for by their family. However, the mass incarceration of idiots and lunatics from the 1800s onwards had practically rendered these persons invisible. As community care became official policy after the MHA 1959, the old asylums reluctantly began to close and persons with intellectual disability slowly started flowing back to residential areas. This process would not end until the early 1990s. Therefore, given the fact that the actual, physical, presence and visibility of persons with intellectual disability in society was very limited in the years that followed World War II, the question of adult welfare decisions would not be raised until a couple of decades later.

The fourth consequence relates to how adult welfare was finally decided by the courts. Anticipating a little, when the issue of adult welfare came up, the *parens patriae* jurisdiction had already been abolished. The legal expedient of guardianship set up by the MHA 1959 had not proved popular. To make matters worse, the Mental Health Act 1983 would expressly curtail the guardianship regime of the 1959 Act; both the circumstances under which a person could be received in guardianship and the powers of guardians over adults were significantly reduced. The gap in the law had become obvious. On the other hand, the evolution of wardship and family law had already familiarised the courts with a process of answering welfare issues for children. The coast was therefore clear for the courts to apply, by way of analogy, the familiar process of dealing with children welfare to adult cases as well.

However, adults with intellectual disability, although similar to children in their vulnerability, are also very different from minors in several important respects. The gradual expansion of the case law relating to adult welfare reflects these difficulties, which eventually led to the passing of the Mental Capacity Act 2005.

The Current Law on Best Interests

In Re D *and* Re B: *Wardship, Sterilisation and Best Interests*

Real change in the legal interpretation of welfare and best interests in the case of intellectual disability only occurred when changes in both society and social welfare policy began to take place in the early 1970s. The most basic of these social changes was the reception of the civil rights movement and normalisation ideas, which became a bastion for the claims of the disabled for equality. The decay of large mental institutions, where mentally ill and persons with intellectual disability were housed, and the need for reform brought about changes in welfare policy. These causes, as well as the proposals of the Percy Report, initiated the revival of community care, which consisted of ushering persons with intellectual disability back into the community by providing care and housing within residential areas. Community care suddenly made persons with intellectual disability visible, and it was natural that cases of concern for their rights would begin to be brought in court.

However, the first cases which evolved around the welfare of persons with intellectual disability dealt with minors under the wardship jurisdiction. And this happened because the educational framework set up after World War II continued a tradition of providing special education and making specific allowances for children with learning disabilities, so that an early framework of care had already developed around them. Moreover, wardship proceedings were an accessible and appropriate forum to air these issues; Legal Aid was available in wardship proceedings, and a sufficient body of case law had already accumulated which had settled the law.

In Re D[29] deserves specific mention, not only because it opened the debate on the best interests of a child with intellectual disability, but also because the case evolved around the issue of non-consensual sterilisation. For the next twenty years or so, the legality of sterilisation procedures for both minors and adults with intellectual disability would become the driving force behind the interpretation and evolution of best interests in English law.

Briefly, the facts of the case are these: the mother of a child with moderate intellectual disability, D, aged 11 years old, had decided very early on that she would have her daughter sterilised. D started menstruating from the age of 10. This prompted her mother to ask D's paediatrician to have D sterilised, and the doctor agreed. D was attending a specialist school for children with learning disabilities, and the consultant educational psychiatrist at the school opposed the sterilisation and applied for D to become a ward of court, also inviting the Official Solicitor to become D's guardian *ad litem*.

Even though the opinion of D's paediatrician was firm that D needed to be sterilised, the medical evidence given by other medical experts pointed the other

29 *In Re D (A Minor) (Wardship: Sterilisation)* [1976] Fam. 185.

way, and the sterilisation was not authorised. Yet the special merit of the judgment is that it is not solely based on the evaluation of the medical evidence presented; Heilbron J evaluated the medical evidence in the light of the possibility of D getting married, or developing in maturity and understanding so as to be able to make an informed choice whether she wanted to be sterilised or not. Moreover, the judgment made reference to a woman's basic right to reproduce, and distinguished non-therapeutic from therapeutic sterilisations:

> The type of operation proposed is one which involves the deprivation of a basic human right, namely, the right of a woman to reproduce, and, therefore, it would be, if performed on a woman for non-therapeutic reasons and without her consent, a violation of such right.[30]

Whereas non-therapeutic sterilisations were a social issue, only therapeutic sterilisations came within the sphere of medical opinion. Heilbron J stressed this point in the following words:

> I cannot believe, and the evidence does not warrant the view, that a decision to carry out an operation of this nature performed for non-therapeutic purposes on a minor can be held to be within the doctor's sole clinical judgment.[31]

Finally, the court made allusion to proportionality; even if D were to be prevented from becoming pregnant, her physical and mental condition could allow her the use of other means of contraception.

With the benefit of hindsight, *In Re D* is not only a humane and compassionate judgment; its reasoning contains propositions in law which are entirely consistent with the protection of human rights prescribed by the Human Rights Act 1998 and afforded by the case law of the ECtHR. Yet the interpretation of best interests was to take a very different turn, as a similar case eventually came to be decided by the House of Lords in *Re B.*[32]

B was 17 years old at the time, and she was living in a community care residential unit. She was beginning to show signs of sexual awareness, exemplified by provocative approaches to male members of staff and other residents, and for this reason B was made a ward of court, with a view to being sterilised. In contrast to the divergent medical opinions given *In Re D*, the medical evidence presented in *Re B* was unanimous that B was unable to understand the link between intercourse and pregnancy, cope with motherhood, receive oral contraceptives or develop her social skills or understanding. Given this unanimity of negative medical opinions, the sterilisation procedure was authorised. Two important objections can be raised against this ruling.

30 Ibid. at 193.

31 Ibid. at 196.

32 *Re B (A Minor) (Wardship: Sterilisation)* [1988] AC 199.

The first objection to the judgment relates to the question of whether the House of Lords overestimated the risk of B's pregnancy. Even though B was becoming sexually active, no substantial evidence was presented to support the view that she would become pregnant in the near future. Her sterilisation was unnecessary at that point in time. However, given the fact that the *parens patriae* jurisdiction over adults had been lost at the time *Re B* was heard, their Lordships hastened to reach their judgment before B turned 18, thus avoiding ruling on a controversial issue in a controversial jurisdiction.

The second criticism of *Re B* in terms of this analysis of best interests is that it did away with the distinction, upheld *In Re D*, between therapeutic and non-therapeutic sterilisations. The leading speech of Lord Hailsham LC also contained remarks about a woman's right to reproduce which effectively denied this right to incapacitated persons, and as such deserve mention in full:

> Moreover, for the purposes of the present appeal I find the distinction they purport to draw between 'therapeutic' and 'non-therapeutic' purposes of this operation in relation to the facts of the present case above as totally meaningless, and, if meaningful, quite irrelevant to the correct application of the welfare principle. To talk of the 'basic right' to reproduce of an individual who is not capable of knowing the causal connection between intercourse and childbirth, the nature of pregnancy, what is involved in delivery, unable to form maternal instincts or to care for a child appears to me wholly to part company with reality.[33]

We believe that the passing of the HRA has forced the above dictum on reproductive rights to part company with legal validity. But to return to *Re B*, the judgment focused exclusively on the question of what were the best interests of B in the present case. The answer to this question would in turn depend on the specific circumstances of the case; this would not allow reaching a decision on best interests based on principle, but rather on the basis of the expert medical evidence presented before the court. This latter fact inevitably would lead, and has led, to the medicalisation of best interests. The reliance of the judiciary on expert opinion obfuscates the possible social dimensions of the issues at hand. This approach was exemplified in the later judgment of the House of Lords in the case of *Re F*.[34]

J *v.* C, Gillick, *and the Children Act 1989*

At roughly the same time as these judgments were being delivered, changes were also occurring in the realm of family law which radically altered the concept of child welfare. Just as persons with intellectual disability were beginning to be increasingly viewed as equal citizens and possessors of equal rights, so children began to be viewed as possessors of rights, rather than being possessions of their parents.

33 Ibid. *per* Lord Hailsham LC at 203–4.

34 *In Re F (Mental Patient: Sterilisation)* [1990] 2 AC 1.

This waning of absolute parental authority is reflected in the seminal case of *J* v. *C*.[35] A child of Spanish parents, who had come to England for work, was entrusted to an English foster family when the parents had to return to Spain. When the child reached the age of 5, the Spanish parents unsuccessfully demanded his return. The case finally reached the House of Lords after another five years had passed. The House ruled that the child should remain with his English foster family, and delivered the authoritative definition of the best interests of the child:

> A process whereby, when all the relevant facts, relationships, claims and wishes of parents, risks, choices, and other circumstances are taken into account and weighed, the course to be followed will be that which is most in the interests of the child's welfare.[36]

After the ruling in *J* v. *C*, the courts have often shown themselves willing to disregard any possessory claims of parents or third parties, in an effort to ensure that the child's welfare will be best served.[37]

The same trend of waning parental authority is reflected in another important case, *Gillick* v. *West Norfolk and Wisbech Area Health Authority*.[38] This judgment held that the parental right to determine whether a minor child below the age of 16 years will have medical treatment terminates if and when the child achieves a significant understanding and intelligence to enable him or her to understand fully what is proposed, but until the child attains such a capacity to consent, the parental right to make the decision continues save only in exceptional circumstances.

Yet, even though during the 1970s and 1980s children were becoming more and more recognised as subjects in law and their welfare was beginning to occupy a central role in decisions made on their behalf, the law did not contain any criteria or guidance as to how the courts should reach their welfare decisions. The revision of family law which led to the passing of the Children Act 1989 mirrors these changes, and also provides the courts with a non-exhaustive welfare checklist aimed at helping the courts to reach decisions on the best interests of the child.

In this sense, there is some guidance as to what constitutes the welfare of the child, or at least there seems to be a consensus as to what the best interests of the child are.[39] It is accepted that the child should grow up to become a responsible and mature adult.

---

35 *J* v. *C* [1970] AC 668.

36 Ibid. *per* Lord MacDermott at 710.

37 G. Douglas, *An Introduction to Family Law*, 2nd ed. (Oxford: Oxford University Press, 2004) at 164.

38 *Gillick* v. *West Norfolk and Wisbech AHA* [1986] AC 112.

39 For a critical evaluation, see H. Reece, 'The Paramountcy Principle: Consensus or Construct?' [1996] CLP 267.

T *v.* T and Re F: Parens Patriae, *Sterilisation of Incapacitated Adults and Best Interests*

The ruling of the House of Lords in *Re B* set the tone for similar judgments in sterilisation cases, a regular flow of which started being brought to the courts. It was therefore only a matter of time before a case involving the sterilisation of an adult with intellectual disability would also be presented at court. This was the case of *T* v. *T*.[40]

T was a young woman with severe intellectual disability, aged 19. Despite the constant care of her mother, she was found to be 11 weeks pregnant. T was described as violent and destructive. She suffered from severe attacks of epilepsy, and her understanding was severely limited. Given the complications that might arise from the continuation of T's pregnancy, both for her health and the health of the foetus, medical experts were of the opinion that an abortion should take place as soon as possible so that these risks would be minimised. At the same time as conducting the abortion place, the doctors contemplated performing a sterilisation on T. T was generally unco-operative with doctors and medical examinations, and had the physical strength to make that point clear; it is reported in the judgment that at one time six nurses were required in order to take a blood sample from her. Given the unanimous opinion of T's doctors, as well as her mother, and her social worker supporting the application, a declaration was made to the effect that it would not be unlawful for the doctors to perform an abortion and sterilisation on T.

In this sense, *T* v. *T* is very similar to *Re B*; the unanimity of medical opinion favouring the abortion and the sterilisation was such that it would have been impossible for the court to fly in the face of medical expertise and decide differently. The process of medicalising the welfare of persons with intellectual disability adult was accepted by the court.

In terms of stating the law, *T* v. *T* is important in that the court ascertained that the *parens patriae* jurisdiction over adults had been lost, and nothing in the MHA 1983 could provide authority for someone consenting on the behalf of an incapacitated adult. Wood J stressed:

> I am content to rely upon the principle that in these exceptional circumstances where there is no provision in law for consent to be given and therefore there is no one who can give the consent, and where the patient is suffering from such mental abnormality as never to be able to give such consent, a medical adviser is justified in taking such steps as good medical practice 'demands' …[41]

The court therefore decided to use its discretion in issuing a declaration of lawfulness in relation to the proposed medical treatment. The criterion of this

40 *T* v. *T and another* [1988] Fam. 52.

41 Ibid. at 68.

lawfulness, the court held, was not necessity, as the concept of necessity was held to be vague; lawfulness was to be decided on the demands of good medical practice – a criterion which, however, is no less ambiguous.

This ambiguity was soon to be resolved by the House of Lords, in a similar case, that of *Re F*.[42] The case involved a 36-year-old woman who had formed a sexual relationship with a male patient, both being cared for in the same mental hospital. The medical opinion was that F was fertile,[43] there was a risk of pregnancy, and pregnancy would be 'catastrophic' to the psychological state of F and her behavioural improvement over the years. Given the fact that medical opinion was unanimous that the proposed sterilisation would be in the best interests of F, the case only reached the House of Lords so that their Lordships could authoritatively state the law governing non-consensual treatment of incapacitated adults.

The House confirmed the abolition of the *parens patriae* jurisdiction, and that no statutory authority was available. It was held that the common law provides that a doctor can lawfully give treatment to adult patients who are incapable of consenting if the proposed treatment is in the best interests of the person, the best interests of the person being those defined by a responsible body of medical opinion, as in *Bolam*. Lord Brandon summarised succinctly when medical intervention is in the best interests of an incapacitated adult in the following passage:

> I would define necessary in this context as that which the general body of medical opinion in the particular specialty would consider to be in the best interests of the patient in order to maintain the health and to secure the well-being of the patient.[44]

With *Re F*, the reliance of the judiciary on medical expertise when deciding the welfare of incapacitated adults became a doctrine in law. In order to understand this development, one has to take into account that *Re F* was likened to *Re B*, and that the reasoning of the latter was applied by way of analogy to the former.[45] Since welfare and best interests had been the major preoccupation of wardship proceedings, this preoccupation was bound to be carried over to adult cases as well. More importantly, the fact that all these cases involved the authorisation of medical treatment led to medical experts largely determining their outcome. From that point, it was a small step to further ascertain the practical supremacy of medical opinion by linking best interests with the *Bolam* test.

42 *In Re F (Mental Patient: Sterilisation)* [1990] 2 AC 1.

43 From the judgment, it would seem that no medical tests had been made to prove this.

44 Ibid. *per* Lord Brandon at 68.

45 See pp. 122–123.

In Re F *and* Re S*: The Inherent Jurisdiction of the High Court to Make Declarations on the Best Interests of Incapacitated Adults*

More recently, two important cases have reached the Court of Appeal which have estranged somewhat the best interests test, not only from its medical background, but also from its medical orientation.

The first of these is *Re S*.[46] This judgment is significant in terms of restating the law on best interests; it is also the first sterilisation decision to be decided by the Court of Appeal since *Re F*. In *Re S*, the court held that the *Bolam* test is in itself of a preliminary nature, since a number of courses of medical treatment can be available to a responsible body of medical opinion. The *Bolam* test therefore only serves to establish the propriety of available medical options. Choosing between these different alternatives in order to serve the patient's best interests is a function of the doctor or of the court, and this decision has to be made on more than just medical grounds; ethical, social, moral and welfare considerations must also be weighed in the balance. The relevant passages from the judgment by Dame Butler-Sloss are significant:

> I would suggest that the starting point of any medical decision would be the principles enunciated in the Bolam test and that a doctor ought not to make any decision about a patient that does not fall within the broad spectrum of the Bolam test. The duty to act in accordance with responsible and competent professional opinion may give the doctor more than one option since there may well be more than one acceptable medical opinion. When the doctor moves on to consider the best interests of the patient he/she has to choose the best option, often from a range of options … In these difficult cases where the medical profession seeks a declaration as to lawfulness of the proposed treatment, the judge, not the doctor, has the duty to decide whether such treatment is in the best interests of the patient … The judicial decision [on best interests] will incorporate broader ethical, social, moral and welfare considerations.[47]

In this sense, between *In Re D* and *Re S*, the case law on the sterilisation issue has come full circle; the issue of best interests, which has dominated the welfare of incapacitated adults, is now conceived of not just as a medical issue or as an issue of expert opinion, but rather has been claimed back by the judiciary. However, it remains unclear to what extent the ruling in *Re S* has been followed by the courts against the authority of *Re F*.

On the contrary, other judgments have been reported which have given the issue of welfare of incapacitated adults a further twist. These primarily relate to the expansion of the inherent jurisdiction of the High Court to grant declarations of lawfulness in other legal situations, such as residence and care orders. The most

46 *Re S (Adult Patient: Sterilisation: Patient's Best Interests)* [2001] Fam. Law 15.

47 Ibid. *per* Dame Butler-Sloss at 27.

important of these is the Court of Appeal's judgment *In Re F.*[48] The court held, as a matter of general principle in the law, that where there is a risk of possible harm to an incapacitated adult, the court has power under its inherent jurisdiction and in the best interests of the person to hear the case and grant the necessary declarations. Several arguments were presented in that case which pointed to the effect that the High Court did not, in fact, have such an inherent jurisdiction, or that the expansion of declaratory relief to issues that were not related to medical treatment would be of dubious legality.

The Mental Capacity Act 2005: Preliminary

This debate was finally settled by the passing of the Mental Capacity Act 2005, which attempted to codify and clarify the law relating to welfare decisions made on behalf of incapacitated adults.

Section 15(1) of the Act authorises the new institution of the Court of Protection to make declarations as to: (1) whether a person has or lacks capacity to make a decision specified in the declaration; (2) whether a person has or lacks capacity to make decisions on such matters as are described in the declaration; and (3) the lawfulness or otherwise of any act done, or yet to be done, in relation to that person.

Yet, as far as persons with intellectual disability are concerned, several uncertainties relating to welfare decisions made on their behalf are no nearer to being resolved, even after the enactment of the Mental Capacity Act. These legislative shortcomings will be analysed extensively later in this chapter. But in order to fully comprehend the difficulties in determining the welfare of adults, a closer look at English family law and the welfare of children is called for.

The Welfare of Children and its Relation to the Welfare of Adults with Intellectual Disability

The Welfare of Children in English Family Law: A Summary of the Current Law

Under s. 1(1) of the Children Act 1989, emphasis is placed on ensuring the best interests of the child, and on making the child's welfare the paramount consideration of courts when taking decisions affecting the child. The focus of the law is therefore no longer to assert the rights of parents over their children.

Moreover, in s. 1(3) of the Act, a welfare checklist is enumerated. This engages the courts to evaluate a range of issues which must be taken into account, including the child's ascertainable wishes and feelings, any risk of harm, the child's age, sex, background and so on. But there is no guidance as to how to rank these criteria in

48 *In Re F (Adult: Court's Jurisdiction)* [2001] Fam. Law 38.

order of importance. And while in some cases the decision may be straightforward, in others value judgments may inevitably affect the outcome.[49]

The other issues that the courts have in mind when determining the best interests of the child are the fact that any delay in deciding the case is considered against the child's welfare, and that the courts must only make an order if they are satisfied that there is a genuine need for them to issue an order.

The interpretation of the expression 'paramount' has caused considerable difficulties, particularly after the incorporation of the ECHR into English law through the HRA 1998, in that the interests of the child are seen to override the rights of the parents under Article 8 of the ECHR. The correct interpretation of the statutory provision would imply that a certain leeway is provided to the court to take into account the separate interests of the parents, and balance these with the interests of the child in order to reach a solution that will still be ultimately determined by what is best for the child.[50]

Glass *v.* UK

These difficulties are exemplified in the case of *Glass* v. *UK*,[51] a recent case of the ECtHR, which involved the medical care of a child with intellectual disability.

David Glass was a severely disabled child, both physically and intellectually. When he was repeatedly admitted to hospital because of respiratory infections, the doctors decided to administer diamorphine to him, against the wishes of his family, as the family believed that diamorphine would shorten his life.

The case eventually reached the ECtHR. The court admitted only the claims relating to Article 8, and unanimously ruled that there had been a violation. The ECtHR noted Mrs Glass's firm opposition to the use of diamorphine. The administration of the medicine contrary to the mother's wishes was therefore sufficient to amount to an interference with David's right to respect for his private life, and in particular his right to physical integrity. The ECtHR did not accept that the interference was legitimate, by disputing its necessity. The ECtHR felt no satisfactory explanation had been given for the failure to approach the High Court, particularly given that two doctors had opined that judicial intervention might be warranted.

In this sense, the ECtHR can be seen as indirectly eroding the paramountcy principle of the welfare of the child, and placing more emphasis on the views of the parents as to what the best interests of the child are. This should signal a change of attitude, both in the medical profession and in the English judiciary, to think twice before overriding parental views in cases of medical treatment, especially in end-of-life situations.

---

49 G. Douglas, *An Introduction to Family Law*, 2nd ed. (Oxford: Oxford University Press, 2004) at 18–19.

50 Ibid. at 165–6.

51 *Glass* v. *UK*, 9 March 2004, [2004] EHRR 15.

However, perhaps the most important issue in *Glass* v. *UK* may be overshadowed by the facts of the case. The issue concerns judicial involvement in life-and-death situations, where the fate of a child cannot depend on whether the family or medical practitioners decide to bring the case to court or not.[52] In cases of disability, the familiar question therefore remains to what extent the voice of the disabled person, or that of her family, is audible in the decision-making process, and what weight this voice carries. This remark becomes all the more poignant in the case of vulnerable adults and the law relating to welfare decisions made on their behalf.

The Welfare of Incapacitated Adults and the Welfare of Minors: A Fallacious Analogy

From the previous section on the historical evolution of best interests, it becomes clear that when questions of adult welfare started being brought to courts, a long tradition of deciding on the welfare of children had already been established. The legal process of deciding the welfare of children was to determine the best interests of the child under the circumstances of each case. This process forms the basis of both the wardship jurisdiction of the courts and the jurisdiction granted to them by the Children Act 1989.

In the case of adult welfare, the equivalent of the wardship jurisdiction had lapsed, and no statutory jurisdiction was available. In order to answer the question of adult welfare and fill in the gap, the common law worked by way of analogy. As the issue of sterilisation of minors had already been cleared, the sterilisation of incapacitated adults was modelled on the previous legal solution. The process remained unchanged; in determining the welfare of an incapacitated adult, the question was, and is, what were the best interests of the person under the circumstances of the case.

The clearest expression of this attitude is to be found in *Re F*, where Lord Donaldson opened his speech with the following words:

> This is the tale of two women, F. and B. Their circumstances are strikingly similar with one exception. F. is aged 36. B., at the material time, was aged 17. The law in relation to B. has been fully explored and authoritatively declared by the House of Lords … We have to explore and determine the law in relation to F.[53]

Similarly, Lord Brandon took the same perspective on the matter and regarded the judgment to be delivered as the adult counterpart of *Re B*:[54]

52 G. Douglas, *An Introduction to Family Law*, 2nd ed. (Oxford: Oxford University Press, 2004) at 93.

53 *In Re F (Mental Patient: Sterilisation)* [1990] 2 AC 1 at 6.

54 *Re B (A Minor) (Wardship: Sterilisation)* [1988] AC 199.

> If F. were a minor of say 17, instead of an adult of 36, and the same problem arose in relation to her, there would be no difficulty in answering these three questions [on adult best interests].[55]

However, answering the question of adult welfare by means of an analogy with the welfare of minors is misleading. For instance, F was thought to have the verbal capacity of a child of 2, and the general mental capacity of a child of 4–5.[56] It does not seem to be very helpful to surmise that a person can actually have more than one mental age, whereas in fact F was a sexually mature woman of 36.[57] The actual, physical age of F and her actual needs do not feature in the judgment. The House equated, probably unconsciously, the estimated mental age of F with the age according to which she should be treated in law.

Current authority in relation to mental capacity makes it clear that this analogy is perfectly acceptable. *Per* Munby J in *Re SA*:[58]

> It is now clear … that the court exercises what is, in substance and reality, a jurisdiction in relation to incompetent adults which is for all practical purposes indistinguishable from its well-established parens patriae or wardship jurisdictions in relation to children. The court exercises a 'protective jurisdiction' in relation to vulnerable adults just as it does in relation to wards of court.

On the contrary, the differences between children and adults with intellectual disability are many. Adults with intellectual disability: (1) have more experience; (2) have other physical needs; (3) with proper support can develop to acquire both more experience or needs; and (4) are bearers of rights which need to be protected and fostered in accordance to their individual preferences and needs. We believe that issues relating to adults with intellectual disability should be resolved on these premises.

To take *Re F* again as an example, there exists no striking similarity between *Re F* and *Re B*, despite their Lordships' belief to the contrary. *Re B* was about an adolescent girl just becoming sexually aware, whereas F was already enjoying a steady sexual relationship. From this point of view, sterilising F would amount to penalising her for her sexuality, whereas clearly, for F, her sexual promiscuity was not a problem, but rather a source of pleasure. Had these differences been taken into account, they would have led to a different, and more correct, reasoning on adult welfare in English law.

---

55 *In Re F (Mental Patient: Sterilisation)* [1990] 2 AC 1 at 54.

56 *Per* Lord Brandon, *In Re F (Mental Patient: Sterilisation)* [1990] 2 AC 1 at 53.

57 Similar criticism of the concept of mental age is raised at Law Commission, *Mental Incapacity*, Report No. 231 (London: Her Majesty's Stationery Office, 1995) at 41, note 33.

58 *Re SA* (Vulnerable Adult with Capacity: Marriage) [2005] EWHC 2942 (Fam.) at para. 37.

The first judgments on adult welfare evolved around medical issues; this narrowed and clouded the debate in an important respect. For persons who cannot look after themselves, it is necessary that some care be thrown round them. This legitimises the provision of care. However, this care has to have a standard, and the standard is that the care provided must be in the best interests of the person. Since the first judgments looked into issues of medical care, it was inevitable that the opinion of medical experts would prevail. Yet, as other cases were brought to the courts where the issue of care was not synonymous to medical care, it became obvious that the criterion of best interests should also include other considerations, such as social or financial factors.

Besides medicalisation, one of the basic problems with adult welfare is that it is not framed within the *parens patriae* jurisdiction; if it was, the courts would have to make welfare decisions in a paternalistic matter, which would only involve the benefit of the adult. This is shown by the application of the *parens patriae* jurisdiction in other common law countries.[59] On the contrary, since the best interests of the person in English law encompass medical, social, personal, financial and all other relevant considerations, the interests of third parties are allowed to influence these considerations.

With the advent of the HRA 1998, the troublesome question in human rights terms has therefore become how to mould these considerations in a principled pattern. Would the ECtHR have found a violation of Article 8 had David Glass been an adult? To what extent can the interests of third parties, or considerations which do not place an emphasis on the individual benefit of the person, be allowed to legitimise interferences with the person's rights?

Within family law, there are the recognised rights of the parents, and there is also statutory guidance which provides some sense of direction. In the case of incapacitated adults, however, the situation is much more complex. As noted in the Introduction, incapacitated persons may have limited, impaired or no autonomy.[60]

The typologies of limited or impaired autonomy comprise adults who have had capacity, but have lost it permanently at some point in their adult life; even if English law does not accept a substituted judgment position, the decision on their welfare or best interests will be based on the person's past, her life plan, past wishes, values and history and so on, rather than on family wishes or carers' wishes or the social or moral values of the court.

Then there is the category of adults with congenital intellectual disability, who may have never had capacity. Since there are no past competent wishes which can guide the decision-making process, the judiciary has relied heavily on expert evidence. It is really this category of persons which has received the least attention and the least protection by the law. Unfortunately, this situation did not change with the passing of the Mental Capacity Act 2005.

---

59 The intransigent position is to be found in Canadian law, particularly in the case of the Canadian Supreme Court of *E. (MRS.)* v. *Eve* [1986] 2 SCR 388, where it was held that the *parens patriae* jurisdiction can only be used for the benefit of the ward.

60 See p. 29.

The Mental Capacity Act 2005

The Background to the Act

In order to comprehend the legal framework which the MCA 2005 has set up in relation to the welfare of incapacitated adults, a close look at the background of the Act is needed. Only those points which bear direct relevance to human rights issues will be highlighted.

Community care and actual integration in the society Although care in the community had been informally provided to persons with intellectual disability from at least since the early 1900s, when much of the implementation of the Mental Deficiency Act 1913 became dependent on voluntary community help, community care as official policy originates from the Percy Commission of 1954–1957. From then on, efforts were made to close down old asylums and mental wards and to provide mental health care within residential areas. This process was to prove slow, but was completed by the end of the 1990s.[61]

The new White Paper on intellectual disability, *Valuing People: A New Strategy for Learning Disability for the 21st Century*, sets the tone of current official policy.[62] The new challenge is the actual, rather than just the physical, inclusion of persons with intellectual disability within society, by providing '... new opportunities for children and adults with learning disabilities and their families to live full and independent lives as part of their local communities'.[63] Consequently, a great deal of emphasis is placed on the rights of persons with intellectual disability, and the legislative efforts which led to the enactment of the Mental Capacity Bill may be seen as part of this incentive.

The Report of the Law Commission on Mental Incapacity As *Re F*[64] was being heard in the House of Lords, the attention of both the public and legal practitioners was drawn to the fact that English law did not contain any specific regulation on the welfare of incapacitated adults. The Law Commission took up the challenge to look into the matter, and as early as 1991 several rounds of consultation began, whose findings were unified and presented in a coherent set of recommendations in 1995 with the publication of the Law Commission's Report on Incapacity.[65]

61 P. Bartlett and R. Sandland, *Mental Health Law*, 2nd ed. (Oxford: Oxford University Press, 2003) at 96–100.

62 For an extensive presentation of the White Paper, see pp. 14–15.

63 Secretary of State for Health, *Valuing People: A New Strategy for Learning Disability for the 21st Century*, Cm 5086 (London: The Stationery Office, 2001) at 2.

64 *In Re F (Mental Patient: Sterilisation)* [1990] 2 AC 1.

65 Law Commission, *Mental Incapacity*, Report No. 231 (London: Her Majesty's Stationery Office, 1995).

The report acknowledged the influence of civil rights arguments on many of its recommendations. It stressed, for instance, the importance of the 1971 UN Declaration on the Rights of Mentally Retarded Persons, which in Article 5 states: 'The mentally retarded person has a right to a qualified guardian when this is required to protect his personal well-being and interests.'[66] Consequently, the report advocated the importance of providing a form of guardianship as protective advocacy and as a civil right of those in need.[67]

Moreover, the Law Commission placed the proposals of the report within a wider social context and presented them as part of it. For instance, the report mentioned that civil rights arguments led to the review of mental health legislation with the passing of the MHA 1983, and that many local and voluntary organisations were adopting charters which stressed the obligations of service providers to consumers of services, and that, as a matter of governmental policy relevant at that time, those who were charged with arranging community care services were under the obligation to consult with those who would use or benefit from them.[68]

This description of various civil rights influences which the Law Commission admitted to have played a part in the drafting of its report reveals the narrowness of the viewpoint that the Commission took when examining the issue of incapacity. There is no mention of any human rights considerations; the mention of rights is linked to the aims of a civil rights agenda, which championed greater participation of consumers of services in the provision of these services within the NHS.

Naturally, one would not have expected the Law Commission to champion human rights causes, because in the period between 1989 and 1995, when the Report was drafted, human rights considerations had not yet emerged. The issue of human rights protection only received imminence a few years later, when the HRA 1998 was passed.

On the other hand, what human rights talk there was in relation to incapacitated adults was dominated by emotionally, and not legally, charged references to the basic right to reproduce within the sterilisation debate. And it is indicative of the absence of human rights considerations in the earlier sterilisation judgments that it was commonly held by the judiciary that the concept of a right to reproduce, when not coupled with informed procreative choice, was meaningless or non-existent.[69]

66 *Declaration on the Rights of Mentally Retarded Persons*, GA Res. 2856(XXVI), UN GAOR, 26th Sess., Supp. No. 29, UN Doc. A/8429, 93 at para. 6.

67 Law Commission, *Mental Incapacity*, Report No. 231 (London: Her Majesty's Stationery Office, 1995) at 14, para. 2.21.

68 Ibid. at 23, para. 2.40.

69 *Per* Lord Oliver in *Re B. (A Minor) (Wardship: Sterilisation)* [1988] AC 199, at 211: 'the right to reproduce is of value only if accompanied by the ability to make a choice.' Lord Hailsham LC, at 204 of the same judgment, expressed similar thoughts: 'To talk of the "basic right" to reproduce of an individual who is not capable of knowing the causal connection between intercourse and childbirth, the nature of pregnancy, what is involved in delivery, unable to form maternal instincts or to care for a child appears to me wholly to part company with reality.'

No mention of these issues is made in the proposals of the report in relation to sterilisations.[70]

As far as the question of best interests is concerned, several of the Law Commission's proposals and remarks are of great interest. It was accepted in the report that where a person has never had capacity, there is no viable alternative to the best interests criterion.[71] The report considered that a welfare checklist should be provided by the law for the benefit of the substitute decision-maker, and that this checklist should include: (1) taking into account the present and past wishes of the person and the factors that the person would consider if able to do so; (2) encouraging the person to participate in the decision-making process; (3) consulting third parties; and (4) providing the less restrictive alternative.[72]

The report then proceeded to explain what the factors are that the person would consider if able to do so. Drawing from the case law of the Court of Protection, the report stated that if the person has never had capacity, and the record of her individual preferences and personality is a blank on which nothing has been written, then the court should assume that she would have been a normal, decent person, acting in accordance with contemporary standards of morality.[73] The factors that the person would consider might also include altruistic sentiments and concern for others.[74]

The fact that the report here adopted propositions held by the courts shows that there had been no independent thinking during the consultation period on the welfare of the very specific group of persons with congenital incapacity. The judiciary is empowered to make a decision on objective grounds, which may, however, fail to meet the subjective developmental needs and aspirations of the person with intellectual disability.

A final mention should be made of sterilisation[75] and organ donation procedures.[76] The report breaks down sterilisations into three categories: (1) those relating to the treatment of a disease in the reproductive organs; such procedures do not require court authorisation; (2) those effected to alleviate the harmful effects of menstruation; these require certification by an independent medical practitioner; and (3) those proposed for contraceptive purposes; these must always have court authorisation. The report also proposed that organ donations should always be authorised by the court.

70 Law Commission, *Mental Incapacity*, Report No. 231 (London: Her Majesty's Stationery Office, 1995) at 84, para. 6.4, and at 87, para. 6.9.

71 Ibid. at 42, para. 3.25.

72 Ibid. at 43–4, para. 3.28.

73 Ibid. at 45, para. 3.30.

74 Ibid. at 45–6, para. 3.31.

75 Ibid. at 84, para 6.4, and 87, para. 6.9.

76 Ibid. at 85, para. 6.5.

A summary of the provisions of the Mental Incapacity Bill The proposals of the Law Commission for reform of the law relating to incapacity fell back in the legislative priorities of Parliament. The issue resurfaced in 1997, when the Lord Chancellor's Department published a Green Paper, Who Decides?,[77] and after further consultation, a policy statement entitled Making Decisions in October 1999.[78] The proposals put forward by these documents were scrutinised and further developed into a Mental Incapacity Bill, presented to Parliament in 2003.[79]

Clauses 1 and 2 of the bill introduced the concept of functional capacity, which focuses on the decision-making process itself. This means that a person with intellectual disability can only be held to be incapable of deciding on her own if she cannot process and balance the information available in a certain way.

Furthermore, if the person is incapable of deciding on her own, then according to clause 4 of the bill, the decision must be made in the person's best interests. The bill provided a checklist of factors that have to be taken into account in order to ensure that the final decision will actually be in the person's best interests.

The bill also introduced the concept of general authority, in clause 6, which renders lawful all the day-to-day decisions made in the best interests of a person with intellectual disability.

Furthermore, the bill instituted the new Court of Protection to ensure the judicial implementation of the bill and deal exclusively with matters of incapacity. Finally, another important provision was clause 19, which dealt with the appointment of deputies by the court. These deputies were to replace the guardians of mental health legislation.[80] They were granted powers to decide on behalf of incapacitated persons, but only for the specific matters where the court has given them decision-making authority.

The Report of the Joint Parliamentary Committee on the Mental Incapacity Bill and the parliamentary debate Following an initial motion in the House of Lords on 12 June, both Houses resolved in July that a Joint Committee was to be set up to hear evidence on the bill, with a remit to report by the end of November 2003.

The Report of the Joint Committee[81] proposed a number of significant amendments in relation to the clauses of the bill. For instance, it was proposed that a number of principles should be placed at the start of the bill to provide conceptual

77 The Lord Chancellor's Department, *Who Decides?*, Cm 3803 (London: Her Majesty's Stationery Office, 1997).

78 The Lord Chancellor's Department, *Making Decisions*, Cm 4465 (London: Her Majesty's Stationery Office, 1999).

79 Bill 120, *Mental Capacity Bill*, 2003–2004 Sess., 2004.

80 This old regulation of guardianship was to be found in s. 7 of the Mental Health Act 1983.

81 Joint Committee on the Draft Mental Incapacity Bill, *Draft Mental Incapacity Bill*, vol. 1, HL Paper 189-I HC 1083-I, Session 2002–2003 (London: The Stationery Office, 2003).

clarity in relation to the principles governing the legislative framework.[82] Other changes in terminology were proposed, not the least among which were the renaming of the bill to 'Mental Capacity Act' and the amending of the term 'general authority'.[83]

On the other hand, the report did not find that the bill was incompatible with the ECHR, in the sense of violating any human rights through the provisions contained therein.[84] The issue of human rights was aired in the work of the Joint Committee, and the some of evidence received deserves specific mention.

Up to the consultation held by the Joint Committee, all consultation papers had related to the issue of best interests, by way of a dichotomy between substituted judgment and the best interests test, as applied by the English courts. These propositions concluded that the substituted judgement test was in some ways better than the best interests test, but also took cognisance of the fact that substituted judgement is untenable in some cases, for instance in relation to persons with congenital intellectual disability. For these reasons, several of the elements of the best interests and substituted judgment tests were combined to form the basis of the concept of best interests included in the bill.

However, a different, third way to conceptualise best interests was proposed to the Committee by Professor John Williams, Head of the Law Department of the University of Wales, Aberystwyth. He supported the view that the principle of best interests could be improved or replaced by a human rights calculation. The report mentions in passing this proposal, and rejects the solution of a human rights calculation as a too onerous an improvement of the best interests test. However, the human rights calculation proposed by Professor Williams merits closer attention.

In his written submission to the Joint Committee, Professor Williams considered that placing the principle of best interests in statute would ensure consistency in the legal approach to incapacity. On the other hand, he voiced his concern as to whether the principle of best interests might favour paternalism. He stated:

> I am not entirely happy with the term 'best interests' as it does conjure up the image of paternalism. A less concise, but in my opinion a more acceptable term, would be 'in the interests of promoting the human rights of the person'. This would suggest that a liberty-based calculation has to be made which will embrace both the need to protect, but also recognise the individual's autonomy. I accept that the individual's autonomy may be seriously compromised by their incapacity; however it must still be part of the calculation.[85]

82 Ibid. at 17–18, paras 43–4.

83 Ibid. at 33 para. 111.

84 Ibid. at 18–21 paras 45–61.

85 Joint Committee on the Draft Mental Incapacity Bill, *Draft Mental Incapacity Bill*, vol. 2, HL Paper 189-II, Session 2002–2003 (London: The Stationery Office, 2003) at MIB 564.

Professor Williams had the opportunity to expand on this point when giving oral evidence before the members of the Joint Committee, intrigued by his proposal. His critique of the principle of best interests was based on two points.

First, Professor Williams claimed that best interests are vague and lead to justifying intuitive decisions:

> I think 'best interests' rather like 'welfare of the child', is a term we use and it is quite a useful term in one sense, but it is also a term that on occasions can lead to the suspension of thought and certainly the lack of thought process behind the decisions: 'It is in the person's best interests to treat them, and there we are'. It is an immensely complex thing to actually try and work out what is in somebody's best interests because there is a best interest in being protected, there is a best interest in having your autonomy protected regardless of what is happening to you.[86]

Second, he supported the view that the principle of best interests, as applied, is a bastion of paternalism:

> My worry with incorporating or using the best interests test in new legislation is that it will bring with it, if you like, all the baggage that the current common law definition has … 'Best interests' gives the impression of being very paternalistic, of doing what is best for you: 'Don't worry, dear, we will always act in your best interests', and it is much more subtle than that.[87]

On the other hand, Professor Williams defended his view on substituting the principle of best interests with a human rights calculation. He emphasised:

> What I am keen to see is that under the law local authorities, health authorities and individual professionals do what I would choose to call a human rights calculation in deciding whether intervention is or is not appropriate. Again, yes, autonomy and protection are very, very difficult things to define but we have to take them on board … It is the full calculation, looking at both sides of the equation and coming to a decision.[88]

The human rights calculation proposed by Professor Williams is a balancing act between two competing interests: protection of autonomy and protection of welfare. Whereas the principle of best interests tends to favour the protection of welfare against the protection of autonomy, the human rights calculation proposed changes this mentality by inviting carers and others to favour autonomy against welfare.

---

86 Ibid. at Q 522.
87 Ibid. at Qs 522–3.
88 Ibid. at Q 522.

The members of the Committee pressed Professor Williams hard for a more accurate description of how this human rights calculation should work in practice. The Committee also advanced the point that the human rights calculation might be even more difficult, and in certain respects more vague, than the principle of best interests. Professor Williams replied:

> I do not think that a reference to 'human rights' would be any more difficult to understand, and in some respects would be easier to understand, because it would set out quite clearly what is the internal debate within the European Convention on Human Rights, namely the struggle between autonomy and protection. In any system we have, if people do not take that on board then I think we are failing vulnerable adults, it has to be part of the equation.[89]

However, given the little time available and the complexity of the issue, it is hardly surprising that the Committee remained distrustful of this proposal. The report gives full support to the principle of best interests, requiring only some marginal clarifications of its content.

The proposal of the report to go along with the principle of best interests is unfortunate. The Committee was not convinced by the arguments of the minority of the submissions that the principle of best interests is paternalistic and can lead to abuse. On the contrary, very important submissions, such as those made by the Making Decisions Alliance, which included such powerful organisations as Mencap or Mind, were in favour of best interests, while proposing ways to improve the principle. The Committee had no time to go into the depth of the matter. The third proposal, voiced by Professor Williams, clearly did not convince the members of the Joint Committee that it could be workable.

Apart from the consultation held by the Joint Committee, sporadic references to human rights concerns were made during the parliamentary debate, but these received minimal attention, as the debate centred on concerns about euthanasia, which were fuelled by several provisions of the bill. In relation to best interests, however, an important submission was made by Lord Brennan during the second reading of the bill which identified several problem areas within its provisions. In relation to best interests, Lord Brennan remarked:

> The third area of complexity relates to 'best interests'. Clause 4 deals with a process of acquiring evidence, but it does not give us the criteria for what are the best interests, personal or financial, that will dictate a decision, yeah or nay, in favour of particular medical decisions. No criteria are given. Subsections (5) and (10) are on the periphery of criteria but do not give them. If the Bill does not tell us what best interests are-whether they depend on the opinions of the family, the

89 Ibid. at Q 527.

> quality of life, intolerability, which are nebulous concepts – who is to determine them and how? That is a serious question.[90]

However, no changes were made to the clauses relating to best interests.

The Provisions of the Mental Capacity Act 2005 and Human Rights Concerns

The Mental Capacity Act which emerged from the parliamentary readings of the bill is in many important respects still the brainchild of the Law Commission's Report. The two structural pillars of the Act remain the test of functional capacity and the concept of best interests. On the other hand, the concept of advocacy was strengthened by the inclusion of independent mental capacity advocates in the Act to ensure that incapacitated persons will participate as fully as possible in any decision made on their behalf.[91] There was also some tinkering with the structure of the Court of Protection, in order to ensure easier access to the court.

Concern and guidance over human rights issues is to be given by means of Codes of Practices. It is questionable whether the guidance provided will be able to supplement the provisions of the Act in a way that will in truth promote the independence, choice and inclusion of incapacitated persons. This is especially so in the case of persons with intellectual disability, as for them it will also be harder, or indeed very hard, to establish their wishes and feelings in relation to important issues about which a decision has to be made.

To use the terms of the MCA 2005, it may not be practicable to do so. For instance, in cases of emergency relating to medical treatment where the person with intellectual disability is speech-impaired, finding an expert in developmental psychology who may have the expertise to tease out the true meaning of the disabled persons' gestures or grunts or dislocated words may be difficult, expensive and cumbersome.

By not providing some obligatory standard of conduct in relation to these difficult cases, the door is left open for paternalistic attitudes which may influence the decision made on behalf of the incapacitated person; what is more, this paternalism may eventually take the form of ascertaining the values and feelings of the person in ways which in fact substitute the preferences of the person with the subjectively value-laden judgment of the decision-maker.

This is not to say that all the wishes of the person are always to be respected. As the MCA 2005 rightly accepts, any decision made on behalf of the incapacitated person should serve her welfare. For instance, medical treatment may have to be provided when a person with intellectual disability has broken her arm, even though she may have a morbid fear of doctors. Yet, on the other hand, no real

---

90 H.L., *Parliamentary Debates*, 5th ser., vol. 668, col. 85 (10 January 2005) (Lord Brennan).

91 S. 35 of the MCA 2005.

safeguard is provided against possible misjudgements of carers in relation to the exercise of their decision-making capacities.

Ultimately, the picture that arises from the Mental Capacity Act 2005, in relation to its actual provisions, is that it is a piece of legislation which reflects long and laborious thinking on the welfare of incapacitated adults. Within this group, however, several of the special problems associated with congenital intellectual disability are not adequately addressed by the Act. Given the historical evolution of how English law has treated adults with intellectual disability, one can realise that the wrongs of the past are not really mended by the MCA 2005.

In terms of the general thinking behind the MCA 2005, the fact that the basic proposals which constitute the backbone of the Act were formulated in an era when human rights considerations were virtually non-existent marked the path that the Act was to take. For the Joint Committee on the Mental Incapacity Bill, it was enough that it could be shown that the provisions of the bill did not violate any rights contained in the ECHR.

In this sense, the relation between the MCA 2005 and human rights is essentially a negative one; it can be showed that no violation arises. Yet the propositions of Professor Williams for a human rights test gave the Commission another option in relation to human rights: to set up a framework of provisions, grounded firmly in human rights considerations, which would actively promote the human rights of incapacitated persons. Unfortunately, these proposals were presented rather late to have significant impact in the very long consultation period of what was to become the MCA 2005.

Sterilisation Procedure and Organ Donation

The law governing the sterilisation of adults with intellectual disability was summarised in the evolution of the concept of best interests in English law. The enactment of the Mental Capacity Act 2005 did not change much in this legal framework.

Before the passing of the MCA 2005, the authority on the law was officially *Re F*.[92] This judgment made clear that medical treatment may be administered lawfully to a person incapable of consenting to the proposed treatment in so far as the treatment is in the best interests of the incapacitated person. The House also held that the essential precondition for the treatment being in the best interests of the person was for it to be supported by a responsible body of medical opinion.

Several years later, the Court of Appeal was to hear the sterilisation case of *In Re S*.[93] In that judgment, the Court of Appeal interpreted the dictum of *Re F* as stating that the test for establishing the best interests of the person included, firstly, establishing whether the proposed treatment was supported by a responsible body

92 *In Re F (Mental Patient: Sterilisation)* [1990] 2 AC 1.

93 *In Re S (Adult Patient: Sterilisation: Patient's Best Interests)* [2001] Fam. 15.

of medical opinion; however, since there may be more than one medical option available which a responsible body of medical opinion would endorse, the choice of medical treatment to be administered should, secondly, be determined by not just medical, but also by broader ethical, social, moral and welfare considerations.

The approach to best interests taken by the Court of Appeal has found its vindication in the MCA 2005, as the question of best interests is to be determined by a large number of factors, among which the criteria given by the Court of Appeal feature prominently.

Yet even if the legal basis for the authorisation of sterilisation procedures remains more or less in line with the case law, at least with the judgment delivered by the Court of Appeal in *Re S*, two important procedural aspects of the law have been changed by the MCA 2005. The first is that the authorisation of sterilisation procedures will be effected by the Court of Protection, and according to the procedures of that court. The second is less obvious, but far more important. It is stated in s. 19 of the MCA 2005 that in cases of serious medical treatment proposed by NHS bodies, the Secretary of State may prescribe that an independent mental capacity advocate will be consulted for her views on the matter. It is almost certain that in the Codes of Practice to accompany the MCA 2005, both sterilisation procedures and organ donations will be included in the category of serious medical treatment.

In this sense, the procedural protection granted to persons with intellectual disability in sterilisation procedures will be immensely strengthened. Instead of the common judicial triangle of the court, the patient, and the doctors or carers, a fourth person with expertise in advocacy will have a role to play in the judicial process, thereby increasing the presence of the person with intellectual disability in the hearing of the case.

Even though it remains to be seen what practical impact advocacy may have on the authorisation of organ donations or sterilisation procedures, it is unfortunate that the substantive law relating to organ donations was not amended by the MCA 2005.

The law concerning organ donation was set down by *Re Y*.[94] For this reason, a short description of the case is appropriate. The mother of a woman with intellectual disability regularly visited her daughter, Y, at a home, and the daughter was apparently fond of her mother's visits. Unfortunately, Y's sister fell gravely ill and required a bone marrow donation by Y in order to survive. In contrast to the mother, however, the ill sister did not have any contact with Y. In this sense, the question was whether the donation of bone marrow to the ill sister could be said to be in the best interests of Y so as to be authorised by the court.

The court effectively saved the day by claiming that the donation would benefit Y, by stretching the concept of best interests. As mentioned before, Y was close to her mother, and derived some psychological benefit from her visits. The reasoning of the judgment was that, were the sick sister not to have a successful bone marrow

94 *Re Y (Mental Patient: Bone Marrow Donation)* [1997] Fam. 110.

transplant, the mother's role as a primary carer until the sister died and thereafter, her role in looking after the child of the sick sister, would impact on the mother's ability to spend time with Y. Therefore, the psychological benefit of maternal visits would be lost on Y. For this reason, the donation was authorised.

The best interests of the individual in *Re Y* were defined by her relationship with her mother and the complicated fact that not donating the bone marrow to a third person would impact on that relationship. In this sense, the conceptualisation of the best interests of Y included very broad considerations of welfare. The law on best interests in relation to organ donations was couched by *Re Y* in such wide terms that the judgment begs the question whether, after all, adequate protection is given to the human rights of persons with intellectual disability donor, since almost anything can be proven to provide some benefit to a person with intellectual disability.

The Joint Report on the Mental Incapacity Bill did not engage in a critical examination of the dictum in *Re Y*, and as with sterilisations, no specific mention of organ donations is made in the provisions of the MCA 2005. In a very real sense, therefore, the MCA 2005 unquestioningly accepted the judicial dicta in cases such as *Re S* and *Re Y*, and used these as illustrations of what the law on best interests under the Mental Capacity Act 2005 is.

Again, as with sterilisations, the MCA 2005 only changed the procedural aspects of the authorisation of organ donations. It is almost certain that organ donations will also be included in the category of serious medical treatment requiring, according to s. 19 of the Act, the consultation of an independent mental capacity advocate. For this reason, as with sterilisations, the voice of the incapacitated person and her wishes will be more adequately heard in the judicial proceedings. This dissipates, to an extent, the fear that non-regenerative organ transplants may be authorised under the statutory regulation.

A Summary Evaluation of the Development of English Law Relating to Intellectual Disability

The evolution of English law, both common and statutory, on best interests forms part of a wider context of social and political changes, and more importantly, of ideologies of equality.

Women became the first major group of disadvantaged persons to fight for their rights and to successfully claim the institution of measures designed to assure their equal treatment in relation to men. The end of World War II saw the rejuvenation of liberal ideas and policies, which led to the acceptance, under the civil rights movement, that other disadvantaged social groups should be granted equal rights by the law. Mentally ill people and persons with intellectual disability were among these groups.

The Mental Capacity Act 2005 forms part of this gradual process of granting rights, and of making the voice of disadvantaged groups more audible within the legal system and within society. However, the shortcomings of the Act make it plain that the provisions of the MCA 2005 are only one step forward in this continuous effort to provide equality.

Most importantly, the MCA 2005 fails to respond to the challenge of the times in which it has been enacted. The passing of the HRA 1998 and the subsequent orientation of English law to a more rights-centred approach is absent from the Act. Even though the MCA 2005 can be credited as being the one piece of legislation in the paternalistic history of English law in relation to incapacitated persons which actually empowers them to take part in the decision-making process relating to their welfare, this empowerment is caught in the modes of the past. To the extent that there is no right of the incapacitated to be heard, and their voice is to be consulted only if it is practicable to do so, the MCA 2005 cannot provide a guarantee of equality, or a catalyst for further changes in the law.

In this sense, we argue that the best interests test does not hold enough substantive material which could generate a more principled and thorough examination of issues relating to decision-making in respect of incapacitated persons, and especially those with intellectual disability.

For this reason, we will now embark on a comparative examination of German law in respect of incapacitated persons, in the hope that such an analysis may provide pointers as to how a more principled approach, firmly protecting the human rights of persons with intellectual disability, can be constructed within English law.

Chapter 6
German Law Relating to Intellectual Disability, Incapacity and Welfare

In order to approach the issue of intellectual disability in the German legal system, it is necessary to navigate the course of the investigation with the help of the Grundgesetz, the German Basic Law on the one hand, and the BGB, the German Civil Code, on the other. These two pieces of legislation form the backbone of the German legal system.

The BGB came into force in 1900. It was, for its time, a piece of progressive legislation in what was predominantly a repressive political atmosphere after the failure of the 1848 revolution; yet it contained, and in many ways asserted, the growing social and financial importance and confidence of the middle class. The classic example of this attitude is the groundbreaking, for the 1900s, right to personality, protecting the autonomy and privacy of the individual by granting a legal claim of compensation against the person who violated the right.

Moreover, the BGB was very much a product of its time in relation to its intellectual affinities; the great industrial revolution, scientific progress, belief in reason, but also the profound learning of German scholars versed in Roman law, are clearly reflected in the provisions of the Civil Code. In this sense, the BGB can be regarded as an expression of Enlightenment ideals as much as anything else.

On the other hand, the German Basic Law represents, both symbolically and normatively, the new beginning of German society and the German legal system after the end of World War II. And as an immediate reaction to the atrocities of the Nazi regime, the Constitutional Assembly of Bonn anchored human dignity as the foremost legal principle of the German legal system, in Article 1 of the Basic Law, and clothed the until then civil right to personality in the constitutional cloak of Article 2 of the Basic Law. Yet this new beginning did not equate, in constitutional terms, with a complete rupture with the past.

On the contrary, the constitutional traditions of the lands comprising Germany and, most importantly, the Constitution of Weimar influenced the provisions of the Basic Law. A striking example of this, which will also come up in a later section in this chapter, is the regulation of the right to family under Article 6 of the Basic Law; as family is placed under the protection of the state, the latter is thereby legitimised to intervene in family life. Such a regulation should have been unthinkable given the many and grave interferences of the Nazi regime to family life, had it not been for a similar regulation in the Constitution of Weimar; in this way, the nascent Republic of Western Germany preserved part of its constitutional history while also ensuring that it had sufficient control over social and political life to uproot the vestiges of Nazi ideology.

Intellectual disability as a legal issue surfaces only indirectly in both the Basic Law and the Civil Code. Even though the general constitutional rights are naturally granted to disabled persons, it was felt that a specific provision should be inserted in the Basic Law relating to disability. This was accomplished by Article 3 III 2 of the Basic Law, which guarantees equality to disabled persons.

The issue of intellectual disability features in the Civil Code as part of the regulation of matters of incapacity. When the Civil Code was enacted, the prevailing belief in reason and the influences of Roman law led to the establishment of a legal framework for incapacitated persons heavily influenced by notions of Roman law tutelage. The person under tutelage was denied capacity to consent to any contract or any other legally binding act; she was appointed a tutor who would decide these matters on her behalf.

Even though this legal regulation of incapacity came to be increasingly criticised and was viewed as unsatisfactory by many, it was not until 1992, when the reunification of Germany prompted many changes in the law, that a new framework for incapacitated persons was enacted: the system of legal carership.

A more detailed analysis of the carership system is provided later in this chapter. For now, however, two important points are of note. The first is that the carership system cannot be understood, or function in legal terms, outside its wider context, that of the Civil Code and the Basic Law. This systematic interpretation permeates every facet of the German legal system. It is accepted in German academic writing that the principle behind the carership system is rehabilitation. In this sense, any specific regulations among the carership provisions must be read in this light.

Moreover, since the carership system forms part of the Civil Code, the general principles and rights underlying the BGB must also form part of the interpretation of the carership provisions: most notably, freedom of contract, and the right to personality. And finally, these two levels of interpretation must also conform to the ultimate, and legally highest, principles and rights of the Basic Law: in this context, the principle of human dignity and the constitutional right to personality. These tiers of legal analysis, argumentation and interpretation form a substantively rich basis to draw from in order to apply the law correctly. This may naturally prove difficult in certain cases, yet the basic stepping-stones of the process are clearly set down.

The second point that needs to be highlighted relates not to substance, but to procedure. Within these constitutional and civil law frameworks of rights and principles, which work in parallel with the system of carership, the courts are directly involved and are called upon to establish the legal relationship between the carer and the person under carership. The courts therefore create a personal, legal, bond between the carer and the person under carership, which relates to specified issues, fixed for a specified time. This achieves great clarity in the law; one always knows who is authorised to decide what and for how long. Moreover, carership functions within the context of constitutional and civil law, and in disputed matters the courts are again authorised to intervene and clarify the law.

Procedurally, therefore, it is a great safeguard against possible abuses that the courts appoint carers, and authorise them to carry out specific tasks. For instance, the guardianship court may appoint a carer to look after the personal, but not financial, affairs of a person. Moreover, the law provides a further safeguard: the court intervenes in disputed matters within the area of responsibility entrusted to the carer.

Even this brief sketch of the constitutional and civil law frameworks of German law enables one to understand that many tiers of principles and rights are at work within the carership system. In this sense, the claim of this chapter is that procedural formality and the existence of several procedural steps of substantive safeguards inherent in German law enable a structured discussion or disagreement before the courts as to how a person with intellectual disability can lawfully be treated. As will become evident in a later section, even though no specific criteria have been set down in relation to the interests or the welfare of the person, both the procedure and the substantive provisions of the Civil Code and the Basic Law provide with an excellent starting point to air these issues through a principled approach. From there on, finding the right answer in law becomes an issue of interpretation. However, this is much different from the pragmatic, case-by-case approach of the English courts, where no principles, let alone specific criteria, have been set down.

Having made this claim, it is now time to turn to the analysis of the law. The first section briefly explains the legal and social policies in relation to intellectual disability. The second section analyses how these policies and principles are reflected in the constitutional right of equality for disabled persons, entrenched in Article 3 III 2 of the German Basic Law. the next section presents an analysis of the carership system and tries to answer how the welfare of persons with intellectual disability has been interpreted by the German legal system. The welfare of adults with intellectual disability is then contrasted to that of children in the fourth section, which shows that because the constitutional framework within which the welfare of children is argued is markedly different from that of adults, the solutions given are much different; in contrast to the English position, no fallacious analogy has been drawn between adults with intellectual disability and children in German law. The next section deals with the regulation of sterilisation in respect of person with intellectual disability adults, and the final section summarises the findings of this comparative analysis of English and German law.

Social and Legal Policies Relating to Disability

Rehabilitation

In the previous section, reference was made to rehabilitation as the principle underlying carership law. Rehabilitation has also been the driving force of German social welfare law from the end of World War II until the economic depression of the 1980s. Rehabilitation was traditionally accepted as part of the doctor's duty of care towards her patients, in the sense that the doctor should not only provide the patient with adequate medical care, but also find ways for the patient to overcome the effects of her illness or disability and become, once again, an active and full member of society. As a social welfare principle, rehabilitation has gradually evolved in an aim to support sick and disabled persons so that they may lead a life which is dignified, by means of all those measures that help persons develop their potential and strengths and find a suitable place in society.[1]

Since the general economic depression of the 1980s, the social welfare state is constantly shrinking, and the idea now is to integrate the disabled into society, rather than providing each and every disabled person with exhaustive rehabilitative training. For instance, instead of training every disabled person to climb stairs, one can provide them with wheelchairs and ramps, which will also be used by the elderly and mothers with babies.[2]

Carership

Given Germany's constitutional framework, it is accepted that the law has a duty to support persons who are in need of help because of physical or mental illness, intellectual disability or old age. Even though financial difficulties have forced the German state to curtail the actual provision of rehabilitative treatments on a grand scale, rehabilitation as state policy remains rooted in the German legal system, as it is considered a major pillar of the welfare state.

A clear expression of this are the legislative changes which took effect in 1992, abolishing the outdated law on tutelage of adults and replacing it with the legal institution of carership.

On the one hand, carership law is founded on the principle of rehabilitation: the carer has a clear duty to facilitate the rehabilitation of the person under carership. The view is also held in academic writing that this duty even extends to carers entrusted with only the financial affairs of the person under carership. According to this view, carers over financial matters have to regulate the finances of the person in a way that not only accommodates the wishes of the person, but also makes it possible to finance rehabilitative treatment in order to cover the eventuality that the person under carership may wish it.

On the other hand, carership law places great emphasis on the wishes of the person subject to it. Any measures restricting the rights of the person under carership are confined to what is absolutely necessary. This regulation grants protection to the constitutional right to personality within the framework of carership law.

---

1 S. Strassmair, *Der besondere Gleichheitssatz aus Art. 3 Abs. 3 Satz 2 GG* (Berlin: Duncker and Humblot, 2002) at 44.

2 Ibid. at 66.

The Constitutional Right of the Disabled: Article 3 III 2 GG

The General Equality Clause of Article 3 GG

German constitutional law includes several provisions that guarantee the principle of equality. Article 3 I is the general equality clause, laconically guaranteeing equality before the law. Equality under the law is not expressly protected by Article 3. To this effect, German academic writing and the German Constitutional Court have interpreted Article 3 I in conjunction with Article 1 III, which binds the legislature, the executive and the judiciary to respect constitutional rights and freedoms. Moreover, Art 3 II 1 and Article 3 III 1 prohibit discrimination on the basis of specific characteristics. According to the consistent case law of the German Constitutional Court, it is inferred from these provisions that absolute equal treatment or a blanket prohibition on all discrimination is not covered by the Basic Law. On the contrary, the principle of equality has been interpreted as prohibiting not only the unjustified differentiated treatment of the substantially similar, but also the unjustified similar treatment of the substantially different.

Article 3 III 2

Within this wider context, the prohibition of discrimination on the grounds of disability, entrenched in Article 3 III 2 of the Basic Law, was inserted in the Constitution during the constitutional revision which took place in 1994 after the reunification of Germany. It was felt at the time that a specific mention of disability was needed in order to stress and amplify the protection that Germany, as a social welfare state, grants to vulnerable persons, and thereby strengthen their position in society and the law.

Disability, in the sense of Article 3 III 2, is a non-temporary handicap of the physical, intellectual, or mental functions. 'Disabled', in the meaning of the regulation, includes all who, because of a continuous disability caused by their physical, intellectual or mental state, cannot acquire a position in society. The prohibition of discrimination is also taken to extend to those discriminatory regulations which, even though they are not based on disability but other criteria, have a discriminatory effect against the disabled. The total prohibition of any discrimination against disabled persons in relation to the non-disabled is not guaranteed by this regulation, however. At any rate, such discriminating measures cannot be direct.

Article 3 III 2 does not create any duty of the state to create a situation of practical equality in relation to non-disabled persons. On the other hand, it does not also prohibit the taking of any positive measures to help the disabled, but leaves this open for the legislator to decide. Most importantly however, the prohibition of discrimination is understood as stressing the equality and the equal importance of disabled people under the law, as well as guiding state action in contributing to the equality of all people.

Even though the disabled person may not have a claim-right against the state for the provision of support or rehabilitative treatment, she does have a negative right to fight against any discriminating measures before the Constitutional Court in cases where legislative measures have contravened the prohibition. The disabled person also has a positive right against the state. In those cases where the state provides financial or other support to vulnerable groups, excluding the disabled, the person can ask that the same support be provided to the group of disabled persons as well.

In this sense, it would seem that the practical importance of Article 3 III 2 is very limited, even though it is important as an interpretative principle and as guidance to the legislature. However, this is not the case, as the prohibition of discrimination on the grounds of disability not only works vertically, affecting the relationship between the state and the individual, but also has a horizontal effect on legal relationships between individuals. Whereas it is accepted that the constitutional legislator explicitly wished this prohibition to have horizontal effect, its extent is disputed in German academic writing.

The prevailing view is that Article 3 III 2 only has indirect horizontal effect. This means that a person, acting as an individual in her private capacity, can actually discriminate against disabled persons; her constitutional liberties allow her that much. But in more general situations, such as employment contracts or general clauses in contracts where goods or services are being offered, the prohibition of discrimination against the disabled applies, because in these cases the private interests of the person become abstract and undefined. The indirect horizontal effect binds the judiciary when interpreting legislation, employment contracts or general clauses; the interpretation of these legal documents has to be made in light of Article 3 III 2.

On the other hand, a minority of academic writers support the view that this prohibition has, at least partially, direct horizontal effect. This interpretation reads Article 3 III 2 in conjunction with Article 1 of the Basic Law, which protects human dignity and has direct horizontal effect. It is argued that the prohibition of discrimination on the grounds of disability plainly aims to protect the human dignity of the disabled person, to the extent that the disability is part of her identity or her personality. In this sense, just as with any private legal action which violates human dignity, discriminating against the disabled is prohibited by Article 3 III 2, taken in conjunction with Article 1 of the Basic Law. This interpretation is more coherent with the aims of Article 3 III 2, which are to serve the social integration and participation of disabled persons.

The Case Law Relating to Article 3 III 2

Article 3 III 2 of the Basic Law has been used to resolve two strands of case law which have enjoyed great coverage and criticism in German media. The first issue relates to holiday contracts offered by big travel agencies. There have been cases where the traveller complained that during her stay in the hotel booked by the agency she was annoyed by the fact that persons with intellectual disability were also staying in the hotel. In several instances, before Article 3 III 2 was passed, the courts did find, based on the terms of the holiday agreement, that this was a flaw in the provision of the holiday package.

However, under Article 3 III 2, the sight of disabled persons during one's holidays does not constitute a flaw of the holiday offer, since a private legal agreement to provide a holiday place free of disabled persons is not valid, as it is against the Constitution.[3] A flaw could only be accepted in the case of repeated noise-making, which would have to be of very great intensity. This protective treatment in favour of disabled persons is justified constitutionally as a compensation for the practical inequality in society that the state tries to iron out. Relative case law has accepted that in such cases, there has to be a higher degree of tolerance in relation to disabled persons.

The second strand of cases relates to complaints about the emission of noise from neighbouring homes or gardens where persons with intellectual disability are playing or talking.

The most notable case of this strand of case law comes from the OLG Köln.[4] The court here accepted that there has to be a high degree of tolerance towards disabled persons. But the court did not place the emphasis on the loudness of the emissions and cries of the persons with intellectual disability, but rather on the exasperation that these cries caused for a normal person. In this sense, the criterion by which the emission of noise could be deemed lawful was not the intensity of the cries, as in the similar case law on holiday offers. This objective criterion was dropped in favour of the annoyance these cries could cause to a normal person – a purely subjective point. The judgment raised a storm in Germany, since from the viewpoint of disabled persons, these cries are their efforts to communicate. In this sense, the main criticism of the judgment concentrated on freedom of expression, as Article 3 III 2 combined with Article 5 I (freedom of expression) of the Basic Law protect the equal right of the disabled to communicate. The German Constitutional Court did not answer the question whether the degree of annoyance can be determined by the exasperation caused by the cries of persons with intellectual disability, since it rejected the case as inadmissible.[5]

3 AG Kleve [2000] NJW 84.

4 OLG Köln [1998] NJW 764.

5 S. Strassmair, *Der besondere Gleichheitssatz aus Art. 3 Abs. 3 Satz 2 GG* (Berlin: Duncker and Humblot, 2002) at 265.

§§ 1896f BGB: Carership Law

The Previous System of Tutelage over Adults and the Need for Reform

Since the German Civil Code came into force in 1900, and until 1992, matters relating to the legal representation and protection of incapacitated adults were being regulated under the legal framework of tutelage. The influence of Roman law and the prevailing intellectual climate of the time, which was both authoritarian and attached great importance to reason and intellect, resulted in the drafting of regulations which were deeply discriminatory. Even the linguistic framing of the provisions was discriminatory. Moreover, the tutelage of adults resulted at least in the partial incapacity of the person to form binding legal transactions. Tutelage could therefore not be regarded as compatible to the principle of proportionality. The provisions of tutelage, which made no exception in reducing the person's capacity, were also not required in order to protect the person or legal transactions.

For many reasons, both political and financial, the reform of the tutelage system did not acquire legislative priority until Germany was reunited. The legal and constitutional changes which were required were many, and the new carership system was enacted as part of this general legislative programme, to take effect from 1992.[6]

The carership system became widely accepted, thus revealing how deep the need for a protective legal framework for vulnerable people had been. In fact, the carership system became too popular: the courts were constantly presented with cases relating to carership issues, especially those relating to the remuneration of carers. Moreover, the financial cost of the carership system became, at one point, too great to be supported by the German social welfare system. For these reasons, a legislative reform took place in 1998 which simplified procedural issues and introduced cost-reducing modifications to the system.[7]

The Constitutional Framework of Carership

In German constitutional theory, the carership system is viewed as an expression of the law's duty to support persons who need help because of physical or intellectual disability, mental illness or old age. This duty reflects the constitutional principle entrenched in Article 20 I of the Basic Law stating that Germany is a social welfare state.

Yet the direct constitutional anchoring of the carership system is much more technical. The constitutional basis of carership can only be understood in relation to its legal function, which is to ensure the legal equality of every individual as a legal personality in cases and to the extent that this person does not have autonomy.

---

6 *Betreuungsgesetz vom 12. September 1990*, BGBl. I, 21 September 1990, 2002. A translation is provided in the Appendix.

7 *Betreuungsänderungsgesetz vom 25. Juni 1998*, BGBl. I, 29 June 1998, 1,580.

In constitutional terms, carership ensures that everybody is granted the dignity recognised to every person, through which everybody is recognised by the law as a legal personality. This recognition of legal personality does not depend on whether the person is actually autonomous or not, and in this sense achieves equality in the law. But to the extent that the person cannot make use of the possibilities that the law opens to everybody because of factual circumstances, this recognition of legal personality is devoid of importance. If the individual cannot make use of these rights because of reduced autonomy, the state is obliged to permit and make possible to the individual the exercise of these rights under the same conditions as everybody else. In this sense, carership is not an infringement of the rights of the person, but on the contrary serves to create the legal personality of the person as a requirement for the exercise of the person's rights. Naturally, this does not mean that the legal personality created by carership exhausts its potential only in facilitating the formation of contracts.

Since the state is obliged by Article 1 I 2 of the Basic Law to protect human dignity, this means that the state not only has to ensure the physical existence of the person, but also her legal personality, and therefore her legal equality. The constitutional justification of carership is therefore based on Article 1 I 2 (duty to protect human dignity) and Article 3 I of the Basic Law (equality before the law).

In other words, if the abstract aim of the carership system is to provide support and protection to vulnerable persons, the tangible way by which this aim is achieved is by the appointment of a carer over the person. The carer then acts as a legal representative of the person under her care, and looks after those matters that the person is incapable of taking care of herself. In this sense, the person under care, although incapacitated, still continues to be actively engaged in legal transactions through her legal representative, the carer. In this way, the legal personality of the incapacitated is kept alive, upheld, shaped and expanded by the carer. This achieves factual equality in the legal system in relation to the recognition of legal personality to all persons: both those capable of consenting and the incapacitated have a valid legal personality and are active participants in the legal system.

This analysis may seem like hair-splitting in common law terms, yet in terms of German constitutional theory, it is of fundamental importance. The recognition of legal personality to all persons, without exception, is constitutionally guaranteed by the principle of human dignity, which is entrenched in Article 1 of the Basic Law and forms the very foundation of the German legal order. Transcribed in constitutional terms, the carership system ensures that the human dignity of the incapacitated person is upheld in a way which equates the incapacitated with those capable to consent.

Carership law meticulously follows the principle of proportionality, and places great emphasis on respecting the wishes and the will of the person under carership. The carership framework ensures that any measures infringing the liberties of the person under care are restricted to what is absolutely necessary. In terms of procedural safeguards, the person under care is protected most of all by the fact that the person has to be heard before the appointment of carership.[8]

The responsibilities of the legal carer are described in §§ 1901–8 BGB. The carer must, in accordance to these regulations, take all necessary steps to look after the legal affairs of the person. According to § 1901 para. 1 BGB, the welfare of the person is the deciding factor. This regulation makes it clear that the welfare of the person includes the ability to lead her life according to her wishes and ideas, as far as her abilities allow her to do so. The carer must comply with the wishes of the person, as far as those are not against her welfare and as far as these wishes are made known to the carer.[9]

In this sense, the respect granted to the wishes of the person complies, in constitutional terms again, with the right to personality entrenched in Article 2 I of the Basic Law. At first glance, therefore, the apparent tension between the wishes of the person and her welfare should be resolved in favour of the constitutional right, which trumps parliamentary legislation. In relation to persons with intellectual disability, this would not only seem problematic, but would also run contrary to established notions of the duty of care. In order to examine the issue more thoroughly, an extensive discussion of the carership system is required.

The Legal Structure of Carership

The appointment of a carer The carer is either appointed on demand by the person wishing to be received into carership, or by the court on its own. The court can only appoint a carer on its own when the person in incapable of consent. In cases of only physical disability, the appointment of carer by the court without prior demand of the person is not made.

The precondition for the appointment of a carer is that the adult cannot look after her own affairs in all or in part, because of mental illness, such as alcoholism or drug abuse, or because of physical or intellectual disability. The appointment of the carer follows the principle of necessity. This is the reason why carership is characterised by the law as subsidiary in relation to other private or public means of support or help.

The appointment of a carer as means of subsidiary help is especially out of the question when the person has already given power of attorney to another person to look after her affairs. If the affairs that need to be covered by the appointment of carership are already covered by the power of attorney, carership is not necessary and will not be authorised. Where this is not the case, a carer is appointed. A carer will also be appointed when there are suspicions that the power of attorney is not valid, or when the person cannot supervise the person given the power of attorney adequately. However, the appointment of a carer is always necessary when the

8 W. Schlüter, *BGB-Familienrecht*, 10th ed. (Heidelberg: C.F. Müller, 2003) at 276.

9 Ibid. at 266–7.

person is in need of a legal representative. This is the case when the person is incapable of consenting to contracts, or when the person's capacity is in such doubt that nobody is actually entering into any contracts with her.

The principle of necessity not only bears on whether a carership can be authorised, but also on how the responsibilities of the carer are to be defined. According to § 1896 II 1 BGB, the responsibilities of the carer are to cover only those affairs that the person cannot look after herself, such as the cleaning of her home, her health issues or support in divorce procedures. This regulation is flexible, so it can take into account the different kinds and severity of the person's illness or disability.[10]

The representation of the person under carership In relation to those affairs that are entrusted to her, the carer represents the person under her care both outside the courts and inside them. The carer is the legal representative of the person. However, the appointment of the carer does not have any negative effect on the capacity of the person to consent, if the person has such capacity. This does not change the fact that the person can be incapable of consenting according to German law when the person cannot freely form her own will because of a state of mind which is caused by illness.[11]

Reservation of consent In cases where the person receiving carership would not be adequately protected by being represented by her carer, the court can reduce the person's capacity to form contracts. According to § 1903 I BGB, the court can declare that the person under carership requires the consent of the carer in order to make a proposal for contract which would be relevant to the affairs that the carer is looking after, if that is necessary in order to avoid a substantial danger to the person or her property. In relation to those legal transactions where the court has reserved consent, the person under carership can only form contracts with the consent of her carer.

In this sense, §§ 1896 and 1903 BGB allow for a progressive reduction of the person's capacity to consent. The guardianship court has to examine whether and to what extent the person is need of a carer because of physical or intellectual disability or mental illness. Independently from this question, the court has also to decide whether and to what extent the capacity of the person to consent has to be reduced in accordance to § 1903 BGB. With this regulation, the court can reduce the capacity of the person according to the circumstances of the case, following the principle of proportionality. For instance, the court can reduce the capacity of the person to consent to contracts above a certain value. For these contracts, the consent of the carer is needed.

According to § 1903 II BGB, the reservation of consent cannot extend to marriage or personal relationships. It is questionable whether this regulation is

10 Ibid. at 277–8.
11 Ibid. at 278–9.

successful. Under German law, persons incapable of consent are incapable of marrying (§ 1304 BGB). The marriage of persons incapable of consenting can be annulled (§ 1314 I BGB).[12]

The principle of personal carership Carership law wants to avoid persons being represented anonymously by professional carers, who had been appointed as tutors to more than a hundred persons before the carership reform took place. Personal contact, and most of all personal discussions, could not take place under such circumstances. A relationship of trust could not be formed. This is the reason why the law, in § 1897 I BGB, states that the carer must preferably be a natural person who is capable of legally looking after the affairs of the person and personally caring for her. The ideas and wishes of the person under carership have to be respected as far as possible in relation to the appointment of her carer. If the person does not or cannot propose anyone as carer, the court, before reaching its decision, must take into account the family and personal ties of the person and the possibilities of conflicts of interests.

The person to be appointed as carer must do so, generally speaking, without requiring a fee. If a person undertakes carership as part of her profession, she can only be appointed as a carer if there is no other person capable of doing so without a fee. If the appointment of a natural person is not possible, the law allows for hospitals or charities to become carers, or if that is also not possible, the responsible social work department.[13]

The duties of the carer The duties of the carer are described in detail in §§ 1901–8 BGB. Under these regulations, the carer is obliged, to undertake all action required to legally take care of the person's affairs. According to § 1901 II BGB, the welfare of the person is the deciding factor. The regulation makes it clear that the welfare of the person also includes the possibility to live, according to the person's abilities, in accordance to the person's wishes and ideas.

The carer must follow the wishes of the person as far as these do not contravene the person's welfare and are to be reasonably expected by the carer. This is the case even when the person is incapacitated. The law also makes it clear that wishes of the person under care, expressed before the appointment of a carer, are only not to be followed if the person does not want them to be fulfilled any more.[14]

§ 1901 BGB primarily aims to regulate the internal relationship between carer and person under carership, whereas § 1902 regulates the external relationship between the carer as the legal representative of the person and the rest of the legal order. The application of § 1901 BGB does not depend on whether the person lives in her usual home or in a community home or is confined. Moreover, § 1901 BGB continues to apply even in cases where the person is capable of consenting and

12 Ibid. at 279–80.

13 Ibid. at 280.

14 Ibid. at 280–82.

legally capable of forming contracts according to her own wishes and ideas. If the person has been appointed a carer because the person cannot look after part or all of her own affairs, § 1901 BGB still applies to the carership relationship between carer and the person under carership.[15]

§ 1901 II contains a general principle of the law which was in force even before carership law came into force.[16] This principle also applies to the external legal relationships between the person under carership and third parties, and is the guiding principle for the duties of the carer.

Para. II 2 is an important regulation which can also be used, in that the person under carership will continue to live, as long as possible, in her home. Especially after a spell in hospital, it becomes increasingly difficult to let the person return to live in her old home. Social welfare practice shows that this can be done successfully with the help of ambulant aid. Moreover, the regulation makes clear that the increase of the person's property cannot be regarded as serving the welfare of the person without further examination if the person under carership wishes to spend more money and live with certain luxuries.[17]

Para. 3 regulates the relative preference of the wishes of the person and the duty of the carer to discuss important issues relating to affairs of the person under carership. Para. III 1 states that the carer must fulfil the wishes of the person under carership, and defines under which requirements and to what extent the carer should do so. The wishes that the carer must fulfil may not only be in the present, but also in the past. The taking into account of the wishes of the person under care is a general principle of the carership law. The duty of the carer to discuss important decisions regarding the welfare of the person is the core of the legislative notion of personal carership. It must be understood as the widest possible involvement of the person in the decisions affecting her welfare.

Whereas paras 2 and 3 of § 1901 BGB relate to the relationship between the carer and the person under carership, para. 4 completes the duties of the carer and contains important guidance as to how the carer should fulfil her duties. Para. 4 obliges the carer to use every possibility within the duties entrusted to her, so that the illness or disability of the person under carership will be cured, or at least its effects will diminish in intensity. In this sense, the carer is an important factor in achieving the rehabilitation of the person under carership. But the carer, even if she is only entrusted with the financial affairs of the person, should strive to achieve these rehabilitation aims, in that the carer should encourage the person to regain control of her own affairs.[18] However, para. 4 does not mean that these rehabilitation aims should be achieved without, or even against, the will of the person under carership.

---

15 W. Bienwald, *Betreuungsrecht Kommentar*, 3rd ed. (Bielefeld: Giese King, 1999) at 299.

16 Ibid.

17 Ibid. at 300.

18 Bt-Drs 11/4528 at 134.

Finally, para. 5 of § 1901 BGB regulates an informational duty of the carer, which has, however, found little application in courts.[19]

In a nutshell, therefore, § 1901 BGB contains several orientation points for the carer, which make it plain that the carer is considered by the law as the representative of the person's interests, and not those of third parties. On the contrary, the welfare of the person is the deciding factor for the exercise of carership duties. The carer must look after the affairs of the person in a way that serves the welfare of the person. The welfare of the person is the limit at which the wishes of the person under carership are no longer to be followed.

The welfare of the person cannot really be defined *in abstracto*. However, as some indication of its contents, the law states that it is also part of the person's welfare to lead her own life according to her own wishes and ideas. In this sense, the carer must allow that the person under carership actually leads her own life according to her own capacities and to the extent compatible with her welfare. The carer is therefore not authorised to interfere in cases where the person is living in a socially abnormal way for that reason alone. In this sense, the welfare of the person cannot be defined only objectively, but also subjectively, according to the wishes of the person.[20]

The wishes of the person under carership can relate to every detail of the care that the carer provides, such as housing, moving house, treatment by a specific doctor and so on. However, it is not the duty of the carer to judge the correctness of such wishes in relation to whether she or a third party would actually decide similarly. The wishes of the person under carership bind the carer even if these are not addressed to her. This is especially important in everyday situations where the person under carership lives in a home. The carer should always investigate whether the person under her care has expressed any wishes to third parties.[21]

It is clear that the legislator has in mind, as a starting point, that in general, the wishes of the person do not contradict the person's welfare. However, this can be totally different in cases of illness, when the wishes of the person may be influenced by fantasies or dreams. Wishes which are plainly against the welfare of the person cannot be followed by the carer. How that is decided, in what circumstances, or how wishes fall into this category have been left undecided by the legislator. The criterion for determining the welfare of the person can be the selfsame person under care, when the carer makes a decision stepping in her shoes.[22]

The potential of the person to lead her own life according to her own wishes and ideas, within the framework of her capabilities, is an important part of what the law understands to be the criterion for every action of the carer: the welfare of the person under her care. The forming of one's life plan based on one's own

19 W. Bienwald, *Betreuungsrecht Kommentar*, 3rd ed. (Bielefeld: Giese King, 1999) at 300–302.

20 Ibid. at 303–4.

21 Ibid. at 306.

22 Ibid. at 306–7.

self-determination, within the framework of one's capabilities is the object and the aim of carership. In this sense, the planning of one's life based on one's self-determination cannot be characterised as being against the welfare of the person, even if the person's ideas are not considered correct by the carer or third parties.

The prerequisite for self-determined life planning is to have the corresponding capabilities. The person must be in the position to form her own wishes and ideas and use them as an orientation point or as a basis for her life plan. This does not mean that the person's life plan must cover all aspects of the person's life. Even when the person can only plan a part of her daily life, this must be respected. Within her life plan, the person is under no other restrictions by the carer, just like any other person not under carership. Wishes that the person expresses within the framework of her life plan cannot be regarded as against the person's welfare.[23]

The carer must fulfil the wishes of the person under carership. However, if the fulfilment of such wishes are not to be reasonably expected from the carer, the carer can ignore them. With this regulation, the legislator has tried to make sure that extravagant wishes of the person under care cannot be taken into account: for instance, wishes that cannot be fulfilled by the financial means of the person or by social welfare, or wishes that reach the limits of illegitimate behaviour can be ignored.

There is doubt in academic writing as to how this reasonableness is to be decided. For this question, it is important on the one hand to identify what is expected from the carer to do, and on the other hand to examine whether the carer can actually provide what is asked of her. If the carer is expected to follow a wish of the person which cannot be ignored, then the second criterion applies: whether the carer is available, in terms of time and personal involvement, to fulfil the wish of the person under carership.[24]

The duties of the guardianship court The carer, in the exercise of her duties, is under the constant control and supervision of the guardianship court. Of course, the independence of the carer is not affected by this regulation. The carer is not an organ of the guardianship court, nor is she turned into one by this regulation. However, if the carer is not executing her duties, the court must take action and issue orders to her. In extreme cases, the court can dismiss the carer and replace her with someone else. Moreover, the carer requires the authorisation of the court for several important or dangerous decisions, such as medical interventions that may endanger the life of the person under carership.

As many of the regulations of carership law show, the court can only examine whether the carer is actually exercising her duties – whether the carer is acting against the law, or whether the carer is acting in a way incompatible with the

23 W. Bienwald, 'Zur Umsetzung des Betreuungsgesetzes in der Praxis' [1992] Fam. RZ at 1,127–9.

24 W. Bienwald, *Betreuungsrecht Kommentar*, 3rd ed. (Bielefeld: Giese King, 1999) at 307–8.

welfare of the person. These regulations stress the independence of the carer, which ensures the constitutional liberty of the person under carership. The guardianship court can only intervene in this liberty if the carer is ignoring a wish of the person that has to be followed, or if the carer is harming the property or the person and this behaviour is not based on a self-determined wish of the person under carership. The guardianship court is therefore not allowed to make any decision on what would be better for the person under carership, but only on whether the decision of the carer is legally permissible.

The guardianship court is also bound to serve the welfare of the person under carership, just as the carer is. From the moment a carer is appointed for the person, the role of the guardianship court is to control the carer, or authorise carership acts such as medical interventions. The welfare of the person under carership legitimises the interferences in her liberty in these instances. Moreover, the court is also obliged, just as the carer is, to follow the wishes of the person.

Consent to medical interventions According to § 1904 I BGB, the carer is required to have the authorisation of the guardianship court in order to consent to a medical examination, a therapeutic treatment or other medical intervention when there is a substantial danger that the person under care may die or suffer severe and long-lasting health damage because of the medical intervention. Only if delay creates further danger can the carer go ahead with medical intervention without the authorisation of the court. The carer can be allowed to consent to these medical interventions only if the person under carership is incapable of consenting. As long as the person under carership can understand the nature, the meaning and the importance of the medical intervention and can make up her own mind responsibly, the person can consent or withhold consent as a bearer of the constitutional right to bodily integrity, according to Article 2 II of the Basic Law. The competency of the carer to consent is subsidiary in relation to that of the person under carership.

The regulation of § 1904 BGB is not successful, and has therefore had very little practical importance. In many cases, it cannot be certain whether a medical intervention caries any danger for the person under carership. Moreover, the authorisation of the guardianship court does little to protect the person under carership, since the judiciary usually follows the opinion of medical experts who are brought before the court.[25]

The duration of carership In order to make sure that the carership will only last as long it is necessary, § 1908 d I BGB states that carership must be removed or reduced if the circumstances that necessitated its authorisation no longer exist. However, in any case, the appointment of a carer must be limited in time. The longest period is five years. A continuation is admissible.[26]

25 W. Schlüter, *BGB-Familienrecht*, 10th ed. (Heidelberg: C.F. Müller, 2003) at 282–3.

26 Ibid. at 285.

Wishes and welfare in the case of intellectual disability The analysis of the carer's duties towards the person under her care have already pointed to how German academic writing has interpreted the relationship between welfare and wishes of the person under care with respect to the constitutional rights that underpin this relationship. It is time to provide a fuller analysis of the constitutional reasoning behind welfare and wishes.[27]

The liberty rights of the individual serve as classic negative rights against interference by the state. They protect the liberty of the individual to define on her own her interests and aims – in other words, the autonomy of the person. This constitutional protection does not depend on the use that the person actually makes of these rights, on whether the person uses these rights or not, on whether these decisions seem logical or irrational to the eyes of third parties, or on whether the person is actually hurting herself or her property.

Therefore, in cases where the state would become active in the constitutionally protected areas of liberty of the individual against her will, the state would in fact be replacing the decision of the individual with an extraneous decision, and would thereby violate the rights of the person. However, it is accepted that the state can stop the individual from harming others in the exercise of her liberty. The state is not allowed to make the person better or discipline the sick. In this sense, protection from self-harm against or without the will of the individual affected is generally prohibited. In those cases where such infringements of the person's liberty can be allowed, these must be covered by a general law and must also be suitable, necessary and proportional to protect the rights of third parties or the general public.

For these reasons, one can conclude that the appointment of a carer by the guardianship court is a state intervention in the liberty of the individual if the appointment is authorised without or against the will of the individual. As long as the appointment of the carer is not accompanied by a reservation of consent, the appointment of the carer infringes the liberty of the individual only potentially. The infringement is performed through the decisions of the carer, which serve the welfare of the person under care without or against her will. This means that the infringement of the liberty of the individual is transferred by the state to the carer, but this does not equally mean that the state is not bound to respect the constitutional rights of the person. The individual measures that the carer makes without or against the will of the person would also constitute infringements in the person's liberty.

Since carership and welfare decisions of the carer aim at serving the welfare of the person, carership against or without the will of the person would be constitutionally invalid.

---

27 See V. Lipp, *Freiheit und Fürsorge: Der Mensch als Rechtsperson* (Tübingen: Mohr Siebeck, 2000) at 118.

However, the German Constitutional Court has already decided that involuntary carership is constitutional. This means that these state interventions are not actual infringements of the constitutionally protected areas of liberty of the individual.

If the function of liberty rights is to guarantee the individual an area of autonomy against interventions by the state, this requires the practical, actual capacity of the person to autonomy. As far as the person has no self-determination, then the state is not actually taking the freedom of the person away when it regulates that the decisions of the person are not be taken into account, and in the place of these decisions, the state actually puts forward its own decisions regarding the person's affairs. In this case, the state is not actually infringing the liberty of the individual, and therefore does not require any justification based on the rights of third parties or of the public. For this reason, the German Constitutional Court has rightly decided that the limited self-determination of the person allows the state to make care interventions even in areas where, in the case of healthy people, the state is forbidden to interfere. The opposed will of the person is legally indifferent. Constitutionally speaking, force, such as brushing aside the natural will of the person, is to be distinguished from the autonomous choice over the use of liberty. Every kind of state force infringes the area which is protected by the liberty right. However, an infringement of these liberty rights exists only when the self-responsible decision of the bearer of the rights is not taken into account, since the constitutional protection of liberty requires the autonomy of the bearer of rights.

For these reasons, the appointment of a carer, against or without the will of the person, and specific measures taken by the carer do not constitute infringements in the liberty rights of the person under care when the capacity of the person under care is limited.

This position has two consequences. On the one hand, the carer protects the area of liberty of the person under carership against state intervention, in that the carer also undertakes to exercise negative liberty rights of the person under her care against the state. State intervention, in the form of the guardianship court, in these areas of liberty against the will of the carer constitutes an infringement in the liberty rights of the person under carership. This is not the case only in situations where the decision on the person's rights has been made by the carer but is not to be seen as an expression of the liberty of the person under carership because, for example, the carer is not following a wish of the person under her care which must be respected.

On the other hand, as far as preventive measures are concerned, several regulations of the carership law make it clear that the carer may only decide against the natural will of the person under her care to the extent that the limited autonomy of the person necessitates it, since such measures are often irreversible.

In the case of persons with intellectual disability under carership, their wishes, to the extent that they do not touch upon diminished autonomy, are to be respected by the carer. In cases of doubt, however, the person's right to self-determination should be respected.[28] A hypothetical example would be a person with Prader-Willi syndrome, which is commonly associated with voracious appetite, who suffers from diabetes. The wish of the person to be given money, which will invariably be spent on sweets, can safely be ignored. On the other hand, supposing that the person has a good sense of direction, her wish that the carer should arrange for her a taxi drive to and from the zoo should be respected.

The decisive question here is how the person with intellectual disability would decide, if she were in a position to make that decision, with full understanding of all the facts and consequences of the act in question. The ideas, preferences and so forth of the person under care are substantively important in this respect. If that does not lead to any answer, then more general criteria must be used. In this case, academic writing accepts a definition of the person's welfare as the summing up of the person's development interests: for instance, the welfare of the person under carership includes, as an open-ended legal term, the entirety of the person's interests to preserve or develop health or property.[29]

The Welfare of Children in German Constitutional and Civil Law

The Constitutional Basis of Child Welfare: Article 6 GG

In the previous section it became clear that the way in which the welfare of adult persons under the carership system is perceived within the German legal system is ultimately shaped by the interpretation of the constitutional rights and principles that underpin the regulations of carership in relation to the constitutional right to personality that the person under carership enjoys.

In relation to child welfare, the legal and constitutional background is radically different; the issue turns on the right to marriage and family, and on what constitutes legitimate interference in that right. The vantage point of the analysis is therefore primarily the discussion of a negative right held by the parents against state interference. The constitutional rights that children also enjoy do not form a prima facie part of this equation. To the extent that children display growing maturity, however, their influence on how their welfare is decided grows as well, and accordingly, the decision-making capacity of the parents and the legitimate interferences of the state lessen in their extent and intensity.

On the other hand, this seemingly simple interpretation of a negative right which defines how the welfare of children is perceived in German law is much more complex, as the right to marriage and family is not only a negative right, but a constitutional guarantee as well. Marriage and family, as legal institutions,

28 D. Schwab, '1901 BGB' in MüKo, vol. 8, 4th ed. (Munich: C.H. Beck, 2002) at 1,925.

29 Ibid. at 1,923–4.

are placed under the special protection of the state; this protection legitimises interferences or regulations of the right to family, which would seem odd had they been applied to a classic negative right.

The constitutional history of Article 6 of the Basic Law stretches back to the Constitution of Weimar, which was the first ever constitution in Europe to guarantee the protection of marriage, family, motherhood, parental rights, children born outside marriage and young persons. The aim of these constitutional provisions was to place marriage as practiced in Western countries under the special protection of the Constitution, and at the same time to reject communist perceptions of marriage.[30]

Under Article 6 of the Basic Law, the content of family and upbringing are not defined by the state, but they are left to the persons enjoying this constitutional right to decide.[31] The way the parents wish to care for the physical well-being and mental and intellectual development, education and upbringing of their children is protected in the parental right of Article 6 II 1 as an independent right in relation to the right to family life. The parents especially have the right to specify the name of the child, or to decide whether the child will be cared for by one or both parents, or by another person.

However, Article 6 not only protects marriage and family in the interest of the individual liberty of the married partners and other family members, but also for the sake of the individual's liberty within the family and for the sake of its perpetuation.[32] For this reason, Article 6 II 2 obliges the state to supervise the exercise of parental rights which are guaranteed in Article 6 II 1 – the care and upbringing of the child.[33]

According to the German Constitutional Court,[34] the welfare of the child is central to this supervisory role. To the extent that the parents can provide a material and ideal family environment, they have the entire responsibility for determining the living and development conditions of the child.[35] The child, according to the court, is a being who has her own human dignity and her own right to the development of her personality, but cannot really defend herself from any threat to the development of her personality. This is why the court understands the supervisory role of the state to prevent the child's development being damaged by misuse of parental rights, or mistreatment.

---

30 R. Gröschner, 'Artikel 6' in H. Dreier, ed., *GG Kommentar*, vol. 1 (Tübingen: Mohr Siebeck, 1996) at 487.

31 Ibid. at 488.

32 Ibid. at 488–9.

33 B. Jeand'Heur, *Verfassungsrechtliche Schutzgebote zum Wohl des Kindes und staatliche Interventionspflichten aus der Garantienorm des Art. 6 Abs. 2 Satz 2 GG* (Berlin: Duncker and Humblot, 1993) at 17.

34 BVerfGE 24, 119 at 120.

35 R. Gröschner, 'Artikel 6' in H. Dreier, ed., *GG Kommentar*, vol. 1 (Tübingen: Mohr Siebeck, 1996) at 520–21.

The control of the state on the exercise of parental care has nothing to do with the interests of society or the state. On the contrary, the duty of the state is to protect the child as a bearer of rights. This duty of protection starts to apply when the parents fail in the exercise of parental care and the welfare of the child is endangered. This means that state protection has a subsidiary role in relation to the primary right of the parents to exercise parental care. In this sense, the state can only intervene when the welfare of the child is endangered or damaged. Questions of good or better in relation to how the child is brought up cannot be answered by the state. The state does not guarantee the child the best or optimal upbringing, but only protects the child from damage to her welfare.[36]

Usually, academic writing develops lists of indicators as to what is endangering the welfare of the child. The state can then intervene and offer help, at first providing support to enable the parents to exercise their parental rights correctly. If these measures do not have any effect, the state can even remove parental responsibility, according to Article 6 III of the Basic Law.

The Welfare of the Child in the BGB

Setting aside the provisions concerning marriage and divorce as irrelevant to this analysis, the critical regulation of parental care is to be found in §§ 1626 BGB f. Parental care in the German Civil Code was completely restructured several years ago. The law concerning parental care and parental contact with the child, as well as the legal provisions concerning court jurisdiction, were either completely changed or substantially overhauled. Moreover, the legal differences between children born in marriage and children born outside marriage were abolished. The target of the reform was to strengthen the right of the parents to provide parental care without unnecessary outside interference from the state.[37]

The reasons for the reform of the law concerning parental care were both internal and external to the German legal system.[38] The internal causes of the reform have to do with the case law of the German Constitutional Court. In a series of cases, the BVerfG found that several of the provisions of the BGB were unconstitutional, for instance the provision that the parents could not have common parental care after their divorce, or the provision that there was a different jurisdiction covering the alimony procedures for children born within marriage and those born outside marriage.

The external reason that brought about the reform is the UN Convention for the Rights of the Child, which became part of German law in 1992. Some of the basic principles of the Convention stress the responsibility of the parents for the care of

36 B. Jeand'Heur, *Verfassungsrechtliche Schutzgebote zum Wohl des Kindes und staatliche Interventionspflichten aus der Garantienorm des Art. 6 Abs. 2 Satz 2 GG* (Berlin: Duncker and Humblot, 1993) at 22.

37 W. Schlüter, *BGB-Familienrecht*, 9th ed.(Heidelberg: C.F. Müller, 2001) at 176.

38 Ibid.

their children, according to their welfare, and that there should be no differences between the legal treatment of children born within or outside marriage. German law was thought not to be in complete accordance with both the spirit and the letter of these guidelines, so that reform was necessary to level out these differences and secure the rights of the child.

For these reasons, one of the most important changes in the law brought about by this reform is that, according to § 1626 BGB, parental care for the child is a duty as well as a right which both parents have. This means that the right and duty of parental care continues to exist even when the parents divorce. The state, or in this instance the court, has no jurisdiction in divorce proceedings to intervene in the common parental care unless one of the parties specifically asks the court to restrict parental care to only one of the parties.[39]

In this sense, parental care is a subjective right of the parents whose function is to protect the child and to ensure her development and welfare. The parents exercise this right under their personal responsibility in order to serve the welfare of the child.[40] Parental care includes the care for the person of the child and her property, as well as the representation of the child in legal matters. According to § 1626 para. 2 BGB, the parents must take into account the abilities, the potential and the needs of the child during its upbringing in order to help the child become an autonomous and responsible person.

The care for the person of the child includes, according to § 1631 para. 1 BGB, most of all the responsibility and the right to care for the child, to bring the child up, to look after the child and to determine the child's residence. The caring for and upbringing of the child are the most important parts of parental care, and are designated as natural rights of the parents as well as their foremost responsibility in Article 6 of the Basic Law. Care for the child is mainly understood as feeding, clothing and looking after her health. With the term 'upbringing', the law has in mind the moral, intellectual and physical development of the child. The aims of the child's upbringing are left to be decided by the parents, in accordance to Article 6 para. 2 of the Basic Law. However, both academic writing as well as the case law of the BVerfG stress that, within the confines of the German legal system, which supports a liberal and responsible social behaviour, the upbringing of the child must target her development so as to become a responsible personality.[41]

Moreover, § 1631 para. 2 BGB makes it clear that children have a right to a non-violent upbringing, so that any physical or psychological mistreatment is not covered by parental care. Academic writing also supports the view that parents should take into account the growing autonomy of their children, so that, in accordance with § 1626 para. 2, the parents should discuss questions of parental care with their children and seek commonly accepted solutions.

---

39 The second instance in which the court can interfere with parental care is, according to § 1666 BGB, danger to a child's welfare.

40 W. Schlüter, *BGB-Familienrecht*, 9th ed. (Heidelberg: C.F. Müller, 2001) at 226.

41 Ibid. at 228.

However, § 1626 para. 2 does not include any measures against the exercise of parental care which would contravene the way the law considers that parental care should be exercised. Although the state has, according to Article 6 of the Basic Law, a supervisory role over the right to marriage and family, the only way that the state can interfere with the substantial exercise of parental care is under the strict circumstances of § 1666 BGB.

The Protection of the Child's Welfare by the Family Court

As mentioned above, the court has jurisdiction to intervene in parental care in two circumstances. The first is when the parents divorce and do not wish to exercise common parental care, and one of the parties asks the court to decide which of the parent should have the responsibility for it.[42] The court, according to § 1671 para. 2 Nr. 2 BGB, may decide to give the right to parental care to the party asking for it if this would serve the welfare of the child. The court has to examine which solution under the specific circumstances of the case better serves the welfare of the child.

The first step for the court is to examine whether the common exercise of parental care is impossible under the circumstances, or whether it is probable that there will be conflicts in the common exercise of parental care which will hinder the development of the child. If the court comes to the conclusion that the common exercise of parental care is not possible, it then proceeds to examine which of the parties will better protect the welfare of the child – which parent is best suited and is in a better position to care for the child. If the parents' capacities for upbringing or material circumstances are more or less the same, then the court has recourse to the continuity of the development and upbringing of the child. The child's bonds with her parents and siblings are important in answering this question.

The second intervention in parental care is, in a sense, much more radical, and has to do with the substance of parental care that the child is receiving. This intervention is covered by § 1666 BGB. The state has retained for itself, in Article 6 of the Basic Law, a supervisory role over the family which obliges the state to protect the child from any danger that may ensue from mistreatment or misuse of parental care. However, this supervisory role of the state clashes with the autonomous right of the parents to parental care, and the resulting conflict is regulated in §§ 1666f BGB. § 1666 para. 1 BGB sets out the conditions under which the state must interfere when the personal or financial welfare of the child is endangered. § 1666 (a) BGB stresses the principle of proportionality which has to be taken into account especially when severe measures are being decided, such as the removal of parental care.

The three conditions under which the court can intervene are the following:

42 Ibid. at 221.

1. misuse of parental care, through neglect of the child, through no fault or error or through the behaviour of a third party,
2. which endangers the physical, intellectual or psychological welfare of the child, and
3. where the parents do not wish to address the danger or are not in a position to do so.[43]

The failure of the parents to protect the welfare of their child does not have to be intentional. By the term 'misuse of parental care', the law means cases where parents do not use their right to parental care in a way that protects the child or benefits its welfare or helps the child to develop into a responsible personality. However, since the parents enjoy a certain freedom in setting down the targets for their way of upbringing, the court cannot consider actions of the parents as a misuse of their right to parental care simply because the court considers them as impractical or improper. According to the case law of the family courts, the misuse of parental care must be clear to every sensibly thinking parent.[44] The term 'neglect of the child' covers any passive behaviour of the parents that harms the child's welfare.

The child's welfare is hard to describe, but depends on the aims that the care for the child, and most of all her upbringing, serve. In a liberal state, the state can only define the outlines of those aims – the upbringing of a child to become a responsible person – so that differences of opinion are bound to arise. In most cases, the court can only decide on whether the welfare of the child has been harmed after hearing expert opinion.

The fact that the parents do not wish to protect the welfare of their child or are not in a position to do so is not really a precondition for the court's interference in parental care. It has to do with how and what the court should do in order to safeguard the child's welfare. In doing so, the court is bound to follow the principle of proportionality.

The Case Law on § 1666 BGB Relating to the Welfare of the Child Born to Parents with Intellectual Disability

§ 1666 BGB states that the court, under strict circumstances, can take measures if the welfare of the child is endangered. The measure most commonly undertaken by the courts in reported cases is the removal of parental care, which is usually accompanied by a residence order if the child has not already been removed from the family home by state authorities. The law does not require any culpable failure of the parents to look after the welfare of their child; the endangerment of the child's welfare is a sufficient ground for the interference of the court.

43 Ibid. at 243.
44 Ibid.

This aspect of the law is important in the case of disabled parents who are physically or intellectually disadvantaged in relation to non-disabled parents. Even in their case, it is only the welfare of the child which matters to the court. This does not mean that German law or the courts assume *in abstracto* that disabled parents cannot look after the welfare of their children. On the contrary, parental care from parents with intellectual disability is removed after careful consideration of the facts of each case.[45] Central to the argumentation of these judgments is danger to the child's welfare.

A legal expert opinion highlights this issue well.[46] The case related to a married couple of persons with intellectual disability. The woman would give birth in a few months to a son, who, according to medical opinion, would not be disabled, either intellectually or physically, and the couple would then return to their family home in a workshop facility for persons with intellectual disability. It was not clear to the authorities whether the couple could actually look after the baby during the night time, so the social welfare authority decided that at the beginning, social workers would provide support 24 hours a day.

The opinion states that if parents with intellectual disability live in a supported family home, the protection of marriage and family dictates that the parents should live with their children as family. The only exception to this would be if the cohabitation of parents and children would represent an endangerment to the welfare of the children. From this constitutional protection ensue rights of the parents against the state to provide support. Otherwise, the special protection of family by the Constitution would have simple declaratory value. This positive side of the right to family empowers the parents to claim suitable facilities and support to bring up their child, so that the special protection of family will be realised in their case as well. With this constitutional analysis as a backdrop, the legal question in the case was which of the social welfare authorities should provide the budget.

In a judgment dating from 1998, the OLG Oldenburg removed parental care, as the basic social development of the children in question could not be achieved by the parents, but only in a social care home.[47] Only parts of the reasoning of the case are reported, and this makes it difficult to understand what precisely was wrong about the parental care provided. The court follows the expert opinion of two psychologists who testified that should the children remain at the family home, their psychological and emotional development would remain stagnant and that the children would not have the chance to be brought up so as to lead autonomous lives. The court stressed that its concern was not that the intellectual or educational deficit of the parents might be transferred to the children, but rather, that the children would not have the opportunity to lead a normal life if they continued

45 A judgment of the OLG Karlsruhe [2001] J. Amt. 192 provides an example of removal of parental care, because the parent (here the mother) is mentally ill.

46 DIJuF-Rechtsgutachten [2003] J. Amt. 354.

47 OLG Oldenburg [1998] DA Vorm. 934.

to live with their parents. The court accepted the opinion of both psychological experts, who agreed that these opportunities would be offered to the children at a specific social care home.

The court turned down the arguments of the mother that the court could order positive measures, in accordance to social welfare law, that would help her in bringing up the children within the family. The court did not make such orders, since this provision of support cannot be given when the welfare of the children is already endangered by residing at the family home.

Another recent case from the OLG Brandenburg relates to the issue of positive measures to be provided to the parents to support them in the upbringing of their children.[48] The facts of the case are extremely complicated, but a short summary runs thus: a mother with intellectual disability had three children from different sexual affairs. She was under carership in relation to her financial affairs. The mother relinquished the care of one of her children, which she then wanted back. The child had begun to attach herself to her foster family. The return of the child to the mother, according to the expert psychological opinion, would not serve the welfare of the child. Moreover, according to the opinion of the social welfare authorities, the care of the remaining two children by their mother was only possible, given the intensive support provided to the mother by the welfare authority.

The court analysed in detail the behaviour of the mother in relation to her daughter, now living with a foster family, and concluded that the return of the child to her mother's home would not serve the welfare of the child. The court stressed that the rejection of the mother's claim for the return of her daughter was in accordance to the principle of proportionality. In the present case, and for five consecutive years, social welfare support had been provided, but came to nothing. The court concluded that if measures aimed at developing responsible behaviour from parents towards their children failed, then the separation of the children from their parents was unavoidable. The principle of proportionality does not authorise limitless expenditure in the provision of support to parents so that they may secure their parental rights.

Some federal states are beginning to provide such social services to families. An example is a social welfare scheme providing family care for disabled mothers and their children[49] in Württemberg-Hohenzollern, which enables the mother and the child to live together in a foster family. Both the mother and her children are cared for by the social welfare authority as well as a person within the foster family. In this way, mothers who have little or no skills in bringing a child up but none the less wish to live together with their child are empowered to do so.

From these examples emerge several patterns in the legal perception of the welfare of the child born to parents with intellectual disability. It is clear that the

48 OLG Brandenburg [2003] J. Amt. 603.

49 Rems-Murr-Kreis, 'Konzeption Familienpflege für behinderte Mütter und ihre Kinder' [2003] J. Amt. 338.

courts follow closely medical expert opinions which are presented to court. Whereas the opinions of legal experts tend to examine all possible legal alternatives to the welfarc and disability issue, the courts tend to follow expert opinions from either social workers or medical doctors. This leads most often to the splitting of the family, since there are no other viable alternatives which can enable some family to live together. However, this is now becoming more and more possible through the provision of common family care.

The Regulation of Sterilisation in § 1905 BGB

In order to round up this presentation of the welfare of persons with intellectual disability in German law, a more detailed analysis of the sterilisation issue is needed. Setting aside the long history of eugenics in Germany, which as an intellectual current of thought runs deeper than the period of Nazi Germany, it is important to note that the sterilisation issue was not explicitly addressed after the war, and the sterilisations which took place at the time before the carership law came into force in 1992 moved in a grey zone of legality.[50] Even though academic writing supported the constitutional compatibility of sterilisations, the need for legislative regulation was apparent. The regulation of sterilisations was inserted in carership law, but is criticised in academic writing as a political compromise which does not offer substantial guarantees against involuntary sterilisations.[51]

None the less, the regulation of sterilisation in the BGB is important, in that it grants an absolute veto right to the person with intellectual disability. If the person refuses, by any means, to undergo the procedure, the sterilisation cannot take place.

From a constitutional point of view, sterilisation is a grave intrusion into the right to bodily integrity, protected in Article 2 II of the Basic Law, and can therefore only be authorised under the strict safeguards of that right. However, this does not account for the granting of a veto right against the procedure. The reasons of this regulation are twofold. Firstly, and having regard to the atrocities committed by Nazi Germany, such as the mass sterilisation of persons with intellectual disability, the German legal system displays a great sensitivity in relation to sterilisation issues, in an effort to efface the horrible past. Secondly, and given this legislative sensitivity, the veto right can be seen as an expression of the negative side of the constitutional right to personality – the right to be left alone. Since the person refuses to undergo the sterilisation, she cannot be forced to accept it. In this sense, even if the person does not have capacity to consent to or refuse the sterilisation, the law acknowledges that the person with intellectual disability has a right to object to it, which has to be respected as an expression of her right to personality.

50 B. Pieroth, 'Die Verfassungsmäßigkeit der Sterilisation Einwilligungsunfähiger gemäß dem Entwurf für ein Betreuungsgesetz' [1990] Fam. RZ 117.

51 W. Schlüter, *BGB-Familienrecht*, 10th ed. (Heidelberg: C.F. Müller, 2003) at 284.

§ 1905 BGB

§ 1905 regulates the sterilisation of adults. The carership law accepts as a starting point that a free-willed sterilisation, to which the person has validly consented, does not raise any legal issues. § 1905 regulates cases in which the person under carership is incapacitated and the carer consents on her behalf. The carer can only consent when: (1) the sterilisation does not contradict the will of the person; (2) the person is permanently incompetent; (3) it can be supposed that, without the sterilisation, a pregnancy would take place; (4) the pregnancy presents a danger to the life of or a serious negative effect on the physical or psychological health of the pregnant woman which in all probability cannot be averted, and (5) the pregnancy cannot be averted by any other means. The consent of the carer also requires the authorisation of the guardianship court, and the actual sterilisation procedure can take place only after two weeks have passed since the authorisation has been granted.

Sterilisation is considered a grave intrusion into the right to bodily integrity. Normally, therefore, the sterilisation procedure may be carried out only with the consent of the person with intellectual disability. If the person is an adult and is considered capable of consent, then the person is left to make up her own mind about the sterilisation without interference from her carer or of the court.

But on the other hand, as in the general medical interventions regulated in § 1904 BGB, the person may be incapable of consent because she cannot understand the nature, meaning and consequences of the procedure and make up her mind according to these facts. If the person with intellectual disability is incapable of consent, then § 1905 BGB applies. The sterilisation procedure may be authorised with the consent of a special sterilisation carer and the authorisation of the court only if stringent hurdles are overcome.

The first and foremost of these conditions is to ensure that the sterilisation is not against the will of the person with intellectual disability. If at any time before the sterilisation takes place the person expresses, by any means, her unwillingness to undergo the operation, then the proceedings have to be abandoned. A large proportion of German academic writing on the subject also points out that if the person has medical phobias and dislikes medical treatments, then this could well be interpreted as an objection to sterilisation. In essence, all these mean in law that even though the person with intellectual disability has no right to consent, she still has a right to object to the sterilisation.

The second condition of § 1905 BGB is that the person with intellectual disability will be continually incapable of consent. This element establishes the necessity that someone has to make the decision for the sterilisation on behalf of the person, since she will never be able to reach that decision on her own.

The third condition is the risk of pregnancy. The risk must be grave and imminent. A sterilisation based on the general assumption that some day the person will likely engage in sexual intercourse is not permissible. The abstract possibility of pregnancy is not enough. The same applies to male persons with intellectual disability. A foreseeable risk that the female partner of a man falling within the conditions of carership may become pregnant meets the conditions of the law, and may lead to authorisation of the man's sterilisation.

The fourth condition is that this foreseeable pregnancy will endanger the life or the mental or physical health of the pregnant woman, and that this danger cannot be treated through other means. An example of this would be a pregnancy that will lead to serious depression and possible suicide tendencies, if these psychological effects cannot be treated through proper medication.

The fifth and last condition of the law is the impossibility of preventing pregnancy through other means. This condition is a direct expression of the proportionality principle that applies in all measures that interfere with constitutional rights. Sterilisation has to be considered as *ultima ratio* of the law, as the final and most drastic of all contraceptive measures. If the same contraceptive outcome can be achieved by other less invasive means, these are to be preferred.

The court examines whether the conditions of § 1905 BGB are cumulatively met. It then appoints a natural person as special sterilisation carer according to § 1,899 BGB. If the carer gives her consent to the procedure, the court, in its turn, may after all accept or refuse to authorise the sterilisation. If the court grants its authorisation, the sterilisation may take place two weeks after the authorisation at the earliest, so that other parties can have the necessary time to appeal against the authorisation if they so wish.

The Case Law on § 1905 BGB

As mentioned in a previous section, carership law came into force at the beginning of 1992, and the regulation of sterilisation procedures for persons under carership were not amended in the reform of carership law in 1997. This stability in the law would mean that a considerable and consistent body of case law should have been formed in the interpretation of § 1905 BGB. This is not so in the case of the sterilisation issue. Even though the number of sterilisations authorised by the guardianship courts is small,[52] this does not account for the handful of reported cases on sterilisation.

The case law stretches as far back as 1994, when the AG Grevenbroich refused to authorise the sterilisation of a 38-year-old incapacitated autistic woman.[53] The court rightly held that the general supposition that the woman, who was living in a mixed home, would some day find a partner and would have sexual contact could not justify the sterilisation of the woman. There needed be, the court accepted, a tangible risk of pregnancy.

---

52 Between 1992 and 1994, 239 sterilisations were authorised on a federal level. See Bt-Drs 13/3822 at 4. Complete statistical data can be found at the website of the German Ministry of Justice at <http://www.bmj.de/media/archive/1089.pdf>.

53 AG Grevenbroich [1995] Bt. Prax. 164.

The next case in this strand of case law came from the OLG Düsseldorf in 1995,[54] relating to detailed matters of court procedure. Among other findings, the court held that the sterilisation carer cannot consent to the sterilisation before the court has first given its initial authorisation. The invalidity of the carer's consent cannot be mitigated by the later authorisation of the court. In this judgment, the court was maintaining the high procedural standards that the law had set down in relation to the authorisation of sterilisations. Consequently, the court did not authorise the sterilisation.

A year later, in 1996, the LG Hildesheim also gave a judgment relating to procedural issues.[55] This time, the court held that the sterilisation carer appointed by the court could not be discharged of her duties because she withheld her consent to the sterilisation procedure after she had examined the facts of the case and decided that the requirements of § 1905 I BGB were not met in the present case. This area of responsibility was exercised by the sterilisation carer in accordance with the law. The court was therefore not allowed to interfere in the area of responsibility which was assigned to the sterilisation carer by discharging the carer. Again, in the present case, the court was striving to safeguard the independence of the sterilisation carer against any interference by third parties. The sterilisation was not authorised.

The judgment of the BayObLG in 1997 signals a turn in the case law towards substantive issues that need to be addressed.[56] The court held that the sterilisation was not justified when there were no tangible reasons to expect that the person would become pregnant if no contraceptive measures were to be taken. The probability of a pregnancy must be high, in accordance with the circumstances of the case. The abstract possibility of a pregnancy was insufficient. The court subsequently refused to give authorisation for the person to be sterilised.

Another judgment reported in relation to § 1905 BGB was decided by the OLG Hamm in 2000.[57] This judgment authorised the sterilisation of a woman with intellectual disability, based on a dubious interpretation of the requirements that § 1905 BGB sets down. The court agreed that a sterilisation cannot be authorised against the natural will of the person under carership. But the court held that the natural will of the person has to be directed against the sterilisation as such. If the resistance of the person under carership is directed against other circumstances, these circumstances have to be altered before the sterilisation can take place. In this instance, the person had successfully fought against any medical examination of her fertility. The court found that the resistance of the person was directed against doctors, and not against the sterilisation procedure as such, so that the sterilisation could after all go through if the person's fear of doctors could be appeased – for example, if the doctor who was to sterilise the person was not dressed as a doctor.

54 OLG Düsseldorf [1996] Fam. RZ 375.

55 LG Hildesheim [1997] Bt. Prax. 121.

56 BayObLG [1997] Bt. Prax. 158.

57 OLG Hamm [2001] Fam. RZ 314.

So far, the last case to be reported in relation to § 1905 BGB was decided by the BayObLG in 2001.[58] This judgment reiterates the dictum of a previous judgment of the same court that sterilisation may only be authorised when there is tangible and serious reason to believe that, without the sterilisation, pregnancy will occur. This does not presuppose that there needs be a specific degree of probability for the pregnancy to occur. However, the abstract probability of a pregnancy is not sufficient. For these reasons, the court did not authorise the sterilisation.

Critique of the Case Law

From this small body of case law, two cases are of particular interest and will be analysed extensively. The first is the judgement handed down by the OLG Hamm.

The case involved a 21-year-old girl who was born with Dandy-Walker syndrome. Her brain had not developed properly, and she suffered from severe epileptic crises, for which she received medication and treatment. She could not read or write, and had a vocabulary of only a few words. According to medical opinion, her minimal learning abilities could not be improved. She lived with a step-family of four young men with learning disabilities around her age. The girl had regular periods, masturbated often, and tried to have physical contact with persons she knew, and especially with another of her step-brothers, to whom she tried to get close in the mornings without wearing any clothes. No medical opinion was given as to whether the girl had had sexual intercourse because she repeatedly shunned medical examinations.

Her carer under the carership system made an application to the court for a sterilisation carer to be appointed for the girl, who would eventually be sterilised. The court in the first instance turned down the application. The appellate court reversed the decision, and subsequently a sterilisation carer was appointed for the girl by the first-instance court. The carer gave her consent to the sterilisation, but again the first-instance court refused to authorise the procedure. The case was brought before the appellate court, which finally authorised the sterilisation.

This judicial odyssey between the lower and the appeal courts shows just how hesitant the German judicial system can be towards sterilisation. The appeal judgement follows closely former sterilisation judgments, and stresses that the person to be sterilised must be perpetually incapable of consent, that the person must engage in sexual activities which will probably lead to a pregnancy, and that this pregnancy, should it occur, will be detrimental to the pregnant person.

More interesting, however, is how the court interpreted the right of the person with intellectual disability to object to sterilisation. The court of appeal followed a strict grammatical interpretation of § 1905 BGB. The criterion that the court applied is whether the person shows, by any means whatsoever, that she does not want the sterilisation.

---

58 BayObLG [2001] Fam. RZ 1560.

In the present case, the girl systematically shunned medical examinations and doctors. But she did not object to the sterilisation as an operation causing her to become permanently infertile. Her objection, according to the court, was directed towards the medical examination, and not the sterilisation. Subsequently, having raised no objection to the sterilisation, the girl could undergo the procedure. However, the conditions relating to the sterilisation procedure that caused the girl distress should be alleviated.

This judgment can be criticised on many points.[59] The first point is how the court interpreted the expectation of pregnancy. According to § 1905 I Nr. 3 BGB, sterilisation can only be authorised when it can be expected that without it, pregnancy will occur. In interpreting this requirement of the law, the court maintained that the expectation of pregnancy must be concrete and serious. At the same time, the court accepted that a high percentage of probability is not necessary, but that it is enough if the person is sexually active and fertile, so that a pregnancy is probable.

This correct interpretation of § 1905 BGB was not covered by the facts of the case. As far as the fertility of the person was concerned, the lower courts accepted that the woman had periods and that there were no reasons to believe that the woman could not become pregnant. But, according to the law, the court must examine not whether the woman *could not* become pregnant, but on the contrary, whether she *could* become pregnant. Making sure that the woman is fertile is a prerequisite in deciding whether she should be sterilised or not. This is the case even when the woman has refused to take part in any sort of gynaecological examinations, as in the present case.

The court also accepted that the conditions that cause the woman's resistance to be examined by a gynaecologist must be addressed so that the sterilisation procedure can take place. However, this applies with equal force to the examination of the woman in order to find out whether she is fertile or not.

A further reasoning of the court is also based on shaky foundations: the assessment of another prerequisite for the expectancy of pregnancy, the genital sexuality of the woman. It is certain from the factual basis of the case that the woman sought and found body contact to other persons. From this fact, the lower courts deducted that the woman would at some point discover genital sexuality, if that had not happened already. In other words, it is not certain whether the woman had ever had genital sexual experience, or that she even displayed an interest in genital sexuality. Moreover, the judgment does not deal with the issue whether her living conditions are such as to enable her to actually acquire experience of genital sexuality. For these reasons, a concrete and serious expectancy of pregnancy cannot be justified from the factual basis of the case before the OLG Hamm.

A further prerequisite for the authorisation of sterilisation by the court is that in case of a pregnancy, a danger to the life of the person or a serious worsening

59 S. Pöld-Krämer, 'Sterilisation gegen den Willen der Betroffenen – das falsche Signal!' [2000] Bt. Prax. 237.

of her mental or physical health are to be expected which cannot be dealt with in any other reasonable way. However, the OLG Hamm also accepted that a possible pregnancy would also not serve the welfare of the child. The present definition of § 1905 BGB does not make any references to the welfare of the child, but only the person under carership.

Another important point is the interpretation that the court makes of the definition of the law that the sterilisation cannot take place against the natural will of the person. Generally speaking, the sterilisation procedure requires the consent of the person as an interference with the person's bodily integrity. § 1905 BGB allows the sterilisation of an incapacitated person only under strictly defined circumstances. During the parliamentary discussions concerning the regulation of sterilisation, a total ban on sterilisations was proposed, in view of the mass sterilisations of the Nazi era. In this historic light, the law prohibits any use of force during sterilisation procedures, and acknowledges no exceptions, even in extreme cases. The prerequisite for the sterilisation of an incapacitated person is therefore that the sterilisation does not contradict the will of the person. The law qualifies this will as natural, in order to point out that it does not have to stem from any rational planning. Any form of resistance or denial is enough to exclude the possibility of sterilisation.

And this was the case in the present judgment. The person could not be expected to differentiate her resistance to such a degree that she would not only generally resist medical examinations, but also specifically a sterilisation procedure. Within sterilisation decision-making, the legally non-binding will of an incapacitated person is legally binding. On the contrary, had the legislator required an expression of will specifically aimed at resisting sterilisation, this would actually require from the person with intellectual disability a higher degree of understanding and self-planning than she possessed.

On the contrary, the OLG Hamm, just like the lower court before it, perceived the law as stating that the will of the person must be against the sterilisation as such. The court especially declared that the woman's resistance to gynaecological examinations could not be regarded as falling under the terms of being against the will of the person. The intention of the legislator was to actually prohibit and stop any sterilisation that would be made under force, because 'the application of force gives the sterilisation procedure a whole new dimension'.[60] In the present case, the woman was permanently incapacitated and could not understand the connection between sex, pregnancy and birth, so that it was questionable whether she could actually resist the sterilisation procedure. In this sense, the interpretation of § 1905 BGB by the OLG Hamm would actually exclude persons with intellectual disability from its protection. Parallel to this, the right to the development of personality of persons with intellectual disability, and therefore also their sexual experiences, must be especially protected, because sexuality is by no means a usual part of the life of persons with intellectual disability.

60 Bt-Drs 11/4528 at 76.

Moreover, the opinion of the court, according to which only resistance specifically aimed against the sterilisation procedure was legally binding, and if the resistance of the person was aimed at the conditions under which this procedure would take place, these conditions must change, was also mistaken, but for different reasons. The court seemed to ignore or misunderstand the different living conditions and circumstances of persons with intellectual disability, especially if these persons were severely or multiply disabled. Every person capable of self-understanding can refuse to be sterilised, because she finds the operation frightening or uncomfortable. The right to the free development of one's personality also protects the right to develop and hold such irrational feelings. This is of crucial importance to persons with severe intellectual disability, whose sign language or gestures alone enable them to communicate. Not taking into account their will, expressed in this fashion, signifies lack of respect for their personality as a whole. In the present case, the woman's resistance to any medical examination shows how important for her it was, in the context of medical examinations, to protect herself from body contact with third parties. Sterilisation cannot be the answer to the sexuality of persons with intellectual disability.

The second judgment to be analysed is also the most recent one, and comes from the BayObLG. In this case, the court agreed with the lower courts which had previously decided the case that the proposed sterilisation could not be authorised.

The girl under care did not have any sexual contacts that would lead one to think that she could become pregnant, but also showed no interest in sexual experiences. She lived with her family and worked in a workshop for persons with disabilities. Her life and working conditions did not leave her much scope for starting a relationship that would lead her to becoming pregnant.

It is worthy of note that the opinion of the medical experts brought before the court was that the girl would not on her own look for a sexual relationship. On the other hand, according to the same medical opinions, there was indeed some probability of the girl having sexual intercourse without taking contraceptive measures.

The BayObLG stressed that the abstract possibility of pregnancy does not meet the standards of § 1905 BGB. The risk assessment has to be more rigorous. The danger of pregnancy must be concrete and serious. In this case, the only possibility of the girl becoming pregnant would be if someone took advantage of her. But again, the court accepted that since the girl lived with her family and worked under supervision, that possibility was far-fetched.

This judgment is important in respect of the earlier case of the OLG Hamm which gave authorisation for the sterilisation of a woman with intellectual disability under the same factual circumstances.

In both judgments, both courts stressed that the danger for a pregnancy had to be grave and imminent, so that a precautionary sterilisation could be authorised under § 1905 BGB. A comparison between the two cases shows that the courts interpreted the concept of what a grave and imminent danger for pregnancy was quite differently.

The OLG Hamm found that there was such danger, since the woman with intellectual disability was seeking bodily contact with other persons in the home she was living, and was successful in having such body contact, so that it was very probable, if it had not already happened, that the woman would discover genital sexuality. She was menstruating, and there were no reasons to suggest that she could not become pregnant. In this sense, it was not clear in the factual basis of the case whether the woman had at least an interest in genital sexuality at the time the judgment was delivered.

As the backdrop to this judgment, the interpretation of § 1905 BGB in the present judgment of the BayObLG is of great importance, in that it stresses that the simple expectation that the person will at some point discover genital sexuality does not constitute a concrete and serious expectation of pregnancy at the time the case was heard, as § 1905 BGB requires. From a wish for and experience of bodily contact, such as caressing and kissing, as well as the biological capacity to become pregnant, the court did not infer that the person had her own wish for genital sexuality. For the court, the non-experience of genital sexuality at the time of hearing was the decisive factor in turning down the application for an authorisation of sterilisation.

Furthermore, the BayObLG also examined whether the woman was living under circumstances that would even give her the opportunity to have genital sexuality which was not based on sexual abuse, which was, as is very often, not the case. The court made it clear that the prerequisites for accepting an expectation of pregnancy under § 1905 BGB go far beyond simply accepting that it is biologically possible that the woman can become pregnant and the expectation that the woman will some day discover genital sexuality.

It is in the interest of women with intellectual disability that other courts besides the BayObLG examine whether the woman has experienced or has an interest in genital sexuality at the time of the hearing, and that they also examine whether the woman lives under circumstances that permit her to have genital sexuality.

From this critique of the case law, it becomes obvious how difficult it is to correctly interpret and apply carership law in relation to persons with intellectual disability. Even though the legal regulation of carership is both liberal and protective, the judicial interpretation of certain articles of the BGB lags behind in providing more freedom and choice to persons with intellectual disability.

The Welfare of Adults and the Welfare of Children in English and German Law: Concluding Remarks

In a complex constitutional and legal system such as the German one, the constitutional principles and rights which underpin the actual provisions of the law determine, in a drastic way, how these legal provisions will be interpreted. Yet this analytical process is both argumentative and interpretative in a way which enables the reasoned and structured reaching of a conclusion as to what the law actually is.

In the case of children, it is the right to marriage and family which sets the tone for the interpretation of their welfare. As parental rights are essentially negative, the freedom of the parents to bring up their children is respected to a very great extent. However, as the state has reserved for itself a supervisory role over the family, parental rights can be interfered with when the upbringing of the children is greatly deficient – when the children's development to become mature and responsible citizens is harmed or endangered.

In the case of adult welfare within the carership framework, and especially as far as persons with intellectual disability are concerned, the starting point of the analysis is the right to personality. On the one hand, the carership system can be seen as generally infringing in the constitutional rights of the person under carership, and most of all in her right to personality. On the other hand, the normative content of the right to personality points to the right interpretative direction: what is protected by the right to personality is the self-empowering life plan that the person has chosen and set up for herself. To the extent that this self-determination is absent from a person with intellectual disability, the interferences with the person's rights do not constitute infringements of these rights. Rather, they establish the missing self-determination, thus equating persons with intellectual disability with persons capable to consent. A similar line of reasoning is not to be found in English law relating to incapacity or intellectual disability.

Moreover, the regulation of non-consensual sterilisation procedures for persons with intellectual disability in England and Germany highlights another fundamental difference in approach between the two jurisdictions in relation to welfare decisions.

Even though the application of § 1905 BGB by German courts can be criticised on many points, the correct interpretation of that provision makes it clear that a sterilisation cannot take place when the person with intellectual disability refuses to undergo the procedure. This veto right is granted to incapacitated adults not only because of the social and legal history of eugenics in Germany, but also because it protects the right to bodily integrity.

If one would compare this regulation with the reasoning in an English judgment, for instance that of *Re X*,[61] the difference becomes apparent. X was a person with severe intellectual disability. There existed a tangible risk of pregnancy in her case, and pregnancy was considered to be damaging for her, as well as her eventual separation from the child, because she would be unable to care for the child. Even though 'X hate[d] hospitals and medical treatment, and would undoubtedly be likely to be frightened and upset by any surgical procedure',[62] the sterilisation was authorised. We consider that, in a very utilitarian way, the court here authorised the sterilisation in order to avoid both the psychological harm of pregnancy and subsequent removal of care, as well as the physical stress of a possible Caesarean section to bring the child to term.

61 *Re X (Adult Sterilisation)* [1998] 2 FLR 1,124.

62 Ibid. at 1,128.

In contrast to this utilitarian calculation, the richness of concepts and principles within the analytical reasoning of German law determining the welfare of persons with intellectual disability shows conclusively that basing welfare decisions for persons with intellectual disability on the concept of best interests is, to say the least, a crude and over-simplified way to address the issue.

This conclusion forms the negative side of the claim which this volume advances based on this comparative analysis of English and German law: English law has neither the substantive principles nor the analytical structure to enable a person-centred approach to the problems persons with intellectual disability face, which would provide persons with intellectual disability with greater protection for their rights.

The positive side of this claim is that, in contrast to English law, the German approach to issues of intellectual disability is based both on the principle of human dignity and on the constitutional right to the development of one's personality, which form the backbone of the German legal order. It is precisely because German law draws from the principle of human dignity and places such great respect on the individuality of the person with intellectual disability that German law is in a far better position than English law to provide protection to persons with intellectual disability.

The previous comparative analysis of the national legal systems of England and Germany with regards to intellectual disability and human rights has brought the second part of this volume to an end. Both international human rights law as well as national legal systems have been shown to face interpretive difficulties in protecting the human rights of persons with intellectual disability. National laws are based on autonomy. Similarly, human rights are conditioned by the autonomous choice of the individual. When this autonomy is questioned, respecting the wishes of the person with intellectual disability or protecting the person from abuse requires careful thinking so that coherent solutions may be arrived at. Otherwise, arbitrariness and unfair practices will continue to oppress persons with intellectual disability, in spite of the adoption of the CRPD.

For this reason, the third and final part will attempt to restructure these weak points, based on the human dignity reasoning which was presented at the beginning of the volume. The point here is to demonstrate how a more coherent approach may provide consistent and satisfying answers to the human rights issues that persons with intellectual disability face.

PART III
The Way Forward

Chapter 7
Applying the Human Dignity Reasoning to Sterilisation Procedures under English Law, the MCA 2005 and the Case Law of the ECtHR

The second part of this volume aimed to demonstrate the structural weaknesses different legal frameworks show in addressing the issues that intellectual disability raises in relation to human rights.

In terms of international human rights law, the recent adoption of the CRPD comes as a welcome change. It addresses the inadequate human rights protection which has been given to persons with disabilities under existing human rights documents, such as the ECHR. Yet a careful examination of both the CRPD and the ECHR demonstrates how difficult it is to protect the human rights of persons with intellectual disabilities.

The CRPD makes a general invocation of complex principles, such as human dignity and autonomy. Other provisions of the CRPD require the consent of the person. This begs the question who is to decide on the capacity to consent and how. These few examples show that the CRPD offers little guidance as to how it should be applied to persons with intellectual disability. It therefore requires a careful interpretation in order to offer satisfying solutions to the issues that persons with intellectual disability face.

The ECHR offers even less guidance, as it is a general human rights document which was drafted long before disability became an issue under human rights law. Surprisingly however, the ECtHR has failed to provide adequate human rights protection to the few applicants with disabilities who have succeeded in bringing a case before the ECtHR. The reason behind this marginalisation of disability is that the ECtHR has not developed a coherent interpretation of the principles that underlie the ECHR. Instead of affirming the existence of positive obligations owed to persons with disabilities, the ECtHR has granted a wide margin of appreciation to national authorities. This means that no effective control may be exercised on national practices which violate the rights of persons with disabilities.

Moving to national legal systems, the comparative analysis of English and German law relating to incapacity has thrown light on the conceptual differences between the common law and civil law approach in matters of intellectual disability.

Whereas English law has adopted a system of pragmatic problem-solving on a case-to-case basis, which stems from a meandering evolution of Poor Law and other historical accidents, German law firmly places carership law within the interpretive context of human dignity.

We have claimed that since the German legal framework of carership is structured around the principle of human dignity, which guides the provision of care to persons with intellectual disability, human dignity provides persons with intellectual disability with care which is more carefully tailored to their individual needs and ultimately achieves solutions which ensure a higher respect for their human rights.

Sadly, there have been court judgments in Germany which fail to provide this protection. Stereotypes of disability and the traditional medical model are still prevalent in social practice. ECtHR judgments sometimes reflect these negative attitudes quite clearly. However, this failure does not diminish the actual interpretive worth of human dignity.

The final part of the volume is therefore concerned with discussing in some depth the ways forward to which the principle of human dignity points. This chapter attempts to address the shortcomings of English law in relation to persons with intellectual disability. This chapter also examines how the case law of the ECtHR should change in favour of persons with disabilities. Specific mention is made of the possible impact the CRPD may have on the ECHR. The closing argument of the volume is that the changes in international human rights law which were brought about by the CRPD need to be incorporated into the ECHR by means of an additional protocol. A protocol on disability may provide legitimacy as well as an excellent opportunity for the ECtHR to develop a more favourable stance on issues of disability.

This chapter begins by reconstructing the provisions of the Mental Capacity Act 2005 along the lines of the human dignity reasoning. The main criticisms against the MCA 2005 which have been raised in this volume are the absence of criteria for the best interests test, and also the relatively weak connection of the Act with human rights and the HRA 1998.[1] We claim that the human dignity reasoning requires, as a bare minimum, the abandonment of the best interests test. An additional safeguard would be the provision of veto rights. Persons with intellectual disability may not be deemed competent to consent to treatment, yet this does not mean that they are also incapable of objecting. On the contrary, their objections in relation to their medical treatment or, more generally, to aspects of the provision of social welfare care they receive should sometimes trump other considerations.

The argumentation of this chapter then turns to common law, and picks up the thread of adult sterilisation case law which was presented earlier in the context of the evolution of best interests in English law.[2] The claim of this section is that, to

---

1 See pp. 132–133.

2 See pp. 113–120.

begin with, the sterilisation of persons with intellectual disability is a violation of Article 12 of the ECHR, considered as *lex specialis* in relation to Article 8, which provides a more general protection of private life.

Moreover, this section also claims that sterilisation may be considered as generally incompatible with the critical interests of persons with intellectual disability. After all, life as a parent may be considered a life which may be more worth living for persons with intellectual disability. In this sense, the instances in which a sterilisation of an intellectually disabled adult may be lawfully authorised are dramatically reduced. This line of reasoning is also consistent with Article 23 para. 1 sentence (c) of the CRPD, which states: 'Persons with disabilities, including children, retain their fertility on an equal basis with others.'

Reformulating English Case Law on Adult Sterilisation

As mentioned in Chapter 5 on English law, the most recent formulation of the law concerning sterilisation of adult persons with intellectual disability comes from the Civil Division of the Court of Appeal in the case of *Re S*.[3] In that case, the court held that sterilisation can be authorised if it is in the best interests of the person. Best interests include not just medical, but also social and other issues. The court, and not doctors, has the final say as to whether the sterilisation falls within the person's best interests:

> In these difficult cases where the medical profession seeks a declaration as to lawfulness of the proposed treatment, the judge, not the doctor, has the duty to decide whether such treatment is in the best interests of the patient. The judicial decision ought to provide the best answer not a range of alternative answers. There may, of course, be situations where the answer may not be obvious and alternatives may have to be tried. It is still at any one point the best option of that moment which should be chosen … The judicial decision will incorporate broader ethical, social, moral and welfare considerations.[4]

This reasoning raises certain important issues. Firstly, the question arises whether, or how, the law applicable to non-consensual sterilisation has changed under the HRA 1998. A second question is how the human dignity reasoning can make a difference to the current state of sterilisations in English law.

---

3 *Re S (Adult Patient: Sterilisation: Patient's Best Interests)* [2001] Fam 15. For a discussion of the judgment, see p. 119.

4 *Per* Dame Butler-Sloss at 27–8.

Within the Scope of Protection of Which Article of the ECHR do Sterilisation Procedures Fall?

Under the ECHR, and according to the case law of the ECtHR, any invasion of bodily integrity is covered by Article 8 of the Convention.[5] In this sense, sterilisation may be regarded as an infringement of due respect to private and family life. The intervention can therefore only be justified in terms of Article 8 para. 2 – if it is in accordance with the law and is necessary in a democratic society for the protection of health and morals.

We maintain that subsuming sterilisation as an intervention in private life is both undesirable as well as legally incorrect. Firstly, it is undesirable because of the vagueness of formulation of Article 8. The case law of the ECtHR has gradually expanded the meaning of private and family life, and extended the scope of protection afforded by the right. Deducing human rights protection against sterilisations from Article 8 seems to be an easy way to deal with the issue.

There is also a second reason why it is undesirable to invoke the protection afforded by the respect due to private and family life against proposed sterilisations. This is because the measure of protection afforded by Article 8 fluctuates against certain infringements. The structure of Article 8 incorporates proportionality and the doctrine of margin of appreciation within its mechanism of protection.

According to the case law of the ECtHR, the ECtHR's review is not limited to ascertaining whether a respondent state has exercised its discretion reasonably, carefully and in good faith. In exercising its supervisory jurisdiction, the ECtHR does not confine itself to considering the impugned decisions in isolation, but looks at them in the light of the case as a whole; it determines whether the reasons adduced to justify the interferences at issue are relevant and sufficient.[6] Only if an interference with Article 8 is not supported by sufficient reasons justifying the measure as proportionate to the legitimate aim pursued can it be shown not to be necessary in a democratic society.[7]

Sterilisation cases have not been presented before the ECtHR. This makes it difficult to surmise what the ECtHR would decide as a matter of law. Given the settled case law of the ECtHR that invasions in bodily integrity fall within the scope of protection of Article 8, it is easier to imagine that the ECtHR will grant a broad margin of appreciation to national authorities as to the legality of the sterilisation authorised. The granting of a broad margin of appreciation may be adduced by the fact that there exists no consensus in relation to restrictions imposed on involuntary sterilisations within member states of the Council of Europe. Moreover, national legal regulations relating to sterilisation may also be regarded as part of national health policy, in relation to which national authorities are better placed to decide.

5 *X and Y* v. *the Netherlands*, 26 March 1985, Ser. A No. 91, at para. 22.

6 Ibid. at para. 68.

7 Ibid. at para. 83.

In this sense, the right of respect for private and family life seems to offer little protection to persons with intellectual disability. Therefore, setting aside Article 8, it is time to examine whether any other article of the Convention can provide better protection against non-consensual sterilisations. The first question in that respect is whether sterilisations can be regarded as inhuman and degrading treatment, under Article 3.

However, historical evidence does not support this view. During the deliberations of the Consultative Assembly which drafted the Convention, one of the representatives of the UK, Cocks, proposed a lengthy amendment to the text relating to the absolute prohibition of torture, and another amendment to add the words:

> In particular no person shall be subjected to any form of mutilation or sterilisation or to any form of torture or beating. Nor shall he be forced to take drugs nor shall they be administered to him without his knowledge and consent. Nor shall he be subjected to imprisonment with such an excess of light, darkness, noise or silence as to cause mental suffering.[8]

After opinions by several of the representatives had been heard, the proposed amendments were withdrawn. It was felt that these lengthy amendments would unbalance the text, as well as providing a footing for an *a contrario* interpretation of the text, supporting the view that only the forms of torture specifically mentioned in the text were prohibited.[9]

The course of action adopted was for the Assembly to issue a draft resolution on the condemnation of torture which, *inter alia*, included the prohibition of sterilisation. However, in the subsequent debate relating to this resolution, the representative of Denmark, Kristensen, objected to the prohibition of sterilisation.[10] The representatives of Sweden and Norway submitted similar objections.[11] In this sense, an attempt at a historical interpretation of Article 3 to provide protection against non-consensual sterilisations remains problematic.

On the contrary, a pointer as to what the ECtHR would actually decide on the basis of Article 3 is given by the somewhat similar case of *Herczegfalvy* v. *Austria*.[12] The applicant in the case was a Hungarian national living in Austria who had been convicted for criminal offences. While in prison, his aggressive behaviour deteriorated to the extent that he was not released at the end of his sentence for fear of his committing other violent crimes, as he was diagnosed to be

8 Council of Europe, *Collected Edition of the Travaux Préparatoires*, vol. 1 (The Hague: Martinus Nijhoff, 1976) at 116–17.

9 Ibid. at 154.

10 'In Denmark we have an Act permitting sterilisation, and I think the same may be the case in other civilised countries'; ibid. at 208.

11 Ibid. at 209.

12 *Herczegfalvy* v. *Austria*, 24 September 1992, Ser. A No. 244.

paranoid. During his detention, Herczegfalvy violently resisted medical treatment on numerous occasions, but was eventually forcibly treated against his will. His medical treatment included the forcible administration of food and neuroleptics, while at some point the applicant remained isolated and attached with handcuffs to a security bed for several weeks.

The ECtHR, in examining the applicant's claim that this treatment amounted to inhuman and degrading treatment, held:

> The ECtHR considers that the position of inferiority and powerlessness which is typical of patients confined in psychiatric hospitals calls for increased vigilance in reviewing whether the Convention has been complied with. While it is for the medical authorities to decide, on the basis of the recognised rules of medical science, on the therapeutic methods to be used, if necessary by force, to preserve the physical and mental health of patients who are entirely incapable of deciding for themselves and for whom they are therefore responsible, such patients nevertheless remain under the protection of Article 3, whose requirements permit of no derogation. The established principles of medicine are admittedly in principle decisive in such cases; as a general rule, a measure which is a therapeutic necessity cannot be regarded as inhuman or degrading. The ECtHR must nevertheless satisfy itself that the medical necessity has been convincingly shown to exist.[13]

The ECtHR then went on to say that the evidence presented was not sufficient to disprove the argument of the respondent state that, according to the psychiatric principles generally accepted at the time, medical necessity justified the treatment of the applicant.

If this judicial reasoning is applied to sterilisation cases, the protection afforded to persons with intellectual disability will again be low, since in most instances, at least in English case law, there is unanimous medical evidence that the proposed sterilisation is medically, in the physical or psychological sense, necessary. In this respect, Article 3 cannot really provide intellectually disabled adults with sufficient protection against wrongful sterilisations.

We therefore claim that neither Article 8, which is conventionally thought of as affording protection against invasions to bodily integrity, nor Article 3 can be considered applicable to cases of non-consensual sterilisation. On the contrary, according to our argument, it is Article 12, which guarantees the right to marry and found a family, which is best suited for accommodating sterilisation procedures.

Article 12 reads as follows: 'Men and women of marriageable age have the right to marry and found a family, according to the national laws governing the exercise of this right.'

The subjects of the right are every man and woman of marriageable age. The substance of the right to marry is a free choice between marriage and celibacy,

---

13 Ibid. at para. 82.

based on the free and full consent of the husband.[14] In this sense, some writers argue that persons with intellectual disability have a right to marry, but only to the extent they can be deemed capable of determining their free will to consent to the marriage.[15]

The substance of the right to found a family is the right to have children within marriage. In principle, the procreative choices of the couple have to be respected. Family planning has to be based on the free consent of the husband; any form of forced contraception, sterilisation or abortion is prohibited.[16] The right to reproduce is only the corollary of marriage, and not its essential aim. In this sense, marriage is protected by Article 12 even when it does not involve procreation. But procreation does not fall under the protection of Article 12 unless it takes place within marriage.

The right to marry is not absolute. The formula of Article 12, 'according to the national laws governing the exercise of this right', is suggestive of limitations. The margin of appreciation enjoyed by the states is large: they can regulate marriage, its celebration and legal consequences, according to their national traditions. Far-reaching limitations as to the exercise of the right to marry may result from national law.[17] These limitations concern the formalities of marriage – such as publicity, the marriage licence and the ceremony – and the capacity to marry – such as inability to consent and prohibited degrees. Moreover, this right can also be limited indirectly by administrative measures irrelevant to family law, such as immigration laws or penitentiary systems.

However, as academic writing has rightly suggested in relation to the limitations of Article 12:

> The very fact that Article 12 puts the right first and foremost implies that domestic regulations ... must not be of such a nature that the right itself would be affected in its essence ... If the right to marry is denied to a person because of his limited mental faculties, his state of health, or his financial situation, the relevant national law cannot be justified as not affecting the essence of that right, assuming of course that such persons can be deemed capable of determining their free will to consent to the marriage.[18]

In this sense, the limitations inherent in Article 12 do not cover legal regulations which allow blanket prohibitions of the right to marry of persons with intellectual disability, even though national laws may determine the threshold of capacity for

---

14 P. van Dijk and G. van Hoof, *Theory and Practice of the European Convention of Human Rights*, 3rd ed. (The Hague: Kluwer Law International, 1998) at 602.

15 Ibid. at 604.

16 Ibid. at 613.

17 Ibid. at 602.

18 Ibid. at 603–4.

marriage. Moreover, the issue of non-consensual sterilisations is not covered by the limitations inherent in the right to marry and found a family:

> Article 12 primarily implies a prohibition for the authorities to interfere with the founding of a family, for instance by prescribing the compulsory use of contraceptives, ordering a non-voluntary sterilisation or abortion, or tolerating the performance thereof ... the national laws governing the exercise of this right may regulate the enjoyment of this right, but may not exclude it altogether, or affect it in its essence ... [T]he victim of such a measure is also entitled to invoke Article 3, and in case of abortion perhaps also Article 2. Whether such an interference ... is permitted in the case of medical necessity depends on the question of whether the right to life has to be considered an inalienable right, for which ultimately the authorities bear responsibility.[19]

The Interplay between Article 12 and the Human Dignity Reasoning in the Regulation of Non-consensual Sterilisation of Intellectually Disabled Adults in English Law

Having argued that sterilisation infringes the right of persons with intellectual disability to marry and found a family, we proceed to examine the ramifications of the human dignity reasoning within the legal context of Article 12 of the ECHR in English law.

It has to be repeated here that the principle of human dignity applies on two levels. On the one hand, human dignity urges the political community to decide, on a general level, questions of sterilisation policy. Human dignity raises the question how is it dignified for that particular society to treat and uphold the dignity of persons with intellectual disability in relation to non-consensual sterilisation.

For instance, as was mentioned in Chapter 6 on German law, the historical misgivings towards eugenics and Nazism in Germany have led contemporary carership law to be extremely sensitive to sterilisation issues, and thus prohibit non-consensual sterilisation if the incapacitated person, for whatever reason, refuses to undergo the procedure. Under German law, an added element of force in involuntary sterilisations would mean that the human dignity of the person with intellectual disability, and her constitutional right to the development of her personality, are violated.[20]

English law, even though not burdened with a history of official eugenics policy, has none the less exerted uninhibited paternalism towards persons with intellectual disability through the application of the best interests test by the judiciary. The common law has allowed many a non-consensual sterilisation to take place by blindly following unchallenged medical evidence presented in court.

19 Ibid. at 611.

20 See p. 166.

We suggest that the dignity of the English social community, based on human rights and individual flourishing, requires that it be attentive to the dignity and the critical interests of all individuals. Given the growing social sensitivity regarding issues of disability, it may perhaps be time for the English political community to revise its perception of the critical interests of persons with intellectual disability in relation to procreative matters. After all, only some persons with intellectual disability are sexually active, and sterilisation may be conceived of as a penalty for their sexual activity. Or it could be said that within a proper framework of social care, persons with intellectual disability may be provided with adequate support to raise their children as a family, and life as a parent may advance the critical interests of the person with intellectual disability, as being a life which may be considered to be more worth living.

In this sense, it is not for this volume to give exact counsel to an imaginary law-maker as to how it is dignified for the English political community to conceptualise the right of persons with intellectual disability to marry and found a family, of which sterilisation is an infringement. The important issue is that the human dignity reasoning opens up the debate on how this right should be conceptualised, and this volume places great emphasis on such a deliberative process.

The second level where the human dignity reasoning applies is that of human rights issues which arise between individuals. When a person is entrusted with decision-making capacity, the question arises how she should decide on behalf of the person with intellectual disability in order to safeguard and promote the critical interests and the human dignity of the disabled person in relation to sterilisation procedures. This entails figuring out human rights disputes between carers, or the state, and the person with intellectual disability, which ultimately revolve around the most coherent interpretation of the critical interests of the person with intellectual disability.

As mentioned in Chapter 2, where the human dignity reasoning was presented, the interpretation of the critical interests of a person with intellectual disability is based on the person's individual characteristics. This does not mean, however, that the issue of non-consensual sterilisation has to be decided on a case-to-case basis according to the specific circumstances of each case, as the best interests test would dictate.

On the contrary, the human dignity reasoning leads to a principled, general approach to the issue of sterilisation which can be applied to suit the particular circumstances of each case. This approach is based on the distinction between therapeutic and non-therapeutic sterilisation as a general pointer to what the critical interests of the person with intellectual disability are. Such a distinction does not introduce the medicalisation of the sterilisation issue by the back door if the distinction is conceived of as a demarcating line between what makes the life of a person with intellectual disability more worth living, as critical interests do.

For instance, a severely and multiply disabled person is suffering from heavy menstrual bleeding; if her physical frailty makes it almost impossible for her to have contact with other persons, freeing her from the pain of menstruation by sterilising her advances her human dignity. If, on the other hand, that same person has communicative skills and is fond of the company of other persons, sterilising her may, for instance, compromise her mental health, or cause her depression; sterilisation may have such adverse effects. Clearly, in such a situation, what advances the critical interests of that person with intellectual disability is to hone her social and communicative skills, and support the person in socialising more, and perhaps forming a relationship, rather than hastening to free her from period pains.

The following analysis provides a more detailed blueprint of the interplay between the human dignity reasoning and sterilisation.

As mentioned earlier in this section, Article 12 of the ECHR grants the right to marry and found a family to every man and woman of marriageable age. The national laws can govern – that is, limit – the exercise of this right, but cannot lawfully affect it in its essence. Unfortunately, however, it is certain that some persons with intellectual disability will not have the intellectual capacity to understand the concept of marriage, so that they are incapable of consenting to it. However, does this mean that they cannot marry? Does the test of functional capacity established by the Mental Capacity Act 2005 apply to consent to marriage? Could such a high degree of understanding be required for one of the most basic elements of social life? The principle of respect for human dignity comes into play here. The person with intellectual disability may be incapable of understanding marriage intellectually, but may want it and may be capable of grasping its social and emotional meaning. As it has been aptly put, marriage is a very simple contract which does not require a high degree of intelligence to understand.[21] Moreover, the parties willing to marry are better suited than anyone else to decide whether they can cope with marriage and become husband and wife.

However, current authority under English law sets down a complicated threshold of capacity to marry. What is problematic in this threshold is that capacity to marry includes the capacity to engage in sexual intercourse, as this capacity is understood in criminal law. *Per* Munby J in *X City Council* v. *MB, NB and MAB*:[22]

> Generally speaking, capacity to marry must include the capacity to consent to sexual relations. And the test of capacity to consent to sexual relations must for this purpose be the same in its essentials as that required by the criminal law. Therefore for present purposes the question comes to this. Does the person have sufficient knowledge and understanding of the nature and character – the sexual nature and character – of the act of sexual intercourse, and of the reasonably foreseeable consequences of sexual intercourse, to have the capacity to choose whether or not to engage in it, the capacity to decide whether to give or withhold consent to sexual intercourse (and, where relevant, to communicate their choice to their spouse)?

---

21 *Per* Sir James Hannen P. in *Durham* v. *Durham* (1885) 10 PD 80 at 82.

22 *X City Council* v. *MB, NB and MAB* 2006 2 FLR 968 at para. 84.

We have consistently argued that coherence in the law regulating the rights of persons with intellectual disability is needed. However, caution must be exercised when criteria of the criminal law are introduced into civil matters. Whereas this threshold of capacity is immensely protective against abuse, it may also prove rather intricate or high for persons with intellectual disability. A simplification of the criteria for capacity is therefore needed.

Moreover, marriage to persons with mental disorder in the meaning of the Mental Health Act 1983, a category under which persons with intellectual disability fall, is valid, but voidable.[23] In this sense, English law may not affect the essence of the right to marry for persons with intellectual disability, yet it places a rather complicated threshold of capacity.

On the other hand, the right of persons with intellectual disability to found a family is fraught with problems. A major concern is that sterilisation procedures are authorised by courts without first enquiring into the necessity of sterilisation. In most cases, the fertility of the person is not established medically, but assumed. However, it can be argued that involuntary sterilisation of a person with intellectual disability without first establishing her fertility is an unnecessary interference with her bodily integrity, and thus degrading treatment that falls under the prohibition of Article 3 of the ECHR.

English law has finally accepted a legal distinction between therapeutic and non-therapeutic sterilisation.[24] Non-therapeutic sterilisation is taken to mean sterilisation for contraceptive purposes. Therapeutic sterilisation encompasses all situations where the appropriate and necessary medical treatment has as an immediate consequence, or side effect, the sterilisation of the patient – for example, the removal of an uterus with carcinoma. Whereas therapeutic sterilisation is always permissible without prior judicial permission, contraceptive sterilisations of persons with intellectual disability have to be referred to court. The proposed sterilisation will be authorised if the procedure is in the best interests of the person: if there is likelihood of pregnancy or sexual activity and likelihood of damage deriving from conception or menstruation, then the most advantageous sterilisation procedure will be authorised.

Therapeutic sterilisation does not, in principle, constitute an unlawful interference with the right to marry and found a family. In the case of persons with intellectual disability, welfare decisions concerning their life and health understandably have priority over other rights that may be violated by these decisions. However, there are two caveats which can be adduced from the principle of human dignity.

Firstly, there is the proportionality argument. The therapeutic benefit from the medical treatment must be very important in order to cover for the loss of the reproductive abilities of the person. Sterilisation procedures intending to alleviate

---

23 S. Cretney, *Family Law*, 4th ed. (London: Sweet and Maxwell, 2000) at 42.

24 The law as it stands is succinctly described in Practice Note (Fam Div: Incapacitated Adults: Declaratory Proceedings) [2002] 1 WLR 325.

symptoms of heavy menstrual bleeding would fall into this category. However, the lower the benefit from the treatment, the more reluctantly should it be authorised. In this respect, English law is unclear. It is stated that cases 'anywhere near the boundary line [between therapeutic and non-therapeutic sterilisation] should be referred to court'.[25] Only with difficulty could this statement be interpreted as an argument of proportionality.

Secondly, the wishes of the person with intellectual disability should also be taken into account. If the person has expressed her desire to have children, then a proposed therapeutic sterilisation has to comply with a higher threshold of beneficence in order to be justifiable.

Even before the relevant provisions of the MCA 2005, the common law had showed signs of such judicial sensitivity. In *Re C*, a schizophrenic patient who, for the purposes of the Mental Health Act 1983, is a person suffering from mental disorder, just like persons with intellectual disability, refused to consent to the amputation of his leg.[26] The medical evidence produced deemed the operation necessary to save the patient's life. However, the trial judge was convinced that the wish of patient should be respected.[27] It would be unfortunate for the wishes of persons with intellectual disability to be totally brushed aside when they concern her reproductive abilities. Since the MCA 2005 has incorporated in the best interests test the principle of respect for the incapacitated person's wishes, as far as it is practicable to do so, the statutory regulation points in the same direction in the context of therapeutic sterilisation.[28]

On the other hand, non-therapeutic sterilisation in the context of the right of persons with intellectual disability to marry and found a family presents an impressive array of legal problems. One could argue that non-consensual contraceptive sterilisation is altogether impermissible: not only does it violate the right to found a family in its essence, it is also contrary to human dignity. Recent international treaties could be used to support this argument. Although UK has not, as yet, incorporated into national law the European Convention on Human Rights and Bioethics, Article 6 para. 1 of the Convention states that medical treatment can be given to persons that are incapable of consenting to it only if they derive direct benefit from it. English law, however, permits non-therapeutic sterilisation under a broad understanding of the best interests of persons with intellectual disability.

---

25 Ibid. at 325.

26 Re C (refusal of medical treatment) [1994] 1 WLR 290.

27 The moral irony is that although the operation did not take place, the patient did not die.

28 See s. 4(6)(a) of the Act. A similar approach to treatment issues was taken by the Joint Committee on Human Rights in its comments on the Draft Mental Health Bill. See Joint Committee on the Draft Mental Health Bill, *Draft Mental Health Bill*, HL Paper 181 HC 1294, Session 2001–2002 (London: The Stationery Office, 2002) at 18–19.

In this sense, contraceptive sterilisation cannot, in principle, be authorised in the case of a married person with intellectual disability. Family planning can only be based on the reproductive wishes of the couple. Article 12 allows for national laws to govern the exercise of the right to marry and found a family. Non-consensual contraceptive sterilisation affects the right in its essence, and is therefore generally impermissible.

The welfare of the child is in this sense immaterial.[29] The exercise of the right to found a family does not depend, according to the wording of Article 12, on the abilities of persons with intellectual disability to raise children. If a person with intellectual disability is unable to care for the child, this does not mean that procreative choices should be denied to her. English law is, in this respect, paternalistic. The fact that 'psychiatric evidence as to the patient's likely ability to care for and/or have a fulfilling relationship with a child' is taken into account by the court does not comply with Article 12.[30]

However, the principle for respect for human dignity can, in exceptional circumstances, justify interference with the right of persons with intellectual disability to found a family. Contraceptive sterilisation may be indicated in order to avoid future harm to the person from conception or pregnancy. For example, if the person will be unable to care for the child, but will be extremely attached to it emotionally and psychologically, then a future separation from the child may have a devastating effect on the person's psychology. In this instance, a contraceptive sterilisation might be permissible. Certainly, proportionality is an important factor in deciding this. Sterilisation must be used reluctantly and only to prevent grave and imminent danger of great harm, especially if the person with intellectual disability has expressed a desire to have children.

On the other hand, contraceptive sterilisation given to unmarried persons with intellectual disability seems, at first, to fall outside the ambit of Article 12 that protects the right to found a family within marriage. However, according to the formula of Article 12, national laws should govern the exercise of the right, and not affect it in its essence.

The principle of respect for human dignity supports this line of reasoning. The fact that a person with intellectual disability has not yet married does not *eo ipso* exclude the possibility of marriage: her personality may in time develop emotionally or intellectually in the presence of a caring partner, so that they may marry. Contraceptive sterilisation deprives persons with intellectual disability of their right to found a family if they eventually decide or are given support to use their right to marry.

---

29 This forms part of the German approach to sterilisation of persons with intellectual disability. See G. Little, 'Comparing German and English law on non-consensual sterilisation: a difference in approach' [1997] *Med. L. Rev.* 269.

30 Practice Note (Fam Div: Incapacitated Adults: Declaratory Proceedings) [2002] 1 WLR 325.

These arguments must not be taken to mean that contraceptive sterilisation is in all cases inadmissible, especially when non-therapeutic sterilisation can be beneficial to persons with intellectual disability. Human dignity again comes under consideration: in some instances, contraceptive sterilisation can be justified in order to avoid grave and imminent harm from conception or pregnancy of a sexually active person when no milder contraceptive option is indicated and when the person has undergone sexual training but this has failed.

Harm to the person must be understood not only as physical, but also as psychological. Proportionality forms an inherent part of the reasoning: the higher the danger and imminence of harm and the graver the estimated harm from conception, the easier it is to justify a contraceptive sterilisation. The welfare of the child is again irrelevant here.[31] Still, the sterilisation has to be a last resort. Persons with intellectual disability have to undergo sexual education that will enable them to familiarise themselves with contraceptive techniques and to understand the risks and responsibilities associated with sexual behaviour. However, should they be unable to comprehend, either intellectually or socially, this sexual education, then sterilisation may after all be a permissible option.

Finally, it must be noted that the incorporation of Article 12 into English law via the HRA 1998 calls for the abandonment of the best interests test and the adoption of a human rights approach to non-consensual sterilisation. A legal analysis of the sterilisation of persons with intellectual disability based on Article 12 of the ECHR has the benefit of removing the present debate from its narrow limits of medical law. Sterilisation is not just a form of medical treatment; it is, or can be, a grave intrusion in bodily integrity, and denies the person, usually without recall, the chances to satisfy one of the most deep human urges – to reproduce. The best interests test can, at its worse, be overtly paternalistic. But even at its best, it is a blunt instrument for deciding such a delicate matter as non-consensual sterilisation. The human rights approach has the advantage of being rich in concepts and multi-layered in its reasoning. The fundamental interpretive principles of the ECHR, such as proportionality and respect for human dignity, can provide for equitable solutions and make the law governing sterilisation coherent and simple to follow.

In a nutshell, the human dignity reasoning of this volume, applied to the right to marry and found a family in relation to non-consensual sterilisation, begins by stressing that persons with intellectual disability have a right to marry and found a family. The proposed sterilisation constitutes an interference with this right. This interference can only be justified if it falls under the following variants.

If the proposed sterilisation is therapeutic and the person is unmarried, then in principle it is lawful. Proportionality applies in this case: the greater the benefit from sterilisation, the more justifiable it becomes.

31 See also *Re X (Adult Sterilisation)* [1998] 2 FLR 1124 at 1,128–9 *per* Holman J: 'it is not the fact of itself that X could not bring up a child, and that any child would have to be removed from her, that makes it justifiable or appropriate to perform a sterilisation. That fact alone could never, ever conceivably justify a non-consensual sterilisation.'

If the person is married and wishes to reproduce, then the therapeutic benefit from the procedure must be of greater importance for the sterilisation to be authorised.

If the proposed sterilisation is non-therapeutic – that is, contraceptive – and the person is unmarried, then, in principle, it is inadmissible. In some cases, it can be justified in order to avoid grave and imminent harm from conception or pregnancy of a sexually active person when no milder contraceptive option is indicated and when the person has undergone sexual training but this has failed.

If the person is married and wishes to reproduce, then sterilisation should only be authorised under exceptional circumstances when the procedure is indicated in order to avoid imminent, non-speculative and grave harm to the person from conception or pregnancy. Proportionality again plays an important role: the higher the danger of harm or the graver the harm from conception, the easier it is for contraceptive sterilisation to be justified.

Cohering the MCA 2005 with the HRA 1998

The Shortcomings of the MCA

In the long legislative process leading to the enactment of the Mental Capacity Act 2005, the then Mental Incapacity Bill was renamed the Mental Capacity Bill, following proposals from the parliamentary Joint Committee Report which suggested that the title of this legislative document should reflect the enabling reasoning behind the bill.[32]

The MCA may now have a title evocative of more freedom and inclusion for incapacitated persons, yet, as already mentioned, the legislative reality of the substantive provisions of the Act is rather different: the MCA is based on best interests, not human rights, the best interests test is vague, as best interests are not accompanied by any criteria or aims, and the Act does not actively promote the human rights of persons with intellectual disability.

In the light of the human dignity reasoning analysed in the Chapter 2, the function of any statutory document relating to issues of incapacity and decision-making authority is to enable an open public and political debate as to how the human rights of incapacitated persons, and especially those with intellectual disability, are to be conceived and best protected by the law. The political and social community decides, on the basis of a deliberative process, how it is dignified of that particular society to treat persons with intellectual disability by discussing how the critical interests of these persons are to be interpreted.

32 According to the Joint Committee on the Mental Incapacity Bill, 'The Bill should be seen as enabling rather than restrictive, although it has to strike a delicate balance between respect for individual autonomy and the need to protect the vulnerable'; Joint Committee on the Draft Mental Incapacity Bill, *Draft Mental Incapacity Bill,* vol. 1, HL Paper 189-I HC 1083-I, Session 2002–2003 (London: The Stationery Office, 2003) at 5.

From this vantage point, the MCA 2005 can be regarded as the product of a parliamentary and public debate which focused on very different issues. Even though the consultation period in the final stages of the bill enabled the Joint Parliamentary Committee to draw on the opinions of many persons, lay or academic, deeply engaged in the protection and care of incapacitated persons, the pressing issues of intellectual disability were obfuscated by the raging opposition to the suspicion that the Mental Capacity Bill would legalise euthanasia.

The consequence of this misdirected debate was that the extremely important provisions of the bill relating to best interests and the test of functional capacity, the role which advocacy could play in protecting the human rights of persons with intellectual disability, or the restrictive framework of the ECtHR of Protection either went unchallenged in parliamentary debate or received little attention by both members of parliament and the national press.

In this sense, the criticisms of the MCA which this volume advances can be summarised as follows. Firstly, the MCA sets down an unavoidably restrictive framework as to what criteria indicate that a person has the functional capacity to reach a decision. However liberal the provisions are, there may be cases in which people will be unfairly deemed incapable of making a decision on their own.

Secondly, the MCA adopts a paternalistic solution by accepting the best interests approach. Whenever a person is incapable of making a decision on her own, a decision is to be made on her behalf which must be in her best interests. The Mental Capacity Act 2005 here simulates the approach of welfare in the Children Act 1989 by inserting a statutory checklist of factors which, if taken into account, should enable the decision-maker to reach a decision which will be in the best interests of the person. However, it is doubtful to what extent this checklist is helpful to the person entrusted with decision-making authority, as it is concerned with a process of acquiring evidence as to what best interests are, yet there is no guidance as to how the evidence amassed is to be interpreted.

Finally and more importantly, the MCA is the culmination of a very long consultation period reaching as far back as 1989. In this sense, most of the substantive provisions and regulations of the MCA had crystallised before the passing of the HRA 1998. Moreover, human rights considerations were not seriously taken into account during the various consultations until the Joint Committee was established.

Besides this serious discrepancy with human rights, the MCA is also out of key with the more progressive White Paper *Valuing People*, in which participation and rights for persons with intellectual disability are strongly emphasised.[33] However, in the few months available to it for consultation, the Joint Committee could not have been expected to readjust the reasoning behind the bill, centring it on human rights. In this sense, the fatal flaw of the MCA is that it does not actively promote the human rights of persons with intellectual disability.

33 See pp. 14–15.

Suggested Improvements to the MCA: What Does the Protection of Human Dignity and Human Rights of Persons with Intellectual Disability Require?

In this section, the aim is again to avoid providing a detailed list of proposed changes to an imaginary law-maker containing statutory amendments to the MCA 2005. Rather, this analysis begins by examining the different views and ideas which were submitted to the Joint Parliamentary Committee during the consultation period of the Mental Capacity Bill, to point out the difference in the rationale behind the MCA had the bill been more expressly oriented towards respect of the human rights of incapacitated persons.

During its short consultation period, the Joint Committee found the time to hear 61 witnesses and examine hundreds of written submissions. Among these, the evidence given by Professor John Williams which was presented in Chapter 5 in relation to English law stands out.[34] The summary of his proposals provided here serves as the starting point of this analysis.

The written and oral submissions of Professor Williams are important in that it was the first time the issue of human rights protection was approached from a fresh angle. Until then, the examination of the substantive regulations of the bill had been fragmentary. Each of the proposed sections of the bill was scrutinised as to its compatibility with specific articles of the ECtHR.

For instance, the institution of the new Court of Protection and the regulations as to who may apply to the ECtHR set down restrictions to the right of access to court entrenched in Article 6 of the ECHR. However, the MCA may be considered as a statute setting down a regulatory framework stipulating who may have access to the ECtHR of Protection. In this sense, the MCA is a general law regulating or restricting this Convention right, and as long as the restrictions are not so great as to completely hinder access to court, they are deemed compatible with Article 6.

However, as the submissions of Professor Williams show, even if the MCA is more or less compatible with the ECHR, it does very little to promote the human rights of incapacitated persons. And this is all the more true for persons with intellectual disability.

Professor Williams suggested the replacement of the best interests test with a human rights reasoning. He accused the best interests test of being paternalistic as well as oversimplifying, and as leading to pragmatic solutions rather than principled outcomes. Replacing best interests with a human rights reasoning, Professor Williams argued, stresses the importance of autonomy rather than protection, even if an incapacitated person may have very limited autonomy. Any other solution fails the human rights protection of incapacitated persons.

Within the context of the best interests test, the question in law becomes one of problem-solving. There is a welfare issue concerning a person with intellectual disability – for example, an illness requiring medical intervention. What course of action should be adopted? This line of reasoning places decision-making authority

34 See pp. 129–131.

in the hands of other persons deciding for a person with intellectual disability. In this sense, the best interests test glorifies paternalistic attitudes. Even if the wishes of the person are to be heard, as far as is practicable, this argument does not alter the fact that the person with intellectual disability serves as an object, rather than an active subject, within the reasoning of the best interest test. The person's wishes are just an element of the equation, and form part of the problem that the decision-maker has to address. This is precisely why the best interests test is problematic in terms of human dignity.

Certainly, the MCA 2005 states that the decision-maker is bound to follow the course of action which is the least restrictive of the person's basic rights and freedoms. This provision, however liberal or human rights-oriented, neither alters the substance of the best interests test nor changes the position of the incapacitated person to that of an active participant in the process.

In stark contrast to the best interests test, within the human rights reasoning, the first consideration for every person in contact with persons with intellectual disability should be that this person with intellectual disability is a human rights bearer. This means, for all intents and purposes, that the law under the ECHR acknowledges in that person certain spheres of freedom or liberty in which national authorities cannot intervene without good cause, nor intervene without following a certain procedure.

In terms of human dignity, acknowledging these areas of liberty in the person with intellectual disability asserts at the same time the status of the person as an active and equal member of a political community in which human rights are a cornerstone of its legal system. This is the communicative side of human dignity, which here comes into play in order to emphasise the active role that the community assigns to the person with intellectual disability by enabling the person to exercise her human rights.

Attaching proper importance to human rights and the dignity of persons with intellectual disability inevitably leads us to argue that in certain cases, under specific circumstances, the wishes of persons with intellectual disability should trump any other consideration with regard to their welfare. This means that the law should recognise veto rights for persons with intellectual disability, and not just ensure that their wishes are taken into account during the decision-making process.

On the other hand, reasoning from a standpoint of human dignity also emphasises the importance of upholding the human rights of the incapacitated person. Within a community based on human rights and equality, it is equally important that the life of each member of the community is successful and fruitful. The responsibility for this success lies within the choices that each member of the community makes.

But in the case of persons with intellectual disability, this responsibility may be, in some difficult cases, assigned back to the persons supporting those with intellectual disability to make these choices on their own. And in those cases where persons with intellectual disability are not competent to reach a decision on their own, the responsibility for making a successful choice falls not only on the decision-makers, but also the political community as a whole.

The point here is essentially one of coherence. The choices made on behalf of a person with intellectual disability should best fit in the general political, social and moral framework of the political community to which she belongs. For instance, in English law the Good Samaritan has never been a welcome figure. The common law does not incur an obligation to help persons in need. This may seem an individualistic, egocentric direction of the law, but this distinctive principle is evident in all areas of the law, such as torts and criminal law. In this sense, it is incoherent, incomprehensible and unfair that persons with intellectual disability are obliged to undergo altruistic medical interventions, such as donations of bone marrow, with only a thin reasoning regarding the benefit they may acquire from these interventions as an excuse.[35]

The final point to be drawn from the responsibility that the political community assumes in order to help persons with intellectual disability lead successful lives is the measure and the extent of that responsibility. Chapter 2 argued that the state is under an obligation to provide support to persons with intellectual disability so that they can exercise their human rights on their own, with adequate help.

Taking this responsibility seriously entails that each missed opportunity to provide that support has to be regarded as a loss of liberty, as a breach of their human rights. The political community recognises the dignity of persons with intellectual disability as bearers of human rights and as active members of the community. In order for them to exercise these rights, they need support. Therefore, in the case of intellectual disability, the failure of the state to provide adequate support is as much a breach of human rights as any other positive interference.

In a nutshell, then, it becomes clear that the MCA 2005 should have distinguished the special needs and problems persons with intellectual disability face, and should have specified that persons with intellectual disability have to be given support to fulfil their potential and get as much out of life as possible. The extent of this positive obligation could have been regulated to depend on available funding, yet a minimum of support should have been set down as obligatory by the MCA 2005. Then the MCA could have set down other regulations to complete this framework, for instance that a socially meaningful way of exercising the rights of persons with intellectual disability is for them to participate in research, and set down a list of safeguards for participation in research. Such a regulation of research involving incapacitated persons would be more satisfactory than the current framework of research regulations which the MCA 2005 has adopted.[36] Another option for the MCA 2005 would also have been to accord veto rights to

---

35 As in *Re Y*. See pp. 134–135.

36 For human rights concerns in relation to the current research framework of the MCA, see J. Laing, 'The Mental Capacity Bill 2004: Human Rights Concerns' [2005] Fam. Law 137.

incapacitated persons in relation to invasive medical interventions, participation in research, or housing benefits.

In this sense, the human rights reasoning coupled with human dignity considerations replaces best interests with the following line of thinking, which should have been placed at the heart of the Mental Capacity Act 2005. In order for the welfare issue at hand to be dealt with, interference with the person's human rights is required. The question here is therefore one of law and of coherent interpretation of the person's individual characteristics. What sort of intervention does the law allow in respect to a specific human right? Has the person been given proper support in order for her to reach her own decision? How can the welfare issue be dealt with, with the least interference to the right achieved? Could it perhaps be the case that respect for the person's wishes and the protection of her rights requires that no welfare intervention be made? The solution which protects and advances the critical interests of the person with intellectual disability must be derived from a balanced examination of the above, and similar, questions.

Veto Rights and Positive Obligations of the State towards Persons with Intellectual Disability

It has already been noted that the Mental Capacity Act 2005 is the product of long and laborious consultation periods which originated in 1989, at a time when the passing of the Children Act 1989 had raised concerns about how welfare decisions in general were been made under English law.

In examining the substantive provisions of these consultation papers, it becomes clear that the original recommendations concerning the reform of the law made by the Law Commission were constantly being refined, but that the central structure of what was later to become the Mental Capacity Act 2005 remained unaltered through the years. From an early stage, best interests and a test of functional capacity had been highlighted as desirable legal regulations.

This observation is crucial in understanding that the MCA 2005 is outmoded in relation to two major changes in the legal and political sphere. Chronologically speaking, the first is the passing of the HRA 1998, and the second one is the publication of a new White Paper, *Valuing People*, which encapsulates current governmental policy on intellectual disability.

Governmental policy on intellectual disability is based on four key principles: rights, independence, choice and inclusion. As far as choice is concerned, the White Paper states:

> Like other people, people with learning disabilities want a real say in where they live, what work they should do and who looks after them. But for too many people with learning disabilities, these are currently unattainable goals. We believe that everyone should be able to make choices. This includes people with

> severe and profound disabilities who, with the right help and support, can make important choices and express preferences about their day to day lives.[37]

These four principles are absent from the MCA 2005. Even though the White Paper mentions the legislative activity in the field of incapacity as part and parcel of governmental efforts to provide people with intellectual disability with more rights and inclusion, the MCA 2005 draws no connection or reference to *Valuing People*.

This is all the more frustrating since the Joint Committee Report made it clear that the principles behind the Mental Capacity Bill should be brought together at the beginning of the bill to give a clear idea to every person dealing with these legal provisions of how they should be interpreted and applied.

So the question arises whether these provisions actually present persons with intellectual disability with more choice. The MCA 2005 states that the wishes of the person should be taken into account during the decision-making process. Does this mean that the person with intellectual disability has to be consulted before each decision? Does it also mean that if the person is not consulted, then the decision is void? Does it mean that the incapacitated person has to be heard by the judge hearing the case? What kind of support should be given to the person to help her reach a decision?

It is clear from the standpoint of human dignity that we are advocating that all possibilities should be explored which may enable persons with intellectual disability to have more choice. And in addition to having more choice, they should also have their choices respected.

This means two things. Firstly, persons with intellectual disability should receive adequate support and help to enable them to reach a decision on their own. If such help is not given, or not given in a satisfactory way, the decision made on behalf of the incapacitated person should be void.

If the political community is committed to respecting the dignity and promoting the rights of persons with intellectual disability, there is no better way to achieve this than acknowledging the positive obligation of the state to provide help and support. In recognising in each person with intellectual disability an active member of the political community, the community also has to provide the means by which the person can fully develop her potential. In the case of autonomous people, this responsibility and freedom is their own, since they have a full measure of autonomy. But incapacitated persons require psychological, social, financial and other help in order to contribute to the community through their activities. Such detailed provisions are unfortunately absent from the MCA 2005.

Secondly, the choices the person with intellectual disability makes should, under certain circumstances, trump all other considerations. This is particularly so when the person is opposed to certain interventions. In the case of intellectual disability, capacity has to be understood as both positive and negative. This means that the

37 Secretary of State for Health, *Valuing People: A New Strategy for Learning Disability for the 21st Century*, Cm 5086 (London: The Stationery Office, 2001) at 24.

law should recognise negative veto rights for the disabled regarding certain types of interventions. The example of German law is illuminating here: if the person is afraid of doctors, then the person cannot be sterilised for contraceptive purposes. In the context of English law, an equivalent provision would be that if the person is afraid of needles, for example, then she cannot have bone marrow harvested from her. Recognising such veto rights extends the capacity of persons with intellectual disability to have more control over their lives. And it is at least ironic that an Act concerning mental capacity should overlook this important, negative aspect of decision-making.

Consequently, the MCA 2005 should have done the sensible thing by readjusting its reasoning to the spirit of a legal system which recognises the importance of human rights. This would have required striking down the best interests test as paternalistic and pragmatic, and replacing it with a human rights reasoning which would have allowed for human dignity considerations to filter through the interpretation of the law. We identify three major changes that human dignity requires in respect of the MCA 2005.

Firstly, the MCA 2005 should recognise veto rights of persons with intellectual disability blocking morally and socially ambiguous interventions, such as bone marrow donations or certain kinds of research, which the law will specify. Another veto right is conceivable in relation to care in the community: some persons with intellectual disability may feel more at ease when with their peers rather than other people. This has to be respected, and it must not be assumed that integration should be achieved at all costs.[38]

Secondly, the MCA 2005 should ensure that persons with intellectual disability receive adequate support in decision-making by directly linking the Act to the values and goals of *Valuing People*. Failure to provide such support should be considered a breach of human rights.

Thirdly, the MCA 2005 should incorporate a clear line of legal reasoning based on human rights considerations. This reasoning must begin by asserting that the person with intellectual disability is a bearer of human rights. The proposed welfare intervention interferes with a specific human right of the person. What opportunities has the person had in the past to exercise that right? If she does not have the functional capacity to make the decision, has she been given proper support in order to make that decision for herself? Is she perhaps opposing the intervention, and does this opposition fall under the veto rights the law accords her? What is the degree of necessity of the intervention, and what is the degree of intensity of interference with the human right of the person? By taking all these factors into account, the decision-maker should then be able to answer the question of which sort of intervention would best meet the welfare needs of the person and be the least restrictive of her human rights.

---

38 See, for example, R. Cummins and A. Lau, 'Community Integration or Community Exposure? A Review and Discussion in Relation to People with an Intellectual Disability' [2003] JARID 145.

In a nutshell, this section has examined the vertical relationship between persons with intellectual disability and the state. National authorities are under an obligation to provide adequate support to persons with intellectual disability through positive measures, so that they may become more able to exercise their human rights. Any failure to provide that support, we argue, is not only a violation of their human rights, but also an affront to their human dignity.

However, the question remains what is the horizontal relationship between adult persons with intellectual disability and members of the social community? Are third parties, other than national authorities, under the obligation to provide support to persons with intellectual disability? If so, what is the measure of these obligations? And more importantly, how are the competing interests and rights of persons with intellectual disability and third parties to be balanced? We proceed to answer this question by examining the competing rights and interests of persons with intellectual disability and their family.

The Balance of Rights in Family Life

As a starting point, it is necessary to define the scope of any horizontal obligations. The case law of the ECtHR has to offer some guidance on the issue. In several cases under the heading of Article 8, the ECtHR has accepted that, in sufficiently close relationships, positive obligations may exist, not only between the state and the individuals, but also between the individuals themselves.[39]

In this sense, the degree of closeness of the relationship in question is the determining factor as to whether any obligations arise. Of course, the issue of intellectual disability is socially sensitive. It requires action and positive attitude from each member of the social community, so that persons with intellectual disability will not be discriminated against, but rather be treated with respect. But it seems that only within the family is the closeness of the relationships between family members of such complexity as to found legal obligations which merit closer examination.

It is a common occurrence that a person with intellectual disability lives and remains within her family during childhood as well as adulthood. The parents accept the role of primary carers for the child with intellectual disability who later grow up to be an adult. These parents have been with the person with intellectual disability for all her life, and are usually the best suited to know her needs and care for her.

Within the family, competing rights have to be balanced against each other in a way that achieves more freedom for persons with intellectual disability while safeguarding a minimum of protection. Here, the balance must be struck in favour of liberty. After all, even though this volume has been concerned with the rights and dignity of vulnerable adults, it is important not to lose sight of the fact that they are still adults.

39 *X and Y* v. *The Netherlands*, 26 March 1985, Ser. A No. 91, at para. 23.

State interference may be needed in order to ensure proper respect for the human rights of the person with intellectual disability. In this context, the importance of support provided to the person with intellectual disability through networks of advocacy and self-advocacy becomes crucial. Advocacy acquires in these instances a mediating role between carers and the person with intellectual disability, who may sometimes have strained relationships. This is again a matter of sensitivity, where the stress lies on assessing the person with intellectual disability's needs in a holistic way.

The parents assume a certain responsibility by becoming the primary carers of the person with intellectual disability. In some cases, this responsibility is taken up willingly, in the sense that the parents wish to care for their child even when she has grown up. In other cases, local authorities responsible with providing support to the disabled are unable to do so, for example because of lack of funds, and the parents have to continue caring for the person with intellectual disability.

Whatever the reason for assuming this responsibility of care, the position of the parents as primary carers of the person effectively places them in the same position as national authorities: they have to provide the person with intellectual disability with adequate help and support so that she can lead a successful life by exercising and protecting her human rights. The parents, similar to national authorities, have to provide this support through positive measures. And finally, parents, just like national authorities, should recognise that the person has certain veto rights concerning her welfare. Within this network of care, a persons with intellectual disability, even if she is living with her family, should be granted veto rights blocking certain welfare decisions made on her behalf which interfere with her human rights.

However, the analogy of parents as primary carers in relation to national authorities stops here. The first differentiating legal factor is that the provision of parental support is commensurate to the parents' financial and personal abilities. To the extent that the parents are unable to provide support which would adequately address the critical interests of the person with intellectual disability, local authorities should provide the full measure of that support. This does not mean to say that budgetary constraints of local authorities should not come into consideration; on the other hand, it is clear that the provision of support should be adequate.

For instance, an elderly mother and her intellectually disabled daughter live in a remote Welsh village some 30 miles from the city where the daughter visits a day centre and receives vocational training. The daughter, who has Down syndrome and is obese, has broken her leg. The elderly mother cannot be expected to lift her daughter from the wheelchair or the bed. On the other hand, the daughter must remain mobile and attend classes at the day centre. It is clear that help from the local authority must be provided here, in the form of ambulant aid.

The second legal factor which differentiates the position of parents from that of national authorities is that the welfare decisions the parents reach and the care they provide to their disabled adult child form part of the family life of the parents, under Article 8 of the ECHR. This means, for all intents and purposes, that the parental right of respect for private and family life also covers parental decisions on the welfare of the adult child, so that these welfare decisions acquire special legal protection. This special legal protection creates two different types of human rights issues.

The first issue is to what extent, and under what circumstances, national authorities may intervene in the family life of the disabled adult and the family life of the parents as carers of the disabled adult by challenging the care the parents provide or the welfare decisions they make. This means that if national authorities decide to intervene in the care that a disabled adult receives from her family, then national authorities interfere both with the family life of the parents as well as with the private and family life of the person with intellectual disability.

This line of reasoning necessarily deals with the legitimate interference that Article 8 allows national authorities. Human dignity can here again serve as guidance as to how to interpret what is necessary in a democratic society. The principle dictates that the support and help the parents provide to the person with intellectual disability should be such as to respond to the person's needs or boost the person's aptitudes. For instance, helping the person acquire social skills by learning to say 'Hello, how do you do?' is meaningless if the person is in a poor state of health that does not allow her to leave the house much and meet new people.

On the other hand, providing the person with art lessons if she shows an aptitude for drawing is helpful. In this sense, if the parents do not, or are not in a position to, provide such well-targeted care to the extent that this hinders the child from getting as much out of life as possible, then national authorities may intervene to supply the care needed. As mentioned above, local authorities are under a duty to supplement parental provision of care. To use the previous example again, if the person with intellectual disability has drawing skills but the parents cannot afford the classes, then local authorities should provide financial support to enable the person to learn how to draw.

Another pointer that human dignity can provide in these cases is to interpret the clause necessary in a democratic society in a way which will cohere with other fundamental values of the political community. This is essentially where notions of liberalism or equality come into play. For instance, an adult male with intellectual disability has always been living with his parents and has been raised in a religiously sectarian environment which is very austere. Current notions of liberalism would not allow national authorities to intervene in the private life of this family to remove the disabled person from his home. But if the adult male is sexually active and his psychological development would benefit from his knowing other people and perhaps forming relationships, whereas his family shuns such matters, an intervention by national authorities to allow him social contacts would be correct.

The second human rights issue is how to balance the right of the parents to their private life against the same right of their adult child. The first question is to what extent the parents are obliged to provide their intellectually disabled adult child with help and support. This is an issue not only of the financial potential of the parents, but also one of their sensitivity, available time and understanding.

In most cases, parents of intellectually disabled adults do a remarkable job. Again, arguing from a standpoint of human dignity, the principle certainly does not require that parents make sacrifices for their children with intellectual disability. As mentioned above, however, human dignity does require that the support which the parents cannot provide should be provided by national authorities. In this sense, the parents, as primary carers, have a full measure of responsibility to help and provide support. To the extent that this is not feasible, that part of the responsibility which the parents cannot undertake on their own falls back onto the state. At any time, if persons with intellectual disability do not receive due help and support, this is a breach of their human dignity and of the human rights that they cannot fulfil without that support.

The second question in the balancing of human rights between family members is the extent to which parental decisions should influence the private life of their adult child with intellectual disability. The exercise of parental care naturally allows parents to determine the upbringing of their child according to their conscience and beliefs. This, of course, applies to intellectually disabled children as well. But even when the disabled child turns into an adult, the parents continue to care for her within their family life. This can potentially lead to issues of human rights protection. To use the example cited above, if an adult child with intellectual disability is living with her religiously strong-minded parents who have adamant views as to promiscuity between unmarried people, no real problem arises unless the adult is sexually active and attracted to other persons. But what are the religiously minded parents to do if one of their intellectually disabled adult children is running around the house naked in the morning trying to find her stepbrother?

In such a case, if persons with intellectual disability would benefit psychologically and developmentally from meeting other people and perhaps having sexual experiences, then the person should be encouraged to do so, even if family morals are against it. This is because the human dignity of the person with intellectual disability adult requires that her wishes and critical interests should be respected and allowed to be fulfilled. Even within the family, human dignity serves this enabling purpose so that the person with intellectual disability may enjoy more freedom.

Chapter 8
A New Protocol on Disability?

This chapter concludes this volume by revisiting the case law of the ECtHR, which was shown to be problematic in respect of the protection it has so far accorded to the human rights of persons with intellectual disability.[1] It provides an account of how the human dignity reasoning can improve the approach of the ECtHR to issues of intellectual disability. The possible influence of the CRPD on the interpretation of the ECHR is also examined. We conclude by claiming that, given the growing social and political sensitivity to issues of disability, a specific disability protocol explicitly based on the principle of human dignity and guided by the needs of disabled persons is required.

Addressing the Shortcomings of the Case Law of the ECtHR

The Starting Point: Interpreting the European Convention on Human Rights as a Living Instrument

Recent academic literature on disability rights criticises the ECtHR for not effectively protecting the human rights of disabled persons guaranteed to them by the ECHR.[2] The starting point of this criticism is that there is growing sensitivity, both internationally and at national levels, concerning the rights and social integration of disabled persons, but that this has not filtered through the case law of the ECtHR.

In legal terms, the starting point of the criticism against the ECtHR's disability case law is that the ECtHR has failed to interpret the ECHR as a living instrument in relation to disabled persons. In the fifty years that the ECtHR has been hearing cases, the social, moral and political circumstances of Europe have been constantly evolving, and the ECtHR keeps abreast of these changes by accepting them as a backdrop to the interpretation of ECHR rights.

A classic example of this interpretive approach is *Marckx* v. *Belgium*.[3] The case involved differences in the legal status of children born outside marriage as opposed to legitimate children. The ECtHR noted that there was a consensus of approach in many of the legal systems of member states abolishing such differences. Based on

---

1 See pp. 98–99.

2 See, for example, A. Lawson and C. Gooding, eds, *Disability Rights in Europe* (Oxford: Hart, 2005) at c. 3 and 4.

3 *Marckx* v. *Belgium*, 13 June 1979, Ser. A No. 31.

this common ground, the ECtHR held that no distinction should be made between legitimate and illegitimate family.

More recently, the ECtHR has gone even further down this line of evolutionary interpretation. In *Christine Goodwin* v. *UK*,[4] the ECtHR was unanimous in finding that even though no consensus of approach has been formed by member states, there is a continuing international trend as to the protection and recognition of transsexuals, and the existence of this international trend provided the normative basis for finding a violation. The relevant passage deserves citation in full:

> The ECtHR accordingly attaches less importance to lack of evidence of a common European approach to the resolution of the legal and practical problems posed, than to the clear and uncontested evidence of a continuing international trend in favour not only of increased social acceptance of transsexuals but of legal recognition of the new sexual identity of post-operative transsexuals.[5]

Moreover, the importance of reasoning by analogy within other judgments which the ECtHR has delivered cannot be ignored. In *Chapman* v. *UK*[6] and similar judgments, Gypsies were recognised as an ethnic minority which is entitled to special consideration and protection:

> The vulnerable position of Gypsies as a minority means that some special consideration should be given to their needs and their different lifestyle both in the relevant regulatory planning framework and in reaching decisions in particular cases. To this extent, there is thus a positive obligation imposed on the Contracting states by virtue of Article 8 to facilitate the Gypsy way of life.[7]

This reasoning can surely be extended to persons with intellectual disability as well. Although they are not an ethnic minority, but rather a silent social minority, the long history of their social exclusion and their vulnerability require heightened alertness in safeguarding and promoting their human rights.

These remarks acquire increased significance in relation to issues of disability, whether physical or intellectual. In the past twenty years, a gradual increase in concern over the welfare and the rights of disabled persons can be noted, both at international level as well as in the jurisdictions of many of the member states of the Council of Europe.

4 *Goodwin* v. *UK*, 11 July 2002, [2002] EHRR 447.

5 Ibid. at para. 85.

6 *Chapman* v. *UK*, 18 January 2001, [2001] EHRR 18.

7 Ibid. at para. 96.

At the international level, several UN declarations have been devoted to the protection of the rights of disabled persons.[8] Moreover, a UN convention on the human rights of disabled persons is currently being drafted.[9]

At the European level, a very important event, both symbolically but also in terms of increasing awareness of disability issues, was the proclamation by the Council of Europe of 2003 as the European Year of Persons with Disabilities, in the wider context of which the Declaration of Madrid on the rights of disabled persons was passed.[10] The European Union has issued a framework directive on disability discrimination in the field of employment,[11] and many member countries of the Council of Europe have enacted anti-discrimination legislation relating to disability.

In the light of the above disability legislation at the European level, it can safely be claimed that there exists a European consensus regarding disability protection, especially in the field of countering discrimination.

On the other hand, national legal systems of member states of the Council of Europe have approached the substantive needs of disabled persons quite differently, according to their welfare systems and their budgetary constraints. For instance, systems for disability pensions and classifications of disability vary considerably from state to state.

Nevertheless, following the dictum in *Christine Goodwin*, and given the above international developments concerning disability issues, it becomes apparent that there also exists clear and uncontested evidence of a continuing international trend in favour of disabled persons, attaching a growing importance to the protection of their human rights and their inclusion and integration into society.

Even though there is lack of evidence of a common European approach to the resolution of the legal and practical problems that disability poses, there exists a growing international trend of disability protection. This volume criticises the ECtHR for not taking proper account of this consensus and this international trend when applying the ECHR in relation to issues of disability.

How the Case Law Should Change: The Human Dignity Reasoning Applied to the Case Law of the ECtHR

The case law of the ECtHR concerning disability can be improved in two ways.

The first set of proposals relates to the special characteristics and needs of persons with intellectual disability. When examining a case which involves an

8 See, for example, *Declaration on the Rights of Disabled Persons*, GA Res. 3447(XXX), UN GAOR, 30th Sess., Supp. No. 34, UN Doc. A/10034, 88.

9 For an account of the proceedings of the Ad Hoc Committee entrusted to draft the convention, see R. Light, 'Disability and Human Rights: The Persistent Oxymoron' in A. Lawson and C. Gooding, eds, *Disability Rights in Europe* (Oxford: Hart, 2005) at 9.

10 Available at <http://www.psih.uaic.ro/cercetare/evenimente/Workshop_Iasi_Documents_BLOEMERS/PPP_THE_MADRID_DECLARATION.pdf>.

11 Council Directive 2000/78/EC of 27 November 2000, [2000] OJ L303/16.

intellectually disabled applicant, the ECtHR must take into consideration the special impairments that intellectual disability brings with it. The ECtHR must also examine whether the applicant's rights would have been better protected or not violated had the applicant had no intellectual disability. Limited understanding, poor social skills, high levels of compliance or suggestibility – all these factors may have played an important role in why or how the rights of persons with intellectual disability applicant have been violated or not protected. In these instances, the ECtHR should be more willing to find a violation under an ECHR right.

Not finding a violation under these circumstances amounts to penalising the distinct psychological features of intellectual disability which made the applicant more vulnerable to any abuse of her human rights. An example of this would be the case of intellectually disabled parents, who may be pressed by local authorities to give away their disabled child to a foster family. Even if the parents were capable of consenting, under national law, a violation of Article 8 should be found in their case, especially if the parents have a high degree of compliance and the pressure from the local authorities was considerable.

The ECtHR should also expand its reasoning under Article 8 with regard to the positive obligations inherent in an effective respect for private or family life, which may involve the adoption of measures designed to secure respect for private life even in the sphere of the relations of individuals between themselves. In the case of intellectual disability, the absence of any positive measures which would enable persons with intellectual disability to enjoy more fully their private and family lives should be considered a violation of Article 8. Given the social sensitivity of disability issues, private and family life should be interpreted in a broad manner.

An illustration of this would be the absence of legislation instituting day centres for vocational or recreational activities for persons with intellectual disability in a certain area. Naturally, other policy considerations are relevant in this respect. However, the state here has a margin of appreciation, but only as to how these day centres will be equipped and manned. Similarly, the ECtHR should also find a violation under Article 8 even if legislation has been enacted which provides for the establishment of day centres and specifies the technical standards of care, but this legislation is not being materialised, for instance due to lack of funds.

The second way in which the case law of the ECtHR should change with regard to intellectual disability is in terms of the human dignity reasoning. As explained in Chapter 4, the principle of human dignity forms part of the philosophical underpinning of the ECHR, both in terms of the drafting history of the ECHR as well as its teleology.[12] No one is therefore better placed to interpret ECHR rights from the viewpoint of human dignity that the ECtHR itself.

In the case of intellectual disability, the human dignity reasoning can strengthen the claim for positive measures as an inherent part of the scope of ECHR rights. Persons with intellectual disability require help and support to become more able

12 See pp. 81–86.

to exercise their rights. They require such help as is necessary, according to their own personality, health needs and developmental possibilities, to get as much out of life as possible. National jurisdictions should provide that support through positive measures, or by empowering persons with intellectual disability with veto rights concerning welfare decisions made on their behalf.

But most importantly, the interpretation of the ECHR through the human dignity reasoning asserts the position of persons with intellectual disability as bearers of human rights who are vulnerable and in need of greater protection. This may render the case law of the ECtHR more sensitive to the problems that persons with intellectual disability face. This position can therefore support the argument that the ECtHR should regard intellectual disability as a special case, in which the status of the applicant as intellectually disabled signals to the ECtHR that stricter scrutiny as to whether an interference with an ECHR right is justified, notwithstanding a certain margin of appreciation of national authorities. The use of strict proportionality control in cases involving intellectually disabled applicants coheres with the need for greater protection that the human dignity reasoning has proposed.

The Margin of Appreciation Issue

The practical side of this line of argumentation is that it provides the normative basis for the finding of violations of ECHR rights, allegations of which would normally be turned down by the ECtHR. A good example can be derived from the factual circumstances surrounding the case of *Nasri* v. *France*.[13]

Nasri was an Algerian national who as a young child was brought to live with his family in Paris. He was born deaf and mute. When his parents applied to a special state institution for deaf and mute persons to have their child educated there, their application was turned down as Nasri was assessed to have very low intelligence, and would not be able to cope with and benefit from specialist education. As a result of the family's financial difficulties and Nasri's aggressive behaviour, he did not receive much by way of education; he did not learn sign language, and remained severely illiterate, subsequently having serious problems with the law.

In similar cases where special education and training is denied to persons with intellectual disability, effectively leaving them with no other alternatives but illiteracy and crime, national authorities fail to foster their autonomy to such a degree that the right for respect of their private life under Article 8 is violated. To use the jurisprudential language of the ECtHR, national authorities are under a positive obligation to provide such basic education, the content and form of which may naturally be decided by national authorities according to their general educational traditions.

---

13 *Nasri* v. *France*, 13 July 1995, Ser. A No. 324.

But in contrast to other positive obligations owed to non-persons with intellectual disability, national authorities cannot be said to have a wide margin of appreciation here regarding who benefits, why and to what extent from this specialist education, since granting such training to persons with intellectual disability is a prerequisite for them to effectively hold the right to respect for private life, whereas the denial of such education would jeopardise the effectiveness of Article 8. A wider margin of appreciation in relation to such specialist education is only conceivable in relation to its content and form, for instance placing an emphasis on vocational training for those persons with intellectual disability with relevant skills.

In other words, in relation to questions of intellectual disability, the ECtHR cannot grant a wide margin of appreciation to the respondent state, as the issues at stake relate directly to the effectiveness of ECHR rights. The status of an applicant as intellectually disabled must signal to the ECtHR that strict scrutiny of the applicant's allegations is required, and a thorough examination of the case should be made.

The Impact of the CRPD on the ECHR

It remains to be seen whether the ECtHR may eventually develop its case law in relation to applicants with intellectual disability along the lines of a human dignity argument similar to the one this volume advances. However, this begs the question whether the interpretation of the ECHR will change through other means. The recent adoption of the CRPD by the UN General Assembly is looked upon as a major change in human rights law. Can the CRPD provide a clear benchmark so that the protection of ECHR rights afforded to persons with intellectual disability will become more adequate?

The starting point of this analysis is again an argument of coherence. The CRPD is a major UN human rights convention. As such, it not only carries great weight as an international human rights document, but it was also drafted with the participation of many states which have adhered to the Council of Europe and are signatories to the ECHR. Similarly, many of these states have ratified the CRPD and its additional Protocol. In light of these developments, the ECtHR must now radically change its case law, based on its interpretation of the ECHR as a living instrument.

Such an evolutionary interpretation involves a number of changes. Firstly, the ECtHR must hear cases involving applicants with disabilities from the viewpoint of the social model of disability. The expert medical evidence which was followed by national authorities should not go unchallenged. The margin of appreciation granted to national authorities must also be narrow. The ECtHR must proceed to conduct its own assessment as to whether the respondent state has failed to lift barriers which impede persons with disabilities from exercising their human rights in order to determine whether a right protected by the ECHR has been violated.

Secondly, the ECtHR must make creative use of the concept of reasonable accommodation. This line of argumentation has been forcefully developed by De Schutter before the adoption of the CRPD.[14] The emphasis that the CRPD places on reasonable accommodation only serves to reinforce his arguments. In order to overcome the negative effects of the case law of the ECtHR on disability, De Schutter discusses several parameters of reasonable accommodations which may be subsumed under Article 8 of the ECHR.

The first of these is the obligation of the state to implement existing national law concerning persons with disabilities. For example, the failure of Italian authorities to implement existing legal provisions regarding the accessibility of public places should have led to the finding of a violation of Article 8 in the case of *Botta* v. *Italy*. A second obligation of the state is to comply with other international human rights instruments. Of course, this does not mean that the ECtHR is empowered to sanction national practices which violate human rights documents other than the ECHR. On the contrary, here the ECtHR is asked to interpret Article 8 in light of other documents of international law. A third obligation is to include safeguards in the decision-making process so as to 'weigh all relevant interests carefully when making decisions and, in particular, to analyse the impact of proposed measures on more vulnerable groups'.[15] A fourth obligation which De Schutter identifies is non-discrimination even in cases where there is only an indirect link between the discriminatory measure and Article 8. A final obligation would be not to inflict inhuman or degrading treatment or punishment on persons with disabilities. In other words, denial of reasonable accommodation may be considered inhuman or degrading treatment and amount to a violation of Article 3 of the ECHR.

Moving away from positive obligations, a third way in which the CRPD may influence the interpretation of the ECHR is the concept of progressive realisation. Here, the ECtHR may temper the effects of its evolutionary interpretation of the ECHR by setting progressive standards of human rights protection for persons with disabilities. The concept of progressive realisation appears in Article 4 para. 2 of the CRPD, in the context of socio-economic rights. Importantly, the concept of progressive realisation is used by the UN Committee on Economic, Social and Cultural Rights in order to assess whether states are taking reasonable steps to implement socio-economic rights in an incremental way.[16] In the case of applicants with disabilities, an assessment of alleged violations of the ECHR through an analysis of progressive realisation would be extremely important. It would signal

14 O. De Schutter, 'Reasonable accommodations and positive obligations in the European convention on human rights' in A. Lawson and C. Gooding, *Disability Rights in Europe: From Theory to Practice* (Oxford: Hart, 2005) at 35–63.

15 Ibid. at 49.

16 Colm O'Cinneide, 'Extracting Protection for the Rights of Persons with Disabilities from Human Rights Frameworks: Established Limits and New Possibilities' in O.M. Arnardóttir and G. Quinn, eds, *The UN Convention on the Rights of Persons with Disabilities: European and Scandinavian Perspectives* (Leiden: Martinus Nijhoff Publishers, 2009) at 189–90.

the willingness of the ECtHR to conduct a thorough examination of the applicant's case, rather than falling back on the margin of appreciation.

Finally, the interpretation of the ECHR must be brought in line with the normative content of specific articles of the CRPD. For instance, a case similar to *Botta* v. *Italy* must now be assessed in light of the right to accessibility under Article 9 of the CRPD. The interpretation of the right to respect for private life under Article 8 of the ECHR must now include the right to accessibility. This means that any restrictions on the right to accessibility must be shown to be necessary in a democratic society and be proportional to the aim to be achieved. Such an interpretation offers the ECtHR the opportunity to adopt a far more protective position with regard to persons with disabilities.

The same applies in cases similar to that of *Sentges* v. *The Netherlands*, where the disability-specific provision of personal mobility (Article 20 of the CRPD) can be meaningfully applied in the context of Article 8 of the ECHR. Sentences (a) and (b) of Article 20 read as follows:

> (a) Facilitating the personal mobility of persons with disabilities in the manner and at the time of their choice, and at affordable cost.
>
> (b) Facilitating access by persons with disabilities to quality mobility aids, devices, assistive technologies and forms of live assistance and intermediaries, including by making them available at affordable cost.

By not providing the applicant with a robotic arm, national authorities denied him access to a mobility aid which was absolutely necessary for him to acquire an adequate degree of personal mobility. With the benefit of hindsight, the important new element that these provisions of the CRPD bring into the analysis of *Sentges* is that national authorities did not offer to meet at least part of the cost of the robotic arm. This raises an important question of proportionality. The outright refusal of national authorities to provide the mobility aid was not proportional to the importance of the robotic arm for the mobility of the applicant. Following this line of reasoning, a violation of Article 8 of the ECHR should have been acknowledged in the case of *Sentges*.

In relation to persons with intellectual disability, cases similar to that of *X and Y* v. *The Netherlands* must also be examined in light of Article 23 of the CRPD, which declares in para. 2: 'States Parties shall recognize that persons with disabilities enjoy legal capacity on an equal basis with others in all aspects of life.' Blanket exclusion of capacity in national laws is equivalent to denial of legal personhood of persons with intellectual disability. As such, it represents an additional violation of Article 8 of the ECHR on a different ground than the one found in the case of *X and Y* v. *The Netherlands*.[17]

---

17 For a discussion of the case, see pp. 90–91.

Similarly, should a case involving involuntary sterilisation be heard by the ECtHR, sentence (c) para. 1 of Article 23 of the CRPD must influence the reasoning of the ECtHR. That provision affirms that: 'Persons with disabilities, including children, retain their fertility on an equal basis with others.' In light of this unequivocal declaration, involuntary sterilisations must be rendered difficult to justify in the eventual case law of the ECtHR.

This analysis has shown that the CRPD has an invaluable potential to influence the interpretation of the ECHR by the ECtHR. The CRPD is based on ideas such as the social model of disability, and principles such as dignity, autonomy and respect for the wishes of persons with disabilities. In addition, the CRPD introduces to international human rights law disability-specific solutions, such as the concept of reasonable accommodation or universal design. These concepts, if used creatively by the ECtHR, may provide a sound basis for the evolution of its case law in favour of applicants with disabilities.

Time alone will show whether the ECtHR will decide to update its case law in relation to applicants with disabilities. One way to do this would be to develop a coherent interpretation of human dignity, which would be especially important in the case of applicants with intellectual disability. A second way to update its case law would be by interpreting the ECHR according to the spirit of the CRPD. Yet this volume ultimately argues that such a process, even though not unlikely, may be greatly facilitated if a new, disability-specific protocol to the ECHR were adopted by the Council of Europe. The next section will examine this claim in greater detail.

Intellectual Disability and the ECHR: A New Protocol?

Introduction

Before developing the reasons why this volume proposes that a new, disability-specific protocol be added to the ECHR, it is perhaps best to recapitulate some of the most important elements of the argumentation. The volume has been based on this line of reasoning: the classic notion of human rights as negative rights protecting an area of freedom in which the state cannot interfere misses the point of human rights protection in the case of persons with intellectual disability. Human rights are conditioned by the autonomous choice that the bearer of the right exercises as an individual. Persons with intellectual disability, however, do not have this autonomy – or worse still, their autonomy is questioned. Basing their human rights protection on autonomy is therefore mistaken. On the contrary, these persons require help and support in order to become more able to exercise their rights. Without proper support – that is, interference – persons with intellectual disability cannot enjoy their rights to the full extent, or as far as their disability allows. The crux of the problem is how to do this in a way that is coherent with the theory and practice of human rights.

Within a network of human rights protection such as the ECHR or the CRPD, there can be found interpretive principles, the most basic of which is human dignity, which may guide national authorities as to what kind of support they should provide to persons with intellectual disability. Moreover, the principle of human dignity may also provide guidance as to whether the human rights of persons with intellectual disability have been violated through the actions or omissions of national authorities.

In relation to English law, the human dignity reasoning presented in this volume points to three very specific changes. The first and foremost change is the abandonment of the best interests test, and of the paternalistic connotations it carries with it. The best interests test has been shown to display a fatal flaw: best interests alone cannot actively protect and promote the human rights of persons with intellectual disability. In the majority of cases, best interests can only be shown not to infringe these rights, whereas in certain cases, the problem-solving approach underlying the best interests test leads to human rights violations. On the other hand, the passing of the Human Rights Act 1998 calls for a more proactive and rights-centred approach to issues relating to vulnerable adults. Further, the second change needed in English law is the recognition of the state's obligation to provide, through positive measures, the help and support that persons with intellectual disability require so that they may exercise their human rights meaningfully. Within that context, a wide acceptance of veto rights relating to welfare decisions made on behalf of persons with intellectual disability represents the third important change.

In relation to the case law of the ECtHR, we supported several changes that the human dignity reasoning requires. The first of these is that the ECtHR should find violations of ECHR rights in those cases where national authorities have not provided assistance to persons with intellectual disability through positive measures. The second change is that the ECtHR should scrutinise any interference with the rights of persons with intellectual disability under a stricter, rather than a weak, proportionality test. Such interference should be the least restrictive of the human rights involved. The ECtHR should not grant any margin of appreciation to national authorities regarding the necessity of the intervention. The assessment of the necessity of the intervention should always be carried out by the ECtHR, as a further safeguard against abuse. On the other hand, a margin of appreciation is conceivable merely as to the form and content of the intervention carried out by the national authorities.

These proposals for change, we believe, are consistent with the teleology of the CRPD. In the case of people with disabilities, human rights protection must accommodate both the need for protection of liberty and the obligation for support that people with disabilities require. The CRPD also has an enormous potential to influence the interpretation of the ECHR. The social model of disability, the obligation for reasonable accommodations, as well as specific rights such as the right to accessibility may provide the ECtHR with the opportunity to develop its case law.

However, the question that must realistically be posed at the end of all this legal argumentation is whether it is feasible to expect such changes in the case law of the ECtHR in the future.

A New Protocol for Disability

We have already provided an examination of the case law of the ECtHR in relation to applicants with disabilities. That analysis demonstrates that the ECtHR has interpreted the ECHR in a very cautious manner when issues of disability have arisen. This reluctance of the ECtHR may be explained in several ways.

Even though European socio-political and legal attitudes towards disability affirm the need for non-discrimination and positive action, the ECtHR is unlikely to take a more sensitive stance towards intellectually disabled applicants, mainly for structural reasons.

The first of these relates to the make-up of the ECtHR itself. The panel of judges adjudicating each case changes; the judges appointed at the ECtHR are not permanent; each judge, coming from a different jurisdiction, has a different approach to the legal question at hand. This lack of continuity in the ECtHR means that only with great difficulty can a coherent line of reasoning towards intellectual disability be developed.

The second issue relates to the ECHR itself. Even if the ECtHR decided to change its case law towards intellectual disability, this change would inevitably take effect mostly through Article 8. The right for respect of private and family life is, conceptually, the best suited to provide protection to persons with intellectual disability. But the formulation of the article is not helpful, and the ECtHR could be faced with the charge that it is creating law in favour of disability.

Thirdly, the subsidiary role of the ECtHR in human rights protection means that national authorities and the judiciary will be deemed to be better placed to estimate the nature and extent of any positive obligation towards persons with intellectual disability. Furthermore, even pilot cases/judgments of the ECtHR in favour of persons with disabilities may only have a limited effect, as persons with disabilities are not a homogenous group, and the specificities of each disability may require a less universal approach.

Importantly, these reasons apply with equal force in the case of the CRPD. Moreover, the ECtHR has repeatedly stressed that its jurisdiction is based solely on the ECHR, and cannot therefore extend this jurisdiction in order to adjudicate on the basis of other human rights documents. The case of *Zehnalová and Zehnal* v. *the Czech Republic*[18] is indicative of the reluctance of the ECtHR to appear to be extending its jurisdictional basis outside the ECHR. In *Zehnalová*, the applicants complained about the lack of accessibility of public buildings in their home town. They invoked, among other provisions, Articles 12 (right to social security) and 13

18 Application No. 3862/97, Decision of 14 May 2002.

(right to social and medical assistance) of the European Social Charter. The ECtHR was emphatic in turning this argument down:

> it is not its task to review governments' compliance with instruments other than the European Convention on Human Rights and its Protocols, even if, like other international treaties, the European Social Charter (which, like the Convention itself, was drawn up within the Council of Europe) may provide it with a source of inspiration.

There is therefore room for doubt whether the ECtHR will use the provisions of the CRPD as an interpretive tool in order to update and specify ECHR rights in relation to persons with intellectual disability.

Given these structural difficulties, we argue that a disability protocol may more easily initiate changes in the interpretation of ECHR rights which should ultimately be based on the principle of human dignity. Such a protocol would provide the much-needed overhaul of the ECHR in relation to disability by specifically dealing with the issues that disability raises in respect of human rights protection. A further important point in drafting such a document would be to update the ECHR in relation to the CRPD and imbue the interpretation of ECHR rights in a way which is more attentive to and protective of the rights of disabled persons.

The importance of a disability protocol cannot be stressed enough. The process of its adoption would initiate a dialogue within the Council of Europe which would provide an opportunity to air the issues that disability raises in a practical way. The spirit of such a disability protocol should guarantee the progressive realisation of ECHR rights in order to leave considerable room for the ECtHR to develop in time an effective framework of protection for persons with disabilities in general and intellectual disability in particular.

Furthermore, the immediate result of adopting such a protocol would be, on the one hand, to legitimise the reluctant ECtHR to afford adequate human rights protection to persons with disability. On the other hand, it would facilitate access to the ECtHR for disabled persons and encourage disability-related litigation.

The applicability of the protocol should be limited to those applicants who successfully claim that they have a disability. In other words, the ECtHR should first establish whether a person has a disability under the protocol, so that the disability-specific provisions of the protocol may apply to her case. Disability need only be broadly defined in the protocol. Similar to the CRPD, the protocol may include a definition of persons with disabilities based on the social model of disability.

Again, this is a very important point with regard to the development of the case law of the ECtHR. By including a definition of who counts as a person with disabilities in the protocol, the ECtHR would be forced to develop its own interpretation of disability. It would engage with issues of disability from the viewpoint of the social model. Especially with regard to intellectual disability, this mode of thinking may enable the ECtHR to acknowledge the legal challenges of human rights protection for persons with intellectual disability.

With regard to the substantive content of such a protocol, several options exist. The first point would be to set down the definition of disability and define the applicability criteria of the protocol. Similar to the CRPD, a second important point would be for the protocol to serve an educative role, by stating the principles which underlie its interpretation. The significance of human dignity for the rights of persons with disabilities should be stressed. However, in contrast to the CRPD, the normative content of the principles should be given at least a broad definition. This is especially important in relation to intellectual disability. The protocol should here acknowledge the tension between intellectual disability, dignity and autonomy, and provide general guidance as to how the rights of persons with intellectual disability should be protected.

A further choice for the protocol would be to render the rights of the ECHR disability-specific. Again, it is not for this volume to give detailed guidance as to how the rights of the ECHR should be rendered more tangible in issues of disability. However, rewriting the articles of the ECHR in the style of the UNCRPD – adding an extensive list of paragraphs as to how the rights may be implemented or protected – may be too restrictive in view of the ECtHR's role and style of reasoning.

A third option in terms of substantive content is to adopt new, disability-specific human rights, rather than subsuming issues of disability under the established rights of the ECHR. A characteristic example would be a right to accessibility, similar to that entrenched in the CRPD. Such a course of action would have the advantage that conceptual clarity and continuity would be maintained in the case law of the ECtHR. The general articles of the ECHR would continue to apply, yet specific issues of disability would be brought under the scope of specific articles in the protocol. These articles would then be applied if the applicant convinced the ECtHR of her status as a victim with disabilities.

A fourth point in adopting the protocol concerns the extent of positive obligations inherent in ECHR rights with regard to disabled applicants. Here, what has been said in the previous section on the impact of the CRPD on the ECHR need only be summarised.[19]

The primary positive obligation which must be included in the protocol is the obligation of national authorities to implement existing national law concerning persons with disabilities. On a European level, this positive obligation offers the opportunity to further extract human rights protection for persons with disabilities based on EU anti-discrimination law.

A second positive obligation of national authorities would be to ensure compliance with other international human rights instruments relating to disability.

---

19 O. De Schutter, 'Reasonable accommodations and positive obligations in the European convention on human rights' in A. Lawson and C. Gooding, *Disability Rights in Europe: From Theory to Practice* (Oxford: Hart, 2005) at 35–63.

The ECtHR would thereby be legitimised to interpret the protocol and the ECHR in light of other documents of international law. Again, this positive obligation would further enhance the human rights protection the ECtHR provides to persons with intellectual disability.

A fifth point in the protocol would be to set down the extent of the margin of appreciation to be accorded to national authorities. Again, here the CRPD becomes relevant: member states may commit themselves to the progressive realisation of acknowledging positive obligations towards disabled persons and the full enjoyment of their rights. National authorities may be granted a progressively diminished margin of appreciation as this process continues.

Establishing a mechanism of progressive realisation of the rights of the protocol ensures that member states will not find themselves in violation of the protocol if they show that they are indeed taking practical steps to ensure adequate protection to the rights of persons with disability. Setting up such a flexible mechanism of control ensures two things. Firstly, it signals to national authorities that the ECtHR does not relinquish control of the facts of the case, as would happen if the ECtHR merely accorded a broad margin of appreciation to national authorities. Secondly, it enables both the ECtHR and national authorities to adapt to a new regime of human rights protection. In this sense, the mechanism of progressive realisation may help overcome any initial misgivings surrounding the adoption of the protocol. As the case law develops, however, the ECtHR may be progressively led to find violations of the protocol and the ECHR according to the circumstances of each case.

Given the fact that the protocol would be adopted within the Council of Europe, a final option for its drafting would be to include anti-discrimination norms which exist at the European level. Lawson, writing in relation to the impact of the CRPD on the ECHR, presents this argument eloquently:

> the CRPD might act as a catalyst to the development of a more comprehensive and cohesive European approach. The EC … played a highly influential role in the elaboration of the CRPD and that instrument is now in its turn likely to play a highly influential role in the further development … of disability-related law and policy …

In this sense, the adoption of the disability protocol is an opportunity to cohere the human rights protected by the ECHR with disability-related solutions provided by anti-discrimination law. A characteristic example would be the recent case of the ECJ in *Coleman*.[20] In that case, the ECJ considered that discrimination by association is prohibited under EU anti-discrimination law. This means that any person who is discriminated against because of her being associated with a person with disability enjoys the same disability-related protection under EU law. Applying this solution in the rights of the ECHR and the protocol would amount to a more complete protection in the case of disability.

---

20 *Coleman* v. *Attridge Law* (Case C-303/06) [2008] 3 CMLR 27, ECJ.

Conclusion

Disability is becoming an important issue in international human rights law. In particular, the recent adoption of the UN Convention on the Rights of Persons with Disabilities provides an excellent opportunity to enquire into the protection afforded to persons with disability under the ECHR. Sadly, however, the case law of the ECtHR is far from providing adequate protection to the human rights of persons with intellectual disability. This is because disability is closely linked to positive action, and the ECtHR considers that national authorities enjoy a wide margin of appreciation in this respect. This position is becoming more and more untenable compared to the UNCRPD and the rights it guarantees to disabled persons. For this reason, a new disability protocol should be added to the ECHR to address the extent of positive obligations towards disabled persons. This in turn will offer the ECtHR the opportunity to engage more actively with the rights of persons with disability and offer an adequate degree of protection to their rights under the ECHR.

In closing, this volume has been an attempt to develop a legal framework for support and protection of the human rights of persons with intellectual disability, which also ensures their rightful place as equals in liberal society. We have argued that there are elements and concepts in existing law whose correct interpretation may lead to improvements in the respect for the human dignity and critical interests of persons with intellectual disability. To the extent that the disability rights movement is gaining ground internationally, interesting challenges for both liberalism and the law lie ahead.

Appendix
German Civil Code Fourth Book – Family Law Second Title

Care and Control (Betreuung)[1]

§ 1896. [Appointment of a protector (Betreuer)]

(1) If a person of full age is, by reason of a physical ailment or physical, mental or psychic impediment, wholly or partly unable to take care of his affairs, the Guardianship Court appoints a protector for him upon his petition or on its own motion. Also a person who is incompetent to enter legal transactions may present the petition. Insofar as a person of full age is unable to take care of his affairs by reason of a physical impediment, a protector may only be appointed upon the petition of the person of full age, unless the latter cannot declare his intention.
(1a) A protector may not be appointed against the free will of the person of full age.
(2) A protector may only be appointed for types of problems for which the care and control is required. The care and control is not necessary to the extent that the affairs of a person of full age can be taken care of by a person with a power of attorney, or by other assistants for whom no legal representative is appointed, as efficiently as by a protector.
(3) The enforcement of the rights of the person under care and control against the protector can be determined as one of the types of such problems.
(4) The decision concerning the telecommunications of the person under care and control and their reception, and the opening and checking of his mail are included in the duties of the protector only if the court expressly so orders.

§ 1897. [Appointment of a natural person]

(1) The Guardianship Court shall appoint as a protector a natural person who is suitable to take care of the affairs of the person under care and control within the scope of duties determined by the court and by doing so entrusts the care within the required scope to him personally.

---

1 This translation is cited, with minor corrections and amendments, from S. Goren, *German Civil Code* (Littleton, CO: F.B. Rothman, 1994) at 338–44. Sentences in italics have been translated by the author. The translation states the law up to April 2006.

(2) The co-worker of a care association recognised by virtue of § 1908f, who is exclusively or partly active as a protector (Association protector), may only be appointed with the consent of the association. An analogous rule applies to a co-worker of an authority competent to deal with care matters, who is exclusively or partly active there as a protector (Authority protector).
(3) A person may not be appointed as a protector if he has a dependency relationship or any other close connection with an institution, home or other establishment, in which the person of full age has been placed or resides.
(4) If the person of full age nominates a person to be appointed as his protector, his suggestion should be accepted if it is not detrimental to the good of that person of full age. If he proposes that a certain person should not be appointed, it shall be taken into consideration. The first and second sentences are also applicable to proposals advanced by the person of full age before the process of appointment of a protector, unless he obviously does not want to adhere to these proposals.
(5) If the person of full age does not propose anyone who can be appointed as his protector, then during the selection process for a protector, consideration should be given to the kinship and other personal ties of the person of full age, especially his ties to parents, children and spouses, as well as to apprehension of conflicts of interests.
(6) If a person becomes a protector as part of his profession, he shall only be appointed as a protector, if there is no other suitable person, who is ready to undertake the care without remuneration. If the protector learns of circumstances, from which ensue that the person of full age can be cared for by one or more persons who do not become protectors as part of their profession, he shall so notify the court.
(7) If a person is appointed a protector under the conditions of subsection (6) sentence (1) for the first time in the district of the Guardianship Court, the court shall first hear the responsible Authority as to the suitability of the chosen protector and as to the decisions to be made according to § 1836 subsection (1) sentence (3) second alternative. The responsible authority shall demand the criminal record and information from the index of debtors.
(8) If a person is appointed pursuant to the conditions of subsection (6) sentence (1), he shall inform as to the number and extent of the care he provides professionally.

§ 1898. [Duty to accept]

(1) The person selected by the Guardianship Court is obliged to undertake the care, if he is suitable to be a protector and the assumption thereof can be expected of hum having considered his family, professional, and other circumstances.
(2) The person selected may only be appointed as protector if he has already declared his willingness to undertake the duties of care.

§ 1899. [Several protectors]

(1) The Guardianship Court may appoint several protectors if the affairs of the person under care can better be served thereby. In such case it shall determine which type of tasks will be entrusted to each protector. *Several protectors, who receive remuneration, shall not be appointed, except in the cases regulated in subsections (2) and (4) as well as § 1908i subsection (1) sentence (1).*
(2) A special protector shall always be appointed for the decision on the sterilisation of the person under care.
(3) Insofar as several protectors have been charged with the same type of duties, they may take care of the affairs of the person under care only jointly, unless the court made a different determination or the delay involves jeopardy.
(4) The court may also appoint several protectors in such a manner that one of them shall take care of the affairs of the person under care only to such extent as the other is prevented.

§ 1900. [Appointment of a protective association]

(1) If the person of full age cannot be taken care of adequately by one or more natural persons, the Guardianship Court shall appoint a recognised protective association as protector. The consent of the association is requisite for the appointment.
(2) The association shall entrust the maintenance of the care to individuals. Proposals of the person of full age shall be complied with hereby, to such extent that they are not contrary to important considerations. The association shall inform the court as soon as possible concerning the person to whom the maintenance of the care was entrusted.
(3) If the association learns of circumstances, the outcome of which is that the person of full age can be taken care of by one or more natural persons in an adequate manner, it shall so notify the court.
(4) If the person of full age cannot adequately be taken care of by one or more natural persons or by an association, the court shall appoint the competent authority as protector. Subsections (2) and (3) apply mutatis mutandis.
(5) The decision on consent for sterilisation of the person under care may not be entrusted to associations or authorities.

§ 1901. [Duties of protectors]

(1) The care includes all activities, which are necessary in order to legally take care of the affairs of the person under care, in accordance to the following provisions.
(2) The protector shall attend to the affairs of the person under care in such a manner as is required for the good of the latter. The good of the person under care also includes the possibility to shape his life within the scope of his ability according to his own wishes and ideas.

(3) The protector shall comply with the wishes of the person under care, insofar as they are not opposed to the good of the latter and can be expected of the protector. This is also applicable to wishes which the person under care expressed prior to the appointment of the care person unless he obviously does not want to adhere to such wishes. Before disposing of serious matters, he shall discuss it with the person under care, insofar as this is not contrary to the good of the latter.
(4) Within the scope of his duties, the protector shall so contribute that opportunities are used to cure illnesses or impediments of the person under care, to cause improvements, to prevent any deterioration or to assuage their consequences. *If the care is undertaken professionally, the protector may in certain cases be required by the court to produce a care plan. The care plan should illustrate the aims of the care and the measures needed to achieve these.*
(5) If the protector learns of circumstances which make possible the cancellation of the care, he shall inform the Guardianship Court thereof. The same applies to circumstances which make possible the reduction of the scope of duties or its extension, the appointment of an additional protector or which require an order for the reservation of consent (§ 1903).

§ 1901a. [Written requests for care]

Whoever is in possession of a written document in which a person expressed proposals for the choice of a protector for the eventuality of being placed under care or wishes for the manner of maintenance of the care, he shall deliver it forthwith to the Guardianship Court after learning that a process for the appointment of a protector has been initiated. *Whoever also is in possession of written documents, in which a person grants a power of attorney to another person with regards to the administration of his affairs, shall notify the Guardianship Court. The Guardianship Court may demand the presentation of a copy.*

§ 1902. [Representation of the person under care]

The protector represents the person under his care in judicial and extrajudicial matters.

§ 1903. [Reservation of consent]

(1) Insofar as it is necessary for the avoidance of substantial jeopardy to the person or property of the person under care, the Guardianship Court shall order that any declaration of intention by the person under care which involves the scope of duties of the protector shall require its consent (Reservation of consent). §§ 108 to 113, 131(2) and § 210 apply mutatis mutandis.
(2) A reservation of consent may not extend to declarations of intention, which concern contracting of marriage, testamentary dispositions and declarations of intention for which a person with limited capacity to enter legal transactions does

not need the consent of his legal representative pursuant to the provisions of the Fourth and Fifth Books.
(3) If a reservation of consent has been ordered, the person under care still does not require the consent of his protector if the declaration of intention merely results in a legal advantage. Insofar as the court does not otherwise order, this also applies if the declaration of intention concerns an insignificant matter of daily life.
(4) § 1901(5) applies mutatis mutandis.

§ 1904. [Consents requiring approval]

The consent of the protector to a physical examination, a treatment or medical intervention requires the approval of the Guardianship Court, if there is substantial apprehension that the person under care may die as the consequence of such measure or suffer severe and long-term health injury. The measure may only be taken without approval if a delay involves jeopardy.
(2) Subsection (1) applies also for the consent of a person with a power of attorney. It is only valid if the power of attorney is written and expressly includes the measures referred to in subsection (1) sentence (1).

§ 1905. [Sterilisation]

(1) If the medical intervention consists of sterilisation of the person under care, to which the latter cannot consent, the protector may only give his consent if:

1. the sterilisation is not contrary to the will of the person under care;
2. the person under care will remain incapable of giving consent for a long period;
3. it is expected that without the sterilisation pregnancy would follow;
4. as to consequence of such pregnancy a danger to the life or a danger of serious damage to the physical or mental state of health of the pregnant person is foreseen and it cannot be avoided in any reasonable way; and
5. the pregnancy cannot be prevented by other reasonable means.

A serious danger to the mental health of the pregnant person would also be the danger of a painful and persistent suffering, which would threaten her because measures by the Guardianship Court involving separation from the child would be taken against her as of necessity (§§ 1666 and 1666a).
(2) The consent requires the approval of the Guardianship Court. The sterilisation may first be carried out two weeks after the approval became effective. In case of sterilisation, the preferable method is one which allows renewal of fertility.

§ 1906. [Confinement]

(1) Confinement of the person under care by the protector, which involves deprivation of his freedom, is only permissible as long as it is required for the good of the person under care because:

1. by reason of a physical ailment or mental or psychic impediment of the person under care there is a danger that he may commit suicide or substantial damage to his health; or
2. an examination of his state of health, a healing therapy, or a medical intervention is necessary which cannot be carried out without confinement of the person under care and owing to a physical ailment or mental or psychic impediment the person under care is unable to recognise the need for his confinement or act in accordance with such recognition.

(2) The confinement is only allowed with the approval of the Guardianship Court. Without such approval the confinement is only permissible if a delay involves danger; the approval shall be subsequently obtained without delay.
(3) The protector shall end the confinement, if the conditions thereof are no longer present. He shall notify the Guardianship Court of the termination of confinement.
(4) Subsections (1) to (3) are analogously applicable if the person under care lives in an institution, a home or other facility, without being confined and his freedom is for a longer period or regularly restricted by mechanical means, medication or in some other manner.
(5) The confinement by a person with a power of attorney and the consent of a person with a power of attorney to measures in accordance to subsection (4) presuppose that the power of attorney is written and expressly includes the measures referred to in subsections (1) and (4). In other matters, subsections (1) and (4) apply mutatis mutandis.

§ 1907. [Tenancy and legal relations]

(1) The protector requires the approval of Guardianship Court for a notice to terminate tenancy of a living quarter rented by the person under care. The same applies to a declaration of intention which concerns the cancellation of such lease relationship.
(2) If other circumstances arise on the ground of which the termination of lease is to be considered, the care person shall immediately notify the Guardianship Court if the scope of his functions includes the determination of lease relations and residence. If the protector wants to give up the living quarters otherwise than by notice of termination or cancellation of the lease, he shall also notify the above without delay.

(3) For a lease or tenancy contract by which the person under care is obliged to make recurring performances, the protector requires the approval of the Guardianship Court, if the contractual relation is the last longer than four years or residential quarters are to be rented by the protector.

§ 1908. [Dowry]

The protector may not promise or grant a dowry from the property of the person under care except with the approval of the Guardianship Court.

§ 1908a. [Measures for a minor aged 17]

Measures pursuant to §§ 1896 and 1903 may also be taken concerning a minor who completed his seventeenth year of age, if it is expected that they will be necessary when he reaches majority. Such measures become effective upon the attainment of majority.

§ 1908b. [Discharge of protector]

(1) The Guardianship Court shall discharge the protector when his qualification to take care of the affairs of the person under care is no longer assured or there is some other important ground from the discharge. *An important ground also exists when the protector intentionally has falsely reported a required bill. The court shall discharge the protector appointed according to § 1897(6), when the person under care can be entrusted to the care of one or more persons, who do not become protectors as part of their profession.*
(2) The protector may request to be discharged if subsequent to his appointment circumstances arise by reason of which he can no longer be expected to carry out the functions of a protector.
(3) The court may discharge the protector when the person under care proposes an equally suitable person as new protector, who is willing to undertake the care.

§ 1908c. [Appointment of a new protector]

If the protector deceased or has been discharged a new protector shall be appointed.

§ 1908d. [Cancellation of protective care]

(1) The care shall be cancelled if the conditions thereof cease to exist. If such conditions cease to exist only as regards a part of the duties of the protector, the scope of duties of the latter shall be limited accordingly.
(2) If the protector is appointed pursuant to the application of the person under care, the protective care shall be cancelled upon his application, unless the care

is required ex officio. A person incompetent to enter legal transactions is also entitled to make an application. First and second sentences analogously apply to the limitation of the scope of duties.
(3) The scope of duties of the protector shall be extended, if this becomes necessary. The provisions on the appointment of protectors are applicable thereto mutatis mutandis.
(4) For the reservation of approval, subsections (1) and (3) are applicable mutatis mutandis.

§ 1908e.

(repealed)

§ 1908f. [Recognition as a protective association]

(1) An association competent to enter legal transactions may be recognised as a protective association if it guarantees that it:

1. has an adequate number of qualified co-workers and it can ensure that they will be supervised, given continuing education, and adequately insured against damage they may cause within the scope of their activities;
2. endeavours in a systematic manner to obtain honorary protectors, trains them for their duties, gives them continuing education and advice;
   2a. regularly informs about powers of attorney concerning care and documents containing wishes concerning the provision of care;
3. makes possible an exchange of experiences among the fellow workers.

(2) The recognition is effective for the respective state of the Federation; it may be limited to certain parts of the state. It may be revoked and may be given subject to conditions.
(3) In other respects the law of the state governs. It may provide for additional conditions for recognition.
(4) The recognised protective associations may in exceptional circumstances inform persons with regards to the drafting of a power of attorney relating to care.

§ 1908g. [Official protector]

(1) No penalty payment shall be adjudicated pursuant to § 1837 subsection (3) sentence (1) against an official protector.
(2) The official protector may deposit the money of the person under his care pursuant to § 1807 also with a public corporate body by which he is employed.

§ 1908h.

(repealed)

§ 1908i. [Analogous application of provisions]

(1) In other matters, § 1632 (1) to (3), §§ 1784, 1787 (1) and § 1791a(3) first sentence second half sentence and second sentence, §§ 1792, 1795 to 1797 (1) sentence (2), §§ 1798, 1799, 1802 (1) sentence (1), subsections (2) and (3), §§ 1803, 1805 to 1821 and 1822 nos. 1 to 4 and 6 to 13, §§ 1823 to 1825, 1828 to 1831, 1833 to 1836e and 1837(1) to (3), §§ 1839 to 1841, 1843, 1845, 1846, 1857a, 1888, 1890 and 1982 to 1894 are analogously applicable to protective care. The law of the respective state may rule that provisions which concern the supervision of the Guardianship Court with regard to property law provisions as well as relating to study and work contracts shall remain inapplicable against the competent authority.
(2) § 1804 shall analogously apply. The protector may, however, give occasional gifts as the representative of the person under his care also on occasions when this is to conform with the wishes of the person under his care and is customary and in accordance with the latter's living standard. § 1857a shall find analogous application to protective care by the father, the mother, the spouse or a descendant of the person under care as well as to an association protector and an official protector, insofar as the Guardianship Court does not order otherwise.

§ 1908k.

(repealed)

Bibliography

Government and Parliamentary Documents

Germany

Bt-Drucks 11/4528.
Bt-Drs 13/3822.

United Kingdom

Command papers

Department for Health, *Valuing People Now: A New Three-year Strategy for People with Learning Disabilities*, Gateway Reference 10531 (2009).

Department of Health and Social Security, *Better Services for the Mentally Handicapped*, Cmnd 4683 (London: Her Majesty's Stationery Office, 1971).

Royal Commission on the Care and Control of the Feeble-Minded, Cd 4202 (London: His Majesty's Stationery Office, 1908).

Royal Commission on the Law Relating to Mental Illness and Mental Deficiency 1954–1957, Cmnd 169 (London: Her Majesty's Stationery Office, 1957).

Secretary of State for Constitutional Affairs, *Draft Mental Incapacity Bill*, Cm 5859 (London: The Stationery Office, 2003).

Secretary of State for Health, *Valuing People: A New Strategy for Learning Disability for the 21st Century*, Cm 5086 (London: The Stationery Office, 2001).

The Lord Chancellor's Department, *Who Decides?*, Cm 3803 (London: Her Majesty's Stationery Office, 1997).

——, *Making Decisions*, Cm 4465 (London: Her Majesty's Stationery Office, 1999).

Debates

H.L., *Parliamentary Debates*, 5th ser., vol. 668, col. 85 (10 January 2005) (Lord Brennan).

Law Commission

Law Commission, *Mental Incapacity*, Report No. 231 (London: Her Majesty's Stationery Office, 1995).

——, *Mentally Incapacitated Adults and Decision-making: An Overview*, Consultation Paper No. 119 (London: Her Majesty's Stationery Office, 1991).

——, *Mentally Incapacitated Adults and Decision-making: A New Jurisdiction*, Consultation Paper No. 128 (London: Her Majesty's Stationery Office, 1993).

——, *Mentally Incapacitated Adults and Decision-making: Medical Treatment and Research*, Consultation Paper No. 129 (London: Her Majesty's Stationery Office, 1993).

Parliamentary papers

Joint Committee on the Draft Mental Health Bill, *Draft Mental Health Bill*, HL Paper 181 HC 1294, Session 2001–2002 (London: The Stationery Office, 2002).

Joint Committee on the Draft Mental Incapacity Bill, *Draft Mental Incapacity Bill*, vol. 1, HL Paper 189-I HC 1083-I and vol. 2, HL Paper 189-II HC 1083-II, Session 2002–2003 (London: The Stationery Office, 2003).

Joint Committee on Human Rights, *A Life Like Any Other: Human Rights of Adults with Learning Disabilities*, vol. 1, HL Paper 40-I HC 73-I, Session 2007–2008 (London: The Stationery Office, 2008).

Other

Union of the Physically Impaired Against Segregation, *Policy Statement* (1976).

International Documents

Council of Europe

Council of Europe, *Collected Edition of the Travaux Préparatoires*, vol. 1 (The Hague: Martinus Nijhoff, 1976).

United Nations

Declaration on the Rights of Disabled Persons, GA Res. 3447(XXX), UN GAOR, 30th Sess., Supp. No. 34, UN Doc. A/10034, 88.

Declaration on the Rights of Mentally Retarded Persons, GA Res. 2856(XXVI), UN GAOR, 26th Sess., Supp. No. 29, UN Doc. A/8429, 93.

Secondary Material

Books

English

Arai-Takahashi, Yutaka. *The Margin of Appreciation Doctrine and the Principle of Proportionality in the Jurisprudence of the ECHR* (Antwerp: Intersentia, 2002).

Arnardóttir, Oddný Mjöll and Quinn, G., eds. *The UN Convention on the Rights of Persons with Disabilities: European and Scandinavian Perspectives* (Leiden: Martinus Nijhoff Publishers, 2009).

Ashton, Gordon R. and Ward, Adrian D. *Mental Handicap and the Law* (London: Sweet and Maxwell, 1992).

Bartlett, Peter. *The Poor Law of Lunacy* (London: Leicester University Press, 1999).

——, and Sandland, Ralph. *Mental Health Law*, 2nd ed. (Oxford: Oxford University Press, 2003).

Barton, Len and Oliver, Mike, eds. *Disability Studies: Past, Present and Future* (Leeds: The Disability Press, 1997).

Bayertz, Kurt, ed. *Sanctity of Life and Human Dignity* (Dordrecht: Kluwer Academic, 1996).

Bell, John S. *French Constitutional Law* (Oxford: Clarendon Press, 1992).

Beyleveld, Deryck and Brownsword, Roger. *Human Dignity in Bioethics and Biolaw* (Oxford: Oxford University Press, 2001).

Bouras, Nick, ed. *Mental Health in Mental Retardation: Recent Advances and Practices* (Cambridge: Cambridge University Press, 1994).

Brown, Hilary and Smith, Helen, eds. *Normalisation: A Reader for the Nineties* (London: Routledge, 1992).

Buchanan, Allen E. and Brock, Dan W. *Deciding for Others: The Ethics of Surrogate Decision-making* (Cambridge: Cambridge University Press, 1989).

Cavinet, Guy, Andenas, Mads and Fairgrieve, Duncan, eds. *Comparative Law before the Courts* (London: British Institute of International and Comparative Law, 2004).

Childress, James F. *Who Should Decide? Paternalism in Health Care* (New York: Oxford University Press, 1982).

Clements, Luke and Read, Janet. *Disabled People and European Human Rights* (Bristol: Policy Press, 2003).

Connolly, Michael, ed. *Townshend-Smith on Discrimination Law: Text, Cases and Materials*, 2nd ed. (London: Cavendish, 2004).

Council of Europe. *Collected Edition of the Travaux Préparatoires*, vol. 1 (The Hague: Martinus Nijhoff, 1976).

Cretney, Stephen M. *Law, Law Reform and the Family* (Oxford: Clarendon Press, 1998).

——, *Family Law*, 4th ed. (London: Sweet and Maxwell, 2000).

——, Masson, Judith M. and Bailey-Harris, Rebecca J. *Principles of Family Law*, 7th ed. (London: Sweet and Maxwell, 2002).

Douglas, Gillian, *An Introduction to Family Law*, 2nd ed. (Oxford: Oxford University Press, 2004).

Dworkin, Ronald M. *Life's Dominion: An Argument about Abortion and Euthanasia* (London: HarperCollins, 1993).

——, *Sovereign Virtue: The Theory and Practice of Equality* (Cambridge, MA: Harvard University Press, 2000).

Eide, Asbjørn et al., eds. *The Universal Declaration Of Human Rights: A Commentary* (Oslo: Scandinavian University Press, 1992).

Ellis, Evelyn, ed. *The Principle of Proportionality in the Laws of Europe* (Oxford: Hart, 1999).

Emerson, Eric et al., eds. *Clinical Psychology and People with Intellectual Disabilities* (Chichester: Wiley, 1998).

Finlayson, G. Citizen, *State, and Social Welfare in Britain 1830–1990* (Oxford: Clarendon Press, 1994).

Flynn, Robert J. and Nitsch, Kathleen E., eds. *Normalization, Social Integration, and Community Services* (Baltimore, MD: University Park Press, 1980).

Fortin, Jane. *Children's Rights and the Developing Law*, 2nd ed. (London: Butterworths, 2003).

Fredman, Sandra. *Discrimination Law* (Oxford: Oxford University Press, 2002).

Fulford, Kenneth W.M., Gillett, Grant R. and Soskice, Janet M., eds. *Medicine and Moral Reasoning* (Cambridge: Cambridge University Press, 1994).

Gibson, Walter S. *Hieronymus Bosch* (London: Thames and Hudson, 2000).

Goren, Simon L. *German Civil Code* (Littleton, CO: F.B. Rothman, 1994).

Hale, Dame Brenda et al. *The Family, Law and Society: Cases and Materials*, 5th ed. (London: Butterworths, 2002).

Herr, Stanley S., Gostin, Laurence O. and Koh, Harold Hongju, eds. *The Human Rights of Persons with Intellectual Disabilities* (Oxford: Oxford University Press, 2005).

Hodapp, Robert M., Burack, Jacob A. and Zigler, Edward, eds. *Issues in the Developmental Approach to Mental Retardation* (Cambridge: Cambridge University Press, 1990).

Jones, Richard M. *Mental Health Act Manual*, 8th ed. (London: Sweet and Maxwell, 2003).

Kretzmer, David and Klein, Eckart, eds. *The Concept of Human Dignity in Human Rights Discourse* (The Hague: Kluwer Law International, 2002).

Lawson, Anna and Gooding, Caroline, eds. *Disability Rights in Europe* (Oxford: Hart, 2005).

McLean, Sheila A.M. *A Patient's Right to Know: Information Disclosure, the Doctor and the Law* (Aldershot: Dartmouth, 1989).

——, ed. *Legal Issues in Human Reproduction* (Aldershot: Gower, 1989).

——, ed. *Contemporary Issues in Law, Medicine and Ethics* (Aldershot: Dartmouth, 1996).

Mason, J. Kenyon and Laurie, Graeme T. *Mason and McCall Smith's Law and Medical Ethics*, 7th ed. (Oxford: Oxford University Press, 2006).

Menuge, Noël James. *Medieval English Wardship in Romance and Law* (Woodbridge: D.S. Brewer, 2001).

Merrills, John G. *The Development of International Law by the European Court of Human Rights*, 2nd ed. (Manchester: Manchester University Press, 1993).

——, and Robertson, Arthur H. *Human Rights in Europe*, 4th ed. (Manchester: Manchester University Press, 2001).

Meyer, Michael J. and Parent, William A., eds. *The Constitution of Rights: Human Dignity and American Values* (Ithaca, NY: Cornell University Press, 1992).

Ovey, Clare and White, Robin, eds. *Jacobs and White, The European Convention on Human Rights*, 3rd ed. (Oxford: Oxford University Press, 2002).

Philpot, Terry and Ward, Linda, eds. *Values and Visions: Changing Ideas in Services for People with Learning Difficulties* (Oxford: Butterworth-Heinemann, 1995).

Rae, Scott B. and Cox, Paul M. *Bioethics: A Christian Approach in a Pluralistic Age* (Grand Rapids, MI: W.B. Eerdmans, 1999).

Reinders, Hans S. *The Future of the Disabled in Liberal Society: An Ethical Analysis* (Notre Dame, IN: University of Notre Dame Press, 2000).

Simma, Bruno, ed. *The Charter of the UN: A Commentary*, vol. 1, 2nd ed. (Oxford: Oxford University Press, 2002).

Simpson, Alfred William Brian. *Human Rights and the End of Empire* (Oxford: Oxford University Press, 2001).

Slack, Paul. *The English Poor Law, 1531–1782* (Cambridge: Cambridge University Press, 1995).

Teff, Harvey. *Reasonable Care: Legal Perspectives on the Doctor–Patient Relationship* (Oxford: Clarendon Press, 1994).

Thomson, Mathew. *The Problem of Mental Deficiency* (Oxford: Clarendon Press, 1998).

Van Dijk, Pieter and Van Hoof, Godefridus J.H. *Theory and Practice of the European Convention on Human Rights*, 3rd ed. (The Hague: Kluwer Law International, 1998).

White, Richard A.H., Carr, A. Paul and Lowe, Nigel V. *The Children Act in Practice*, 3rd ed. (London: Butterworths, 2002).

Wright, David and Digby, Anne, eds. *From Idiocy to Mental Deficiency* (London: Routledge, 1996).

French

Bernadet, Philippe, Douraki, Thomaïs and Vaillant, Corinne. *Psychiatrie, droits de l'homme et défense des usagers en Europe* (Paris: Erès, 2002).

Commission européenne pour la démocratie par le droit. *Le principe du respect de la dignité de la personne humaine: actes du Séminaire UniDem organisé à Montpellier du 2 au 6 juillet 1998* (Strasbourg: Editions du Conseil de l'Europe, 1999).

Douraki, Thomaïs. *La Convention Européenne des droits de l'homme et le droit à la liberté de certains malades et marginaux* (Paris: Librairie Générale de Droit et de Jurisprudence, 1986).

Jourdain, Patrice et al. *Le nouveau droit des malades* (Paris: Litec, 2002).

Levy, Catherine. 'La personne humaine en droit' (thèse doctorale, Université de Sorbonne-Paris I, 2000) [unpublished].

Maurer, Béatrice. *Le principe de respect de la dignité humaine et la Convention Européenne des droits de l'homme* (Paris: Documentation française, 1999).

Pavia, Marie-Luce and Revet, Thierry, eds. *La dignité de la personne humaine* (Paris: Economica, 1999).

German

Amelung, Knut. *Vetorechte beschränkt Enwilligungsfähiger in Grenzbereichen medizinischer Intervention* (Berlin: de Gruyter, 1995).

Becker, Ulrich. *Das 'Menschenbild des Grundgesetzes' in der Rechtsprechung des Bundesverfassungsgerichts* (Berlin: Duncker and Humblot, 1996).

Benda, Ernst, Maihofer, Werner and Vogel, Hans-Jochen, eds. *Handbuch des Verfassungsrechts*, vol. 1, 2. Auflage (Berlin: de Gryuter, 1994).

Bettermann, Karl August, Neumann, Franz L. and Nipperdey, Hans Carl. *Die Grundrechte*, vol. 1 (Berlin: Duncker and Humblot, 1966).

Bienwald, Werner. *Betreuungsrecht Kommentar*, 3rd ed. (Bielefeld: Giese King, 1999).

Bonner Kommentar GG (Heidelberg: C.F. Müller, 2003).

Buch, Michael. *Das Grundrecht der Behinderten* (Osnabrück: Der andere Verlag, 2001).

Castendiek, Jan and Hoffmann, Günther. *Das Recht der behinderten Menschen* (Nomos, 2002).

Dederich, Markus. *Behinderung, Medizin, Ethik* (Bad Heilbrunn: Klinkhardt, 2000).

——, *Menschen mit Behinderung zwischen Ausschluß und Anerkennung* (Bad Heilbrunn: Klinkhardt, 2001).

——, ed. *Bioethik und Behinderung* (Bad Heilbrunn: Julius Klinkhardt, 2003).

Dreier, Horst, ed. *GG Kommentar*, vol. 1 (Tübingen: Mohr Siebeck, 1996).

Enders Cristoph, *Die Menschenwürde in der Verfassungsordnung* (Tübingen: Mohr Siebeck Verlag, 1997).

Frost, Andreas. *Arztrechtliche Probleme des neuen Betreuungsrechts* (Berlin: Springer, 1994).

Geddert-Steinacher, Tatjana. *Menchenwürde als Verfassungsbegriff* (Berlin: Duncker and Humblot, 1990).

Häberle, Peter. *Das Menschenbild im Verfassungsstaat* (Berlin: Duncker and Humblot, 1988).

Hillgruber, Christian. *Der Schutz des Menschen vor sich selbst* (Munich: Franz Vahlen, 1992).

Hoffmann, Birgit. *Sterilisation geistig behinderter Erwachsener* (Baden-Baden: Nomos, 1996).

Jeand'Heur, Bernd. *Verfassungsrechtliche Schutzgebote zum Wohl des Kindes und staatliche Interventionspflichten aus der Garantienorm des Art. 6 Abs. 2 Satz 2 GG* (Berlin: Duncker and Humblot, 1993).

Lipp, Volker. *Freiheit und Fürsorge: Der Mensch als Rechtsperson* (Tübingen: Mohr Siebeck, 2000).

Maunz, Theodor and Dürig, Günter, eds. *Grundgesetzkommentar*, vol 1 (Munich: C.H. Beck, 2003).

Meyer, Gaby. *Die Unfähigkeit des erwachsenen Patienten zur Einwilligung in den ärtzlichen Eingriff* (Frankfurt: Peter Lang, 1994).

Münchener Kommentar, vol. 8, 4th ed. (Munich: C.H. Beck, 2002).

Pieroth, Bodo and Schlink, Bernhardt. *Grundrechte Staatsrecht II*, 16th ed. (Heidelberg: C.F. Müller, 2000).

Quambusch, Erwin. *Das Recht der geistig Behinderten*, 4th ed. (Freiburg im Breisgau: Lambertus, 2001).

Schlüter, Wilfried. *BGB-Familienrecht*, 10th ed. (Heidelberg: C.F. Müller, 2003).

Schwab, Dieter et al., eds. *Staat, Kirche, Wissenschaft in einer pluralistischen Gesellschaft: Festschrift zum 65. Geburtstag von Paul Mikat* (Berlin: Duncker and Humblot, 1989).

Sonnenfeld, Susanne. *Betreuungs- und Pflegeschaftsrecht*, 2nd ed. (Bielefeld: Gieseking, 2001).

Speck, Otto. *Menschen mit geistiger Behinderung und ihre Erziehung*, 9th ed. (Munich: Ernst Reinhardt, 1999).

Stock, Anke. *Gleichstellung im Vergleich* (Regensburg: S. Roderer, 2003).

Strassmair, Stefan Manfred. *Der besondere Gleichheitssatz aus Art. 3 Abs. 3 Satz 2 GG* (Berlin: Duncker and Humblot, 2002).

Walter, Joachim, ed. *Sexualität und geistige Behinderung*, 4th ed. (Heidelberg: C. Winter, 1997).

Articles and Case Comments

English

Bartlett, Peter and McHale, Jean. 'Mental Incapacity and Mental Health: The Development of Legal Reform and the Need for Joined-up Thinking' [2003] JSWFL 313.

Bellhouse, John et al. 'Decision-making Capacity in Adults: Its assessment in Clinical Practice' [2001] Adv. Psychiatr. Treat. 294.

Beyleveld, Deryck and Brownsword, Roger. 'Human Dignity, Human Rights, and Human Genetics' [1998] MLR 661.

Carson, David. 'The Sexuality of People with Learning Difficulties' [1989] JSWL 355.

Choudry, Shazia. 'The Adoption and Children Act 2002, the Welfare Principle and the Human Rights Act 1998: A Missed Opportunity?' [2003] CFLQ 119.

Cica, Natasha. 'Sterilising Persons with Intellectual Disability: The Approach of the High Court of Australia in *Department of Health* v. *J.W.B. and S.M.B.*' [1993] Med. L. Rev. 186.

Cummins, Robert A. and Lau, Anna L.D. 'Community Integration or Community Exposure? A Review and Discussion in Relation to People with an Intellectual Disability' [2003] JARID 145.

Delany, Linda. 'Altruism by Proxy: Volunteering Children for Bone Marrow Donation' [1996] BMJ 240.

Dimopoulos, Andreas. 'Intellectually Disabled Parents before the European Court of Human Rights and English Courts' [2009] EHRLR 82.

Edwards, Steven D. 'The Moral Status of Intellectually Disabled Individuals' [1997] J. Med. Philos. 29.

Eekelaar, John. 'Beyond the Welfare Principle' [2002] CFLQ 237.
Feldman, David. 'Human Dignity as a Legal Value' [1999] Pub. L. 682 and [2000] Pub. L. 61.
Fennell, Philip. 'The Law Commission's Proposals on Mental Incapacity' [1995] Fam. Law. J. 420.
——, 'Doctor Knows Best? Therapeutic Detention Under Common Law, The Mental Health Act, and the European Convention' [1998] Med. L. Rev. 322.
Fenwick, Andrea J. '*Re S (Medical Treatment: Adult Sterilisation)*: Retrenching on Risk – Revising the Lawful Boundaries of Sterilisation' [1999] CFLQ 313.
Gostin, Lawrence O. 'Human Rights of Persons with Mental Disabilities' [2000] IJLP 125.
Grubb, Andrew. 'Who Decides? Legislating for the Incapacitated Adult' [1998] EJHL 231.
——, and Pearl, David. 'Sterilisation and the Courts' [1987] CLJ 439.
Gunn, Michael. 'Mental Incapacity: The Law Commission's Report' [1995] CFLQ 209.
——, et al. 'Decision-making Capacity' [1999] Med. L. Rev. 269.
——, et al. 'Medical Research and Incompetent Adults' [2000] JMHL 60.
——, et al. 'Families and New Medical Dilemmas: Capacity to Make Decisions' 2001 CFLQ 383.
Hunt, Jane. 'A Revolutionary Group with a Revolutionary Message' (2001) *Coalition* 22–30.
Johnson, Linda. 'Expanding Eugenics or Improving Health Care in China: Commentary on the Provisions of the Standing Committee of the Gensu People's Congress Concerning the Prohibition of Reproduction by Intellectually Impaired Persons' [1997] J. Law and Soc. 199.
Keywood, Kirsty. 'Gatekeepers, Proxies, Advocates? The Evolving Role of Carers Under Mental Health and Mental Incapacity Law Reforms' [2003] JSWFL 355.
Laing, Jacqueline. 'The Mental Capacity Bill 2004: Human Rights Concerns' [2005] Fam. Law. J. 137.
Laing, Judith M. 'Rights Versus Risk? Reform of the Mental Health Act 1983' [2000] Med. L. Rev. 210.
Lawson, Anna. 'The United Nations Convention on the Rights of Persons with Disabilities: New Era or False Dawn?' [2007] Syracuse J. Int'l L. and Com. 563.
Lee, Robert and Morgan, Derek. 'Sterilisation and Mental Handicap: Sapping the Strength of the State?' [1988] J. Law and Soc. 229.
Letsas, George. 'The Truth in Autonomous Concepts: How To Interpret the E.C.H.R.' [2004] EJIL 279.
Lewis, Penney. 'Procedures that are Against the Medical Interests of Incompetent Adults' [2002] OJLS 575.

Little, George Bradbury. 'Comparing German and English Law on Non-consensual Sterilisation: A Difference in Approach' [1997] Med. L. Rev. 269.
Little, Hilary. 'Non-consensual Sterilisation of Persons with Intellectual Disability in the Australian Context: Potential for Human Rights Abuse and the Need for Reform' [1993] Aust. YIL 203.
MacKay, Don. 'The United Nations Convention on the Rights of Persons with Disabilities' [2007] *Syracuse Journal of International Law and Commerce* 323.
Martin, Norma. 'Case Comment on *Re B*' [1987] JSWFL 370.
Mason, J. Kenyon. 'Conjoined Twins: A Diagnostic Conundrum' [2001] Edin. L. Rev. 226.
Millns, Susan. 'Dwarf-throwing and Human Dignity: A French Perspective' [1996] JSWFL 375.
Morgan, Derek. 'Case Comment on *F* v. *West Berkshire Mental Health Authority*' [1990] JSWFL 206.
Newman, Dwight. 'An Examination of Saskatchewan Law on the Sterilisation of Persons with Mental Disabilities' 1999 Sask. L. Rev. 329.
Norrie, Kenneth M. 'Sterilisation of the Mentally Disabled in English and Canadian Law' [1989] ICLQ 387.
Reece, Helen. 'The Paramountcy Principle: Consensus or Construct?' [1996] CLP 267.
Reed, Lucy. 'The Draft Mental Incapacity Bill' [2003] Fam. Law J. 771.
Reinders, Hans S. 'Introduction to Intellectual Disability, Genetics and Ethics' [2003] JIDR 501.
Rhoades, Helen. 'Intellectual Disability and Sterilisation: An Inevitable Connection?' [1995] Austl. J. Fam. L. 234.
Schachter, Oscar. 'Human Dignity as a Normative Concept' [1983] AJIL 848.
Seymour, John. 'Parens Patriae and Wardship Powers: Their Nature and Origins' [1994] OJLS 159.
Shone, Margaret A. 'Mental Health: Sterilization of Mentally Retarded Persons – Parens Patriae Power: *Re Eve*' [1987] CBR 635.
Stainton, T. 'Identity and Ethical Politics of Prenatal Testing' [2003] JIDR 533.
Suto, W.M.I., Clare, Isabel C.H. and Holland, Anthony J. 'Substitute Financial Decision-making in England and Wales: A Study of the Court of Protection' [2002] JSWFL 37.
Tait, David, Carney, Terry and Deane, Kirsten. 'Legal Regulation of Sterilisation: The Role of Guardianship Tribunals in NSW and Victoria' [1994] Austl. J. Fam. L. 141.
Wheatley, Steven, 'Human Rights and Human Dignity in the Resolution of Certain Ethical Questions in Biomedicine' [2001] EHRLR 312.
Wong, J.G. et al. 'Capacity to Make Health Care Decisions: Its Importance in Clinical Practice' [1999] Psych. Med. 437.

French

Benoît, Jorion. 'La dignité de la personne humaine ou la difficile insertion d'une règle morale dans le droit positif' Rev. dr. publ. 1999.197.

Mathieu, Bertrand. 'La dignité de la personne humaine: quel droit? quel titulaire?' D. 1996.282.

——, 'La dignité de la personne humaine' Rev. dr. publ. 1999.92.

Moutouh, Hugues. 'La dignité de l'homme en droit' Rev. dr. publ. 1999.159.

German

Bayertz, Kurt. 'Die Idee der Menschenwürde: Probleme und Paradoxien' [1995] ARSP 465.

Bienwald, Werner. 'Zur Umsetzung des Betreuungsgesetzes in der Praxis' [1992] Fam. RZ.

Dürig, Günter. 'Der Grundrechtssatz von der Menschenwürde' [1956] AöR 118.

Fechner, Frank. 'Öffentliche Ordnung: Renaissance eines Begriffs?' [2003] JuS 734.

Fratzky, York. 'Kann der Betreuer die Wohnung des Betreuten gegen dessen Willen betreten?' [2000] Bt. Prax. 239.

Herdegen, Matthias. 'Die Menschenwürde im Fluß des bioethischen Diskurses' [2001] JZ 773.

Hoerster, Norbert. 'Zur Bedeutung des Prinzips Menschenwürde' [1983] JuS 93.

Hofmann, Hasso. 'Die versprochene Menschenwürde' [1993] AöR 353.

Hoffmann, Birgit. 'Anmerkungen zum Beschluß des OLG Hamm vom 28.2.2000' [2000] Bt. Prax. 168.

——, 'Anmerkungen zum Beschluß des BayObLG vom 23.5.2001' [2001] Bt. Prax. 240.

——, 'Hilfen zur Erziehung und Betreuung' [2002] Bt. Prax. 246.

Höfling, Wolfram. 'Die Unantastbarkeit der Menschenwürde: Annäherungen an einen schwierigen Verfassungsrechtssatz' [1995] JuS 857.

Lachwitz, Klaus. 'Menschen mit geistiger Behinderung im Spannungsfeld zwischen Selbst- und Fremdbestimmung' [1995] Bt. Prax. 114.

Neumann, Ulfrid. 'Die Tyrannei der Würde' [1998] ARSP 153.

Neumann, Volker. 'Menschenwürde und psychische Krankheit' [1993] Krit. Vjschr. 276.

Pieroth, Bodo. 'Die Verfassungsmäßigkeit der Sterilisation Einwilligungsunfähiger gemäß dem Entwurf für ein Betreuungsgesetz' [1990] Fam. RZ 117.

Pohlmann, Rüdiger. 'Sexuelle Aufklärung geistig behinderter Menschen' [1995] Bt. Prax. 114.

Pöld-Krämer, Sylvia. 'Sterilisation gegen den Willen der Betroffenen: das falsche Signal!' [2000] Bt. Prax. 237.

Rädler, Peter. 'Die Unverfügbarkeit der Menschenwürde in Deutschland und Frankreich' [1997] DÖV 109.

Rems-Murr-Kreis. 'Konzeption Familienpflege für behinderte Mütter und ihre Kinder' [2003] J. Amt. 338.

Stalinski, Dirk. 'Anmerkung zum Beschluß des OLG Hamm' [2000] Bt. Prax. 106.

Vitzthum, Wolfgang Graf. 'Die Menschenwürde als Verfassungsbegriff' [1985] JZ 201.

Wessels, Wolfgang. 'Familiäre Konflikte in der Betreuung' [1998] Bt. Prax. 64.

Index

In subheadings, ID is an abbreviation for 'intellectually disabled' and PD is an abbreviation for 'physically disabled'.